THE JUNKMAN SMILES

A Foochow Pole Junk

THE
JUNKMAN SMILES

By

G. R. G. *Worcester*

With illustrations by the Author

1959
CHATTO AND WINDUS
LONDON

Published by
Chatto & Windus Ltd
London

★

Clarke, Irwin & Co. Ltd
Toronto

Printed in Great Britain by
Ebenezer Baylis & Son, Limited
The Trinity Press, Worcester
and London

Dedication

This book is dedicated to the memory of my late wife, Doris Worcester. With amazing courage she shared some of the adventures and many of the dangers and discomforts recorded in these pages. Although she was suffering from ill health, her fortitude and self-denying work for others in the Japanese Concentration Camp were an inspiration to all who knew her. Soon after our liberation she died in China, the country she knew so well and loved so much.

Contents

Plates

(*There are also many drawings throughout the text*)

Preface

I HAVE been studying, writing about and lecturing on the Chinese Junk for more than twenty years. This has earned me the name of THE JUNKMAN.

When I retired from the Chinese Maritime Customs, immediately after the last war, I came to England and stayed with friends. It was a period of acute food shortage, and I was sent out to stand in food queues. I used to talk to all the housewives, provided they were over 40 years of age, and I well remember one dear old lady who asked me where I came from. 'Madam,' I said, 'I hardly know how to answer your question but, I suppose, it might be said that I come from China.' She looked very hard at me for a moment and said, 'You don't look Chinese to me, I thought you were an American.' Then she went on to tell me that she knew little of China, except that it was very far away and near Tibet. All she knew about Tibet, she continued, was that they had Lamas in temples there; and all she knew about llamas was that they spat at you when you fed them in the Zoo.

Well! We may smile at my worthy old friend but it is surprising how many people there are in England today who know next to nothing of China and the Chinese. This is all very sad, for China has become a Great Power and is soon going to be a factor to be reckoned with in the affairs of many lands.

Generally speaking, the Chinese have very great intellectual ability; they are kindly and hospitable, patient and cheerful; and they have many other good qualities. Yet they can, on occasion, be callous and truculent, unscrupulous, crafty and cruel. They are, moreover, the greatest money-makers and the most successful bankers in the world. Catch a Chinese young, and there is nothing you cannot teach him, good or bad.

All these good and bad qualities make China the greatest potential danger in the world today. She is not likely to imitate the Japanese mistake of trying to conquer South-east Asia, and beyond, by force of arms, but she will do so by unobtrusive and timely infiltration and bribery. But politics are dull and depressing and are quite out-side the scope of this book.

From a nautical research point of view, it is disappointing to find how little is known of China and the Chinese junk, not only by the man in the street, but by literary giants, admirals and professors. Some of them know all there is to know about the ships of Greece and Rome and yet, when it comes to the Chinese junk, whose an-cestry is just as long, they know little more than my old housewife. I say it is disappointing, for we sailors of the West owe a debt of gratitude to the seamen of China. To their countrymen goes the credit of inventing the water-tight compartment, the lug-sail, the balance rudder and many other nautical devices in common use today.

When I say we owe a debt of gratitude to China, I do not mean it to be inferred that a party of Chinese nautical research experts set out from Far Cathay to teach the shipwrights of Europe their job. I mean that many important Chinese nautical devices found their way to the West, where they were copied and improved upon.

There never was a Chinese Nelson; there never was a Chinese yachtsman; no Chinese child ever plays with a toy ship, and there is a Chinese proverb which says, 'To ride a horse or travel in a ship is attended with 75 per cent risk.' Nevertheless, the Chinese as a race are probably the most amphibious people in the world. No land animal, not even the duck, takes more kindly to the art of navi-gation than they do.

The population of China is about 400 million, and it is said that about one-tenth of this number is water-borne; by which I mean that they live on the water in some shape or form. The area of China is about four million square miles, so there is plenty of room for everybody. The Chinese don't go afloat because they have to, but because they genuinely like it; in other words, they are the world's natural sailors.

I am an old sailor myself, and I have served with the Chinese in peace and in war. I have served with them in armed merchant cruisers, and my thirty-three years' service in the Chinese Maritime Customs brought me in touch with every kind of Chinese sailor. I have been out with them in their junks at sea on the treacherous

China coast; I have seen them working their large salt junks through the narrow, winding channels of the Yangtze in winter, and their huge timber rafts in summer. I have seen them mud-larking on the Tung T'ing and Poyang Lakes, battling with the rapids and races of the Upper Yangtze, and coming down mountain torrents on logs of wood on the borders of Tibet; and I can say without the slightest hesitation that the Chinese sailor by and large is the most hospitable, good tempered, brave and efficient in the world. This is, I know, very high praise, but I mean every word of it; and it is chiefly about them that I wrote this book.

When my friends hear that I was in the Chinese Maritime Customs, they always assume that I examined people's luggage. Actually my work was not as interesting as that: with others I was responsible for the surveying and marking of channels, and the safe navigation of various types of ship, from aircraft carrier to sampan, in a route of well over two thousand miles of river, lake and creek on the Yangtze Kiang. Then, as it was discovered that I could write a bit and draw a bit, that I loved travel in the interior, that I could put up with discomfort to achieve my object, and was prepared to take various personal risks, the Inspector-General of Customs, Sir Frederick Maze, took me off all Customs work and put me on to Chinese Nautical Research. And so it came about that I spent eight supremely happy years travelling about the interior of China, studying the boats, the people and their customs.

When my first technical book on the junk was published, the Inspector-General sent for me and said that, in the unlikely event of it being a success, I was to understand that no credit was to go to me. The Chinese Customs, who had put me in a position to gather information, would get any praise that was going. And Sir Frederick was right. I could not have carried out the research I did without the financial backing of the Customs. Moreover, Customs letters of introduction enabled me to visit places difficult of access; and, most important of all, the Customs were behind me when I got into trouble and, twice, into Chinese jails.

My work was carried out during perhaps the most disturbed period of China's eventful history, and in China's recognized storm centres, amid almost continual fighting, civilian bandit raids, enemy occupation, floods and droughts, and finally ended amid the daily apprehensions of two and a half years in a Japanese concentration camp.

Altogether I produced five uninteresting technical books, now out of print, for the archives of the Chinese Maritime Customs. Notes, sketches and ideas were jotted down in all sorts of places: in trucks and cars, in junks, sampans, steamers and aeroplanes; on the tracking-path and in the rapid; on the sea and up the river, in fair weather and foul; in tea houses, markets and innumerable towns and villages far off the beaten track.

A great deal of the material I thus collected was quite unsuitable for a dull, technical tome, and so all these discarded notes and countless sketches were stuffed into a trunk. One day my wife turned out the trunk and said, 'I do wish you would try and weave some of this disjointed material into a book.' Well, here it is.

It must, however, be clearly understood that everything dealt with in this book concerns the old China, the China that has passed away; the wheelbarrow and sedan chair have given up the unequal struggle with the diesel engine and the jet aircraft, the graceful sail has been driven out by the unromantic funnel, and the China that I knew has gone for ever.

If you derive pleasure from rich dinners, small talk, bridge and the latest scandal, you had better keep away from the interior of China; but if your taste is for lovely scenery, a roving life, a clear sky, kindly people, and a little *adventure*, too, then I strongly advise the reader to try the Middle Kingdom.

NOTE

The word 'Foreigner', appearing so often in these pages, has, through long usage, come to designate all those of Western nationality in China. The Chinese themselves used the term Yang-ren, or Foreign People, and some Ning Po-ren, since Ningpo to them signified a vaguely hybrid place where the foreigners, and especially the English, had established themselves. In the interior the simple country people use the paradoxical courtesy title of Yang Kwei Tzu ta-ren, meaning 'His Excellency the Foreign Devil'.

When one has good wine,
A graceful boat,
And a maiden's love,
Why envy the immortal gods?
Li T'ai-po
(A.D. 705–762)

CHAPTER I

Shanghai to the Chusans

THE different methods of transport in China, whether by land or by water, are slow, cumbrous and in most cases uncomfortable and cramped. Both boats and vehicles seem to be designed so as to render it utterly impossible to travel with any speed or comfort. For thousands of years the natives have travelled slowly and uncomfortably, and the Chinese of today are quite prepared to do the same.

Time was when travel by junk or sampan in the bewildering and intricate network of waterways of Kiangsu and Chekiang was the only means of long-distance, cross-country transport, and nobody was in a hurry. But about the turn of the century things began to change, and there came into being a service composed of small launches. Finally a variety of dumb-lighter, carrying passengers, was added. This immediately became popular, and today there are few waterways without their boat trains, so called because the procession, with very short tow-ropes, looks more akin to the coaches of a railway train than to the lengthy water-borne tow. Everything possible is left to chance. The deck is usually unsafe and leaks. The handrails are liable to give way at any moment, and the whole pantechnicon, for so it may be called, is grossly overcrowded. Nevertheless, it generally manages to retain its stability against the most fearful odds. Frequent stops *en route* are made, and at the end of the voyage it would probably be found that not a single passenger who embarked at the beginning of the trip was still on board at the terminus; and yet the density of the human cargo has always remained the same.

I could have gone from Shanghai to Hangchow in four and a half hours in the afternoon express train, in a first-class compartment, with dinner in the dining-car, but I preferred to go the hard way, the way the junkmen would travel. To me the joy of moving down the creeks, with the sights and sounds of Chinese life afloat around one, is a pleasure I would not willingly forgo for any form of rapid transport. So I proceeded (this was in 1948) to the Soochow Creek to join the 4.30 p.m. Shanghai-Hangchow boat train. No rigorous time-table is adhered to, but the 'trains' do leave within one or two hours of the advertised time. This one was due to reach its destination the following night, taking thirty-six hours to cover the 117 miles.

The departure of these 'trains' is rich in human interest, and presents an unrivalled scene of confusion. Hawkers, coolies, loafers, thieves, beggars and tea-boys crowd round the prospective passen-

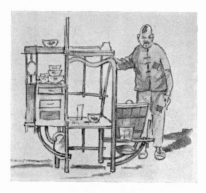

Travelling Kitchen

gers and offer free advice or highly-priced service. The travelling kitchens are everywhere to be seen. Everyone seems to be struggling with one or more pieces of unhandy luggage. But the chief interest centres in the mass of craft of all kinds with which the creek appears to be completely blocked, so that the question occurs, how did the boat train worm its way in among this congestion of junks, sampans and launches; and, having got there, how will it ever extricate itself? But it does.

The Chinese call the boat train the T'o Ch'uan. It takes its name from the word T'o, which oddly enough has exactly the same significance in Chinese as 'tow' in English. The boat is some 70 feet in length, with a beam of 14 feet and a depth of 4½ feet. This size is more or less standard, but there are large differences in the details of fittings and superstructure. In the interest of increased accommodation some boat owners take greater liberties with stability.

In some of the boat trains a slight attempt is made to provide a little primitive comfort for the passengers; sometimes, for instance, one or two bunks are provided for an extra charge. These consist of flat wooden shelves less than twenty-four inches wide, each without any rail or front, and separated from the next by a partition head-board six inches high. The less wealthy lie down on the deck and sleep head-to-head. The average boat train lighter will carry up to 200 passengers, of which sixty are on the upper deck and 140 elsewhere. To say that our craft was overcrowded, overloaded and unsafe would be a gross understatement. But the Chinese do not object to overcrowding; it is their normal condition.

The crew consisted of two deck-hands, two ticket collectors and two tea-boys. These all lived in the baggage room, where they camped out and cooked their food, with apparent comfort, on the passengers' boxes and bundles. Meals of a sort could be had by the passengers at a price, and tea and hot water were also sold at a hand-some profit. Below the deck was the galley, about the size of an or-dinary cabin trunk, for the use of the owner and his family, or any-one rash or rich enough to incur the expense of an ordered meal; this was the province of the tea-boys.

No description of travel in the interior of China would be com-plete without a reference to tea and tea-boys, for the Chinese as a nation remain unrivalled as the greatest tea-drinkers in the world. Tea-drinking is with them both an art and a science, not cultivated or even understood in any other country. They drink it at all seasons, times and places.

The tea plant, a native of Southern China, was known from very early times to Chinese botany and medicine. It is alluded to in the classics under various names: T'u, Shê, Ch'uan and Ming, and was highly prized for possessing the virtues of 'relieving fatigue, delight-ing the soul, strengthening the will and repairing the eyesight.' Not only was it taken internally; it was often applied externally in the form of a paste to alleviate rheumatic pains. The Taoists claimed it as an important ingredient of the elixir of immortality, and the

Tea Junk

Buddhists used it extensively to prevent drowsiness during their long hours of meditation.

The method of preparing tea in those early days was primitive. The leaves were steamed and crushed in a mortar, made into a cake and boiled with rice, ginger, salt, orange peel, spices and sometimes with onions. It needed the genius of the T'ang Dynasty, A.D. 618–907, to emancipate tea from its crude use, and lead it to its final idealization. Tea soon became a favourite beverage among the inhabitants of the Yangtze Valley, and today is carried in special junks.

The poets of China have left us some fragments of their adoration of the 'froth of the liquid jade'. Wang Yü-cheng, for example, eulogized tea as 'flooding the soul like a direct appeal, so that its delicate bitterness reminded one of the after-taste of good counsel,' whatever that may mean.

In those days the preparation of tea needed the hand of a master to bring out its noblest qualities. Each preparation of the leaves had to have its own individuality, its 'special affinity with water and heat'. The 'truly beautiful' had always to be in it. Like painting, tea-making had its changing cults. There were, for example, the classic, the romantic and the naturalistic periods in the history of tea. In course of time tea began to be, in the words of a Chinese master, 'not a poetic pastime, but one of the methods of self-realization'.

The Emperors used to bestow some rare preparation of the leaves on their high ministers as a reward for eminent services; and tea-drinking used, even until comparatively recent times, to be an important phase of the refined scholarly life. Every scholar had to be able to drink tea artistically, and was supposed to be able to tell not only the type of tea used, but also the quality of the water used in brewing it.

Among the Chinese, it is sad to relate, the art of preparing tea and the appreciation of it are on the wane. The romance of the T'ang and Sung ceremonies is not to be found in the modern cup. Tea, today, is a beverage, not an ideal; indeed, tea-drinking has become little more than 'watering the ox'. Iced water, Coca-cola and packaged products are possibly responsible for the mournful decline in the elegant national custom.

Tea-boys are the curse of travel in China. They are to be found in almost every form of conveyance. As their name implies, their work is to supply tea to passengers at exorbitant rates and, for their own personal benefit, to bleed the passengers by every means in their quite considerable power. While disliking them as a class, one cannot but admire their skill in serving tea. They are known as 'Doctors of Tea'. The 'degree' has an ancient history dating back to the Sung Dynasty. During this period there lived an official named Lo Yu, who glorified tea in much the same way as Mr. Ziegfeld 'glorified the American girl'. Among the many feats Lo accomplished during his lifetime was the writing of three thick volumes about the art of brewing tea. When a high official came to his town, Lo visited him and tried to interest him in the development of the tea trade. He talked of the grades of tea, the methods of preparing the various types of tea, the health value of tea, and this and that aspect of the shrub. When the official concluded the interview, he sent Lo a present of 30 cash (the equivalent of about a farthing), said good-bye and called him Doctor of Tea. And Doctors of Tea the tea-boys of China have been ever since. It would be too much to expect the tea-boys of today to be so specialized and learned in their subject. Possibly they know about Lo's famous book, and certainly they know the technical terms for the various types of tea, such as 'Flag and Lance', 'Before Corn Rain', 'Hairy Needle' and so forth. Even laymen know these terms.

Nevertheless the tea-boys deserve their exalted title, not perhaps for their knowledge of the subject, but for their technique in refilling the teapots and in passing and intercepting hot towels, to say nothing of the art of salvaging used tea-leaves and serving them up again after drying. The tea-boys are required to refill the teapots constantly and carefully, lest the customers be hurt by the boiling water. The master tea-boys can refill a pot when standing two or three feet from it and in a way known as 'Phoenix Nodding Three Times'. The shining brass kettle, with a spout three feet in length, is lyrically known as the Phoenix. In executing this pass, the tea-boy first lowers the kettle to the pot, then pours the water and, as the pot is being filled, lifts the kettle three times, and not a drop is ever spilled. A master tea-boy must also be a very skilled catcher. When serving hot towels to his customers, he must be capable of throwing a boiling hot towel over the heads of various passengers in such a way that it lands in the hands of the person requiring it. In returning the towel the customers have not his skill, and so he must be an exceedingly good fielder so as to intercept a badly-thrown towel before it hits an unwary customer.*

When a Chinese is seen asking for a glass of water it may be assumed that he has quite adapted himself to foreign ways, for a typical Chinese gentleman never drinks cold water. He sips boiling

---

* The tea-boys in the theatre are capable of throwing a boiling hot towel from the stalls to any desired person in the dress circle with unerring aim. They do this by balancing the towel on the end of a short stick.

The Hangchow Trader, the junk that rides the bore

tea, green or red. In short, tea drinking is often regarded as the best means of telling a person's character and social standing.

On the journey I am describing, we arrived at Hangchow moderately on time, after a quite uneventful voyage. Hangchow is not, for China, a very ancient city, having been founded in A.D. 606. Before the terrible destruction wrought by the T'ai P'ing rebels, it was one of the cities of China most famous for its wealth and beautiful scenery, the West Lake being specially celebrated for its surrounding hills. It is also noted for its fans, silk, chopsticks and scissors.

With the coming of the motor-road things have greatly changed, and Hangchow has become a popular tourist centre; so I did not stay at the Lake Side Luxury Hotel, which I knew would be full of cocktail-drinking, week-end trippers. Instead, I went to the Chao Ch'in Lu Sze, or Monastery of Manifest Congratulations, which was built during the reign of the Wu-Yüeh Kings of Hangchow in the year A.D. 968.

One of the main reasons for this trip was to enable me to ride the Hangchow Bore in a junk, and to make a detailed study of the Hangchow Trader, a most picturesque junk specially designed for its purpose. The best place to do this was from the sea wall of the ancient town of Haining, twenty-eight miles from the Hangchow City Gate. The distance across country is less, and, since the next day the motor buses were hopelessly full, I set out by wheelbarrow. The wheelbarrows of Chekiang are vastly superior to those of the interior. They are not only of better design, but are larger and carry a far greater load. They are, however, broader at the shafts, and this causes more strain on the coolies who push them. A full capacity load consists of three passengers a side, with their legs dangling down; but, if, as in my case, only one passenger is carried, the driver balances his barrow with the wheel tilted over at such an astonishing angle to the vertical as to constitute almost a direct challenge to the laws of gravity.

The junkmen say that there are three wonders of the world in China: the demons of Tungchow, the thunder of Lungchow, and the great bore of Hangchow. The third they say is the greatest of all.

Nearly everything in the province of Chekiang, from the Bridge of Fifty Thousand Ages on the West Lake to the fresh eggs on sale in the shops, is very ancient; and the oldest of all is doubtless the Great Bore of Hangchow. It is first mentioned in history in the fifth century B.C., and there is a local legend which concerns an old statesman of the Wu Kingdom, named Wu Tzŭ-Hsü, who kept on reproving the Emperor for his policy of appeasement. In time the Emperor grew tired of being continually warned about a problematic invasion of the country, and so he ordered his execution.

Wu Tzŭ-Hsü sent for his eldest son and instructed him that after his death he should cut out his father's eyes and hang them on the East Gate of the city, so that he might see the advancing forces which he predicted would come: 'and,' said the old statesman, 'wrap up my body in the skin of a fish, and I will come in twice daily on the tide to discomfort the Emperor'.

His words came true; the country of Wu was conquered soon afterwards by Yüeh; and it is said that from the day of Wu's death the tide of the Ch'ien T'ang River has grown higher and higher, and that many and many a time the body of that revengeful old statesman has been seen riding in on a huge white horse on the tide, to avenge himself by flooding the country. In desperation, temples in his honour were built up and down the river in an attempt to appease his spirit. Posthumous honours were heaped upon him, sacrifices were offered, letters were written to him and thrown into the river; but it was all too late.

About 400 B.C., the bore was described by the philosopher, Chuang Chou, as being 'like a high mountain, its crest as high as a house, its sound like thunder, its onward rush sufficient to move the heavens and to wash the face of the sun'. As prayers, libations, incense and prostrations all proved fruitless, the local people, unable to stand it any longer, memorialized the Throne.

The Emperor of those days emulated the action of Canute—he ordered the bore to stop; but, as it refused to co-operate, he sent 5,000 archers, the best in the country, with orders to fire a volley at the approaching bore. It was the last volley they ever fired, for they were swept inland into the country and never seen again.

There was only one thing to be done, and they did it. They built a wall. The wall they built was 120 miles long and at Haining 26 feet

Hangchow Trader

high, and for about 1,200 years this wall has protected the millions of people who live in the vicinity of Hangchow Bay.

Facing the sea, Hangchow Bay, 60 miles wide, forms a funnel narrowing to 9 miles. As the rising tide comes in, the funnel naturally narrows the water in the bay and changes it as it advances from a shallow stream to one of considerable depth. Shelters for the junks have been built at various points on the wall to protect them from the force of the bore, and to deflect its approach. These consist of two curving buttresses, about 1,000 feet apart, built out some 30 to 40 feet from the sea wall, and bordered with piling. The wall here between the buttresses is in the form of shelves or platforms, 6 to 8 feet high and extending 20 feet out. The sea-junks come in at high water and are secured to the top of the wall. They exchange cargo with the riverine junks bound for the Grand Canal. As the tide goes out they settle on the shelves.

Then in comes the bore. It can be seen as a thin white streak across the horizon, and its roar can be heard for an hour before it arrives. It is followed by the junks riding in on the after-rush. The wave from the south-east joins that from the east, and nearer and nearer comes the rising water, growing higher and higher; and then with a deafening crash it strikes the outer buttresses and rises to a height of some 15 feet, with a rebound from the wall raising it to 20 or even 30 feet. The white, roaring, bubbling wave at this point breaks into a crest, and with the advance of the tide through the ever-narrowing funnel the crest grows even higher, until it reaches its maximum at the Junk shelter at Haining Pagoda.

Then pandemonium breaks loose from the junks on the shelves. Gongs and drums are banged, and in the midst of this appalling din crackers are fired. They bang and splutter in all directions and add very much to the general excitement. The madly yelling junk-men fend off their boats from the stone wall and then smartly slip their mooring ropes, are afloat in an instant and, bobbing about like cockle shells, are on their way to Hangchow in the wake of the bore. They usually do the twenty-three miles in about two hours. After passing the Pagoda at Haining, the crest of the wave diminishes and finally disappears entirely some ten miles further up river, where there is a width of two miles. Accustomed as I am to thrilling ex-periences, I can still look back on the riding of the Great Bore of Hangchow in a junk as one of my most cherished memories.

Before leaving Hangchow I visited three temples, including the temple of Ts'ang Shên, the God of Letters, who lived about 4,600 years ago, and that of Chu Yi, a God of Literature. To him I made an offering of an ink slab and a new pen, in the hope that it would im-prove my standard of writing. The whimsical Chu Yi has always been a favourite of mine. He is a Taoist Deity, who is said to have lived as a man in Szechuan during the T'ang Dynasty. He equals in authority the three rulers of Heaven, and controls the earth and sea, both very responsible jobs. He always assists those seeking office or testing their abilities in the public examinations. He is invariably depicted as holding a pen and a scroll, on which appear four charac-ters meaning, 'Heaven decides literary success'—which is just about true. Despite his great powers and considerable ability he is a modest god; indeed, he used continually to weep at his own unworthiness; and, when a beautiful princess fell in love with him and conducted him to heaven, he made a speedy return to earth because he wished to study the classics.

Another interesting temple is the one which marks the tomb of Yao Fei, who lived in the twelfth century and is still one of China's national heroes. For some curious reason it is also known as the Temple of the Four Traitors, the most famous of whom was Ts'ao Ts'ao, the most hated man in Chinese history. Although Ts'ao Ts'ao is popularly regarded as being a bad minister and an unscrupulous traitor, actually he does not seem to have been as bad as he has been painted. He was, amongst other things, a great martinet. Many stories are told of the strictness of his discipline. As an instance of this it is said that, when he was leading his army against his foes, he ordered his soldiers to keep away from the rice fields in order to prevent injury to the standing crops. Decapitation, he said, should be the only punishment for persons who disobeyed the order.

All went well until a rabbit made an untimely appearance on the narrow path, causing Ts'ao's horse to gallop away from the road and dash into a rice field. After some time he managed to regain control of his horse and brought it back to the road. A section of the rice crop on the field had been damaged by the trampling horse, and Ts'ao had violated his own orders. Drawing a sword, he announced that he had sentenced himself to death by decapitation. His staff rushed to the scene and prevented his self-punishment, pleading that it was only an accident. 'Orders are orders,' he insisted. Heeding their pleadings, however, he reduced his sentence to, 'Having his hair cut off'.

From Hangchow I went by the various creeks to Shaohsing in one of the deservedly famous foot-boats, the lightning expresses of China. They are long and slender, though by no means light boats, and are said to be the direct descendants of the well-known Post Boats of the T'ang Dynasty; indeed, even until comparatively recent times they were used for the carriage of mails, and later for the express letter service when it was inaugurated. Today, however, their main purpose is the rapid transport of passengers and light luggage. What makes them unpopular is that they are often used by agents when collecting rents. Human nature in China much resembles its European counterpart.

The boat is strengthened by seven bulkheads, the centre one being exactly amidships. From the after bulkhead to the stern the deck is flush with the gunwale and is exclusively used by the oarsman. Two midship wells, with a half bulkhead in each, serve for the passengers, who sit on the bottom of the boat or lie down, as they may desire. The mat roofing is in three parts, which can on fine days be slid back, allowing the passengers to enjoy the fresh air; and on rainy days the boat can be entirely closed in.

The creek routes through which we had to travel were very narrow and infested with robbers. For this reason my boatman insisted on leaving the mat roof behind, and made me lie flat on my face covered entirely with straw, on the bottom of the boat. As an additional precaution he hired a fat lady (for whom I had to pay) to sit on top of the straw and of me. Thus camouflaged, he said, it gave the impression that the boat was an innocent trader.

By stretching things a little it might perhaps be said that the foot-boat resembles a Thames punt, in that the passengers lie out in comparative comfort, and both craft have about the same amount of free-board. Here, however, the resemblance ceases.

The craft is, of course, remarkable for its unusual method of propulsion. Its entire propelling equipment consists of an oar and a four-foot paddle. The oar is shipped on the starboard side and is operated by the oarsmen's feet, as shown on page 27, while the paddle is used on the port side to supplement the oar and to steer. A rudder is provided, but is seldom used. The tiller is short and is operated by movements of the oarsman's back. Indeed, to watch these boats in operation is to believe that it is the one craft in the world that provides the maximum amount of human propulsion for the minimum of effort.

With an almost indescribable movement of his feet, the oarsman works his long oar backwards and forwards, even causing it to feather as it skims forward over the water for the next stroke. Bracing himself against his back rest and bringing up his legs, his knees nearly touching his chin, he puts his whole weight into the stroke, and sends the boat forward at a rapid rate. The movements are repeated quite quickly.

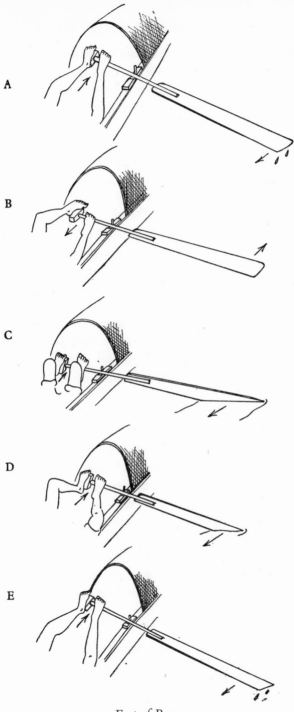

A

B

C

D

E

Feet of Rower

The mechanics employed in returning the oar for the stroke are very interesting. What seems so remarkable is the fact that the oarsman steers and considerably augments his speed with the paddle, yet often does so without appearing to synchronize the action of feet and arms.

The method of rowing might, on paper, seem clumsy and slow; but it is quite amazing how powerful it is in operation. Experienced oarsmen are so nonchalant in their performance that the oar appears to come back to the beginning of the stroke of its own volition. Actually, however, the oar is feathered by both feet and is drawn back to the body by the dexterous use of the big toe of the left foot. The endurance of the oarsmen is quite phenomenal; some have been known to row for twenty-four hours. A trip from Hangchow to Shanghai, 150 miles away, has been recorded in thirty-six hours.

The hulls of many of these boats are painted throughout their length, and here the shipwrights display their artistic ability, and their knowledge of history, religion and mythology, on vividly painted panels. Here may be seen pictures of gods and goddesses, mountains and trees, gardens and flowers, ladies and children, sages admiring the moon, poets seated in pavilions, travellers on hills and fishermen in boats. The more modern craft, however, are painted green with a red conventional device at bow and stern.

There is a grotesque air of ease and leisure about these boatmen. Shaded by an ample paper umbrella, stepped in a bamboo socket, they kick their way along while cooking, eating, smoking, conversing with their passengers, and even playing the flute, without reducing speed. They appear to have an air of superiority over those who toil with their hands. Unhappily, the days of these nimble little boats are numbered. The march of science in the shape of the diesel-driven launch is able to do all a foot-boat can do, and very much more besides.

If Shaohsing, one of the principal cities of Chekiang, had no other claim to fame, it would doubtless find sufficient glory in the fact that it is the burial place of the great Emperor Yü, who traditionally lived and died about the time of Abraham. The wonderful system of

Foot Boat

waterways for which the fertile Shaohsing plain is famous is attributed to him.

Marco Polo, when he visited the neighbourhood, found enough canals to cause him to exclaim: 'Here is the Venice of China.' Until quite recently there were no roads in this part of Chekiang, and the city could be reached by boat only; even now, practically all commerce depends on the slow-moving boats on the canals, which run in all directions.

When we think of Shaohsing, we think at once of its wine. When we talk of wine, we mean only that from Shaohsing. In about 2205 B.C., the Jade Girl, who, before her entry into the court of the Emperor Yü as an Imperial Concubine, was the servant of a goddess in the distant western paradise, is said to have brought from there the formula for making wine. This important secret she imparted to one I Ti at the Emperor's court. The legend is that, when I Ti first produced the drink, he invited a group of friends to sample it. While the latent qualities of the beverage were generally acknowledged, it was felt that something was still lacking. Someone suggested that human blood might be added. Taking his advice, I Ti went out, met a scholar and killed him for his blood, which he added to the wine. There was, however, only little improvement. Next he went out and met a ferocious pugilist, whom he likewise killed, and whose blood also went into the mixture. Yet another person, a poor, shivering beggar, was similarly sacrificed for his blood: and so the wine was perfected. But the ghosts of the three martyrs could not forget their contribution to the product and still continue to hover over wine parties. The scholar appears first, and usually under his influence the party starts in a gentle, leisurely manner, with everybody remaining very polite. Next comes the pugilist, and the influence of this ghost accounts for the noisy and quarrelsome nature of the party, as the feast progresses. Finally the beggar appears, and the guests, drunk, with their vigour spent, become exhausted, spiritless and shivering.

The tradition is that when the Emperor Yü, whose fame is more commonly associated with water than with wine, tasted the new drink, he found it so attractive that he feared excessive indulgence would overpower his senses and cause him to become neglectful of the duties of his high office. He accordingly became a teetotaller and banished I Ti from his court.

Shaohsing lies in the middle of a network of streams and lakes of unusually clear water, which, descending from the surrounding mountains, filters through many layers of sand and gravel. Water is one of the most important factors that go to make the quality of a wine. For this reason Shaohsing wine has become the best and most popular in China and is virtually the standard alcoholic beverage in the country.

Shaohsing is also noted for the excellence of its cormorants. The cormorant is, of course, the hereditary enemy of the fish, and its undoubted skill in catching them has been turned to the service of man and supplements ordinary methods of fishing.

The female cormorant lays three to nine eggs in the first and eighth moons. Those laid in the first season are the only ones retained; those of the second season are not used because the weather is too cold. The cormorant is a careless mother, and it is, therefore, usual to entrust the actual sitting to hens. On hatching, the chicks are placed in baskets filled with cotton wool and kept in a warm place. They are fed on a mixture of bean curd and raw eels' flesh in equal parts.

A cormorant can easily be tamed. At two months, their training commences. A string is tied to one leg, and the other end is fastened to a small stake in the bank. They are made to go into the water at the word of command, the trainer uttering a distinctive call and using a light bamboo stick to enforce his orders. Inasmuch as the birds work only when hungry, they are kept in a constant state of semi-starvation. Small fish are thrown in for them to practise on, and these are eagerly seized. They are then recalled by the trainer, who employs a different call, and are forced to obey by means of the string. When they readily obey, they are rewarded with small fish. The training period lasts for a month or more, then they are given practical experience afloat under the supervision of an old and well-trained bird. The birds are well disciplined and any show of insubordination is immediately checked by having their legs tied by a short string in the form of a loop. A disobedient bird can thus at any moment be hoisted bodily out of the water on the end of the trainer's long bamboo. Sometimes a bird will get an idle fit and swim about playfully instead of fishing. In such an event it is at once recalled to duty by its master, who strikes the water with his pole and shouts at the culprit. The latter invariably accepts the rebuke at once and dives after its prey.

Except to its owner the cormorant is not a docile or friendly bird. Nevertheless they receive most distinguished names: Ancestor of Thunder, Reclining Dragon, Sweet Dew, Blessed Plum, Unblemished Rectitude, Wavy Snow, and so on.

The secret of successful cormorant fishing is, of course, that each bird has a rattan or string tied round its throat, which prevents it swallowing anything but small fish. The trained birds sit on perches until instructed by name to jump into the water. In a very short space of time the bird will return to the surface with a fish in its beak, when it is immediately relieved of its catch by the fisherman. At the risk of being suspected of introducing a fishing story I must add that, when a cormorant is called upon to retrieve a fish beyond its capabilities, a colleague will be detailed to assist in the operation. It is very remarkable, too, that although many different boats may be fishing nearby, these sagacious birds always return to their own masters. The number of cormorants carried by each boat varies, but the usual number is eighteen. On a good day, the fishermen affirm, eighteen cormorants will deliver 250 lbs. of fish.

After fishing for two or three hours the birds are allowed a rest, and at the end of the day the ring round each of their necks is removed, and they are permitted to fish on their own account. It is interesting to note that the fish are always taken by the cormorant head foremost. If the cormorant makes a mistake, the fish is tossed into the air, caught head downwards and immediately swallowed.

Friar Odoric, who travelled extensively in China between the years 1317 and 1330, is said to be the first European to give a description of cormorant fishing in China.

*   *   *

From Shaohsing, its wine and cormorants, I went to Ningpo.

Ningpo is full of the voices of the past and is probably at least 1,200 years old. The junkmen say that the first Ming Emperor gave Ningpo its present name. The inhabitants, being a maritime people, did not like the former name of Mingchow, because of some unpleasant association; and the Emperor came to the rescue and suggested a change. 'There is a city,' he said in effect, 'named Tinghai Ting, "Settle the Sea"; when the sea goes down the waves are at peace; why not call your city Ningpo, "Peaceful Wave"?' So Ningpo it has been ever since.

The city stands on the River Yung, twelve miles from the sea, and about ninety miles south of Shanghai. It is at the point of convergence of an extensive river and canal system, and at the same time occupies a commanding position with reference to the well-known Chusan Archipelago. Owing partly to the wealth and the enterprising character of its people and partly to its favourable position, Ningpo is one of the most celebrated places in China for the extent and variety of its pelagic fishing industry.

*   *   *

From Ningpo I went to Ting Hai T'ing in the Chusan Archipelago in a Chicken Boat. Launches of this type take their name from the fact that they carry live chickens in huge baskets from the islands to the mainland, and on the return journey, believe it or not, carry live chickens in huge baskets from the mainland to the islands.

There is a daily service, weather permitting, and the Chicken Boats are always crowded with passengers and loaded down to the gunwales with their effects. They often have two decks, and from the upper deck tables, chairs, bicycles and wardrobes are festooned along the ship's side on short ropes. When the launch rolls, they all dip deep into the sea; and, when she heels the other way, they are jerked into the air.

The Chinese are always on the move. Country people from the mainland are constantly going to the islands to buy rice, and an equal number of people from the islands go to the mainland for the same purpose. All the passengers have produce to sell, and all seem to travel the longest possible distance to dispose of it. Crowded aboard are also trussed-up pigs, baskets of fruit and piles of vegetables. Old men, young men, old women, young women, babies in arms, children and grandmothers hobbling on bound feet, everybody is huddled together in such numbers that there is barely room to stand, much less sit; and, directly the launch gets out to sea, everybody is sea-sick.

Hawkers, the only people on board able to move, try to avoid stepping on the passengers while they sell sweets, groundnuts, oranges and sunflower seeds. The shells and orange peel soon form a thick carpet. Hour succeeds hour, as the launch pants on with what seems to be hardly steerage way. Quiet is not for a moment to be thought of; and, strange to say, no one seems to desire it. Amid the unending clamour of crying babies, protesting livestock and the clatter and noisy expectoration of the wakeful, many of the passengers manage miraculously to sleep while lying, sitting and even standing, their heads swaying in oblivion.

When after four or five hours' steaming the launch arrives at
Ting Hai T'ing, stowage is broken, and down the gangway they all
pour, while an equal number of newcomers press forward in an
attempt to get on board for the return journey before the disembark-
ing passengers have left. Pushing, shoving, spitting and shouting,
they wriggle their way in and out, until almost simultaneously the
outgoing and incoming passengers reach their objectives. The
launch whistles to recall most of the crew, who have gone ashore to
smuggle drugs, and after what seems an interminable delay the return journey to the mainland begins.

CHAPTER 2

The Chusan Archipelago

THE Chusan Archipelago lies about twenty-five miles off Ning-po. The total number of islands in the group is over one hundred, but Chusan gives its name to the whole area. It is nearly twenty-five miles long and ten broad. Ting Hai T'ing is the capital. Navigation is difficult throughout the Archipelago on account of the very strong current, which runs at seven or eight knots and is extremely variable owing to the numerous windings it has to make.

Although I had considerable experience with the Chusan fishermen working the Yangtze Estuary, I had never seen them in their own habitat; so I was most anxious to visit the Archipelago, and especially Sing ki Mun at its eastern extremity. This is said to be the second largest fishing port in the Far East and the fourth largest in the world. Unhappily, when I was free to go there, the whole group of islands was so over-run with pirates, bandits and kidnappers that even I would not entertain the risk involved; but, as my days in China were fast drawing to a close, I came to the conclusion that, come what may, I must make an attempt to get as close to Sing ki Mun as possible.

From Ting Hai T'ing, therefore, I set out on foot, accompanied by my faithful secretary, for the Roman Catholic Mission on the hill overlooking the harbour, to seek the advice of the priest. Father Givry belonged to a French Order; he was a Breton with a strong nautical background, and he had been out in China for the greater part of his life. His parish consisted of the whole Archipelago, and he spent most of his time in a junk, which he had equipped as a hospital ship, in which he cruised among the units of the fishing fleet. His colleague did the same from Sing ki Mun. In consequence they were much respected not only by the fishermen, but by all the pirates and other wrong-doers in the Archipelago.

Before retiring for the night, the Father told me about the unhappy conditions then obtaining in Chusan. During the late war, he said, the Americans had raised and trained a force of guerillas. These men were recruited from the most experienced Communist bandits in Kwangtung and had been equipped with the most modern arms, the intention being that they should harry the Japanese in the rear and also rescue bailed-out American airmen. The U.S. crews carried, sewn to their clothing, attractive notices in Chinese saying that, in consideration of their being delivered to the U.S. lines, a reward of a thousand gold dollars per head would be paid on demand.

So lucrative and simple did the business become that the guerrillas gave up harrying the Japanese and made the search for American airmen a full-time occupation, going so far as to shoot some of them down themselves.

These happy conditions could not last for ever, and one day the terrible news came through that the Japanese had capitulated. Stopping only long enough to draw their pay to date, and without waiting for the formalities of 'Lend Lease' or 'Rehabilitation Grants to Distressed Peoples', they made off with their arms and ammunition—a most dangerous fighting force. They had the whole country to choose from, but selected Chusàn as a base because to a life of robbery, murder, rape, kidnapping and drug-smuggling, they could add piracy as a side-line.

They soon became such a menace to the mainland that the Government was forced to take action. However, all the troops sent over to exterminate them turned over to the bandits, and the situation became infinitely worse. There was only one thing to be done, and the Government did it. They made the head bandit Chief of Police of the Island, with a proviso that he was to restrain the activities of his followers to reasonable proportions. He carried out his part of the bargain with praiseworthy effect, according to his lights; but it is difficult for a bandit to lead a godly, righteous and sober life.

The result of all this was that, try as they might to be good citizens, the bandits would from time to time, and at quite unpredictable times, suddenly break out and indulge in a wild outbreak of rapacity and lawless practices.

The Father said that one of these ferments had just taken place, and so it was reasonable to suppose that this would be followed by a period of rest and recuperation. Because of this he thought I should perhaps be justified in trying to get through the zone of their activities. He suggested that I should travel in disguise, with one of his converts as a guide, and stay with his colleague at the Mission in Sing ki Mun. This was good news beyond my wildest dreams.

I slept the night in a bedroom of the Mission used by the Father as his dressing-room, and before getting into bed I surreptitiously tried on the clerical robes I found in the wardrobe. At first sight they presented a heaven-sent disguise; but, when I had finished doing up the innumerable buttons of his cassock, I found the bottom one barely below my knees, and as a concealment of identity it would not have misled a Seventh Day Adventist.

The next morning well before daylight I set out in the costume of a fisherman, with no luggage beyond my sketch book and a pencil carried in the mail-bag—to be described later. I had decided that I could not permit my secretary to accept the risk of capture by bandits; and so, very greatly against his will, I left him behind and set out with the convert as my only companion. We stopped for the night at my guide's home. Here, finding a suitable bed for me presented some difficulty. It is customary for elderly Chinese gentlemen of the old school to keep their coffins in their bedrooms. This fact prompted me to ask if any of the inmates or neighbours had a coffin available and, if so, could they oblige me with the loan of it for the night. This seemed a very practical suggestion, and several old men from the village came along and offered to place their coffins at my disposal. I selected one in red lacquer with highly-carved stags and cranes representing official honours and longevity. For reasons outside the scope of this narrative, Chinese coffins are very much larger than those used in other parts of the world. They are more or less standard in shape, the body being slightly rounded at the sides and foot and formed in a curve sloping upwards and forwards at the head. This particular coffin had also a curved roof, which fitted into grooves in the coffin body. Swathing myself tightly in the straw, with my note-books beside me and with the lid of the coffin half shut to keep out the draught, I slept the sleep of utter exhaustion.

The next night we reached the mission at Sing ki Mun. The church was picturesquely sited on a hill commanding the harbour. A large statue of the Virgin Mary on the roof was holding up a hand in disapproval in the direction of P'u T'u, the sacred island of the Buddhists.

I was received with the greatest hospitality at the Mission, but the Father gave me clearly to understand that, if I wished to stay more than one night there, he must report my arrival and the purpose of my visit to the head bandit. He advised that I should turn back; but, having come so far, I felt it would be unthinkable to retreat with the end almost in sight. I therefore agreed to accept his condition. In this I was influenced by Father Givry's opinion that the bandits were enjoying a well-earned rest, and might not therefore take too serious a view of my activities.

I did not sleep much my first night at Sing ki Mun, for, looking out of my bedroom window I was absolutely fascinated by the scene below me, where, in the pretty, land-locked harbour, lay 2,000 fishing junks at anchor in the moonlight. I could see small boats going round the junks with shadowy figures in them. The sound of a one-string fiddle and the clanging of a cymbal with its distinctive note came to me across the water. Finally it died away altogether, and then in the grey shadow of the dawn, as I stood by the open window, I could hear the bustle and chatter of the junkmen preparing for sea.

At breakfast I asked the Father about the particular noises I had heard. He laughed: 'Do you mean to tell me,' he said, 'that you have been studying junks all these years and do not know what that means?' 'No,' I said, 'I don't, but I should like to.' Then he told me that these were the 'ladies of the town' going the round of the junks, and he went on to describe the life of these poor, simple sailors.

The fishermen of the Chusans are a very frugal folk, and have many very fine qualities. Like all good sailors, they start their careers as children, and they live a life of almost unbelievable hardship. As a result they do not live long. Rheumatism, lung trouble and trachoma, as well as poisoned wounds, take a very heavy toll. They are charitable, helping each other in distress; and they are superstitious beyond belief. It can with truth be said that probably no class of people in the world is under so much bondage to superstition and credulity as the fishermen of the Chusans. Their life is one incessant warfare against devils, fairies, dragons, evil spirits and a multitude of snakes, monkeys, foxes and so on. Every disease has its presiding demon; so has every part of the body. Happily all the activities of these malignant spirits can be circumvented in a variety of practical ways. Each must, of course, be propitiated, and each requires a different technique. For example, the fishermen believe that high winds are caused by noxious spirits, which lie in wait to catch the junks. For this reason, when a gale is at its worst, it is the custom to throw overboard a small paper junk in order that the angry spirits of the water may be deceived into thinking that this is the junk which they are pursuing, and thus allow the real one to escape.

The next morning a message came to say that I was wanted at the bandit's headquarters. The priest, very kindly, offered to accompany me. I must confess that it was not a very happy walk; I carried over my shoulder the bag containing my note-books and sketching materials, for I felt that if I were to be captured I would rather have them with me. When we arrived at the headquarters, which was nothing more than a large room in a picturesque farmhouse, we were halted by two lounging sentries in nondescript uniforms, and at length were ushered into the presence of the great man.

He asked my name and several quite relevant questions, and on the whole seemed prepared to be friendly. Then a man who had taken no part in the conversation, and had been sitting meanwhile in the semi-darkness at the back of the room, came forward and asked if I had been stationed at Cheng-ling-ki. When I replied that I had, he said with a very broad grin, 'I have heard of this man: I was responsible for the looting of his house.' He then went on to describe with perfect accuracy what had happened on that occasion. I shall come to this in the next chapter.

The unidentified man then said that, although it was for him all a part of the day's work, yet, now that he had met me, he felt sorry for the inconvenience he had caused. He wished, he said, to make amends, and so suggested that not only should I be allowed to stay in the island for two weeks, but that I should be entertained at dinner that night.

The subsequent party was a great success. We drank toasts in samshu and vodka; and, although it has never happened to me before or since, I have only very hazy recollections of what took place or when the party broke up except from hearsay the next morning, when I received a call from the unidentified bandit who came to express his profound regrets for the events of the preceding evening.

Actually I did not feel very proud of my own share in the festivities; and, when I mentioned this, he hastened to point out that the conviviality of the party had not been the reason for his apology. He had been told, he said, by one of the servants that in the early hours of the morning his 'mean and insignificant carcase' had been found lying on the floor under my 'honourable and exalted body'. The unhappy conclusions, he continued, to be drawn from the relative positions of the prostrate forms could be little else than that he as the host had succumbed earlier than had I, his guest. This, according to Chinese notions of politeness, was a gross breach of the etiquette of hospitality, in that he should have been attending to the desires of his guest, a duty he had obviously not been in a position to do. If, he concluded, the position of the bodies had been exactly reversed, all would have been well, and there would have been no reason for self-reproach.

Such is the external decorum in China to which all, even bandits, seek to aspire.

Thanks to these kind-hearted and hospitable bandits, I was able to spend a very happy and instructive time out in the junks of the Chusans.

* * *

The fishermen of the Chusans are rough and tough and are capable of enduring great hardship. In the winter they have to battle with the fury of the China Sea, possibly the worst in the world. Fogs, which are frequent from March to July, render navigation still more dangerous. Sometimes the weather is so bad that the men are unable to get a hot meal for days on end. In the summer they have to contend with the terrific heat, and then comes the typhoon season. They are at sea sometimes for three months on end; food and water are taken out to them on the fishing grounds, and their catch is brought in either by ice boats or salt boats.

After being boiled in a concoction of mangrove bark the nets are steeped in pig's blood or wood oil to dye and preserve them. In the hot summer, nets are tanned twice during the month, but during the rest of the year once each month will suffice. The ink-fish net has the general shape of a large conical bag with two wings, and it is attached to a long bamboo pole.

As with most sea-going fishing junks in China, the eyeball of the oculus is set low in the white, so as to be on the alert to observe the fish, whereas in the trading junk the eye looks straight ahead so as to perceive and avoid distant perils, invisible to mortal sight. This is the very heart of the oculus country, so it is not surprising to find that in the old days even steamers trading on the coast had eyes painted on their bows and paddle boxes as a concession to Chinese ideas, their use being defended with the remark, ' 'Spose no got eye, how fashion can see; suppose no can see, how fashion can walkee?'

The old *Changwo*, a Jardine steamer, had a spoon bow, and carried large eyes on the bow like a sea-going junk. During the night on one occasion, when she was in port, a party of convivial humorists from a British gunboat lying alongside painted a gigantic pair of horn-rimmed spectacles round the oculi. This fashion in eye-wear, so long established in China, had only just become popular in America. Nevertheless, old or new, the scandalized Chinese crew painted them out the next morning.

The fishermen do not own their junks but hire them from middle-men, who require that they sell their catch only to them, at the buyers' prices. These simple, hardworking fishermen cannot read or write, they know nothing of political economy or the laws of capital and labour; they just manage to eke out a bare existence and no more; and they are never out of the iron grip of the profiteer, the middleman and the shark.

The convert and I eventually returned the way we had come, but this time under official bandit protection. While passing through one of the villages, we noticed a great commotion. It turned out to be my secretary resisting arrest. He had so often in the past rescued me from embarrassing situations that it was a pleasure for me to be able to do the same for him. It appeared that he had been unable to stand the strain of waiting, and had come out to look for me.

Whenever I look at a map of China, my eye instinctively travels to the Chusans, and then I always wonder what has happened to my charming friends the bandits.

CHAPTER 3

Trouble, Bandits and a Flood

To appreciate the events referred to by the unidentified bandit of the last chapter calls for a somewhat lengthy digression; and it is necessary to go back to the unhappy days of Chiang Kai-shek's rise to power.

In January, 1927, a mob of workmen, incited by revolutionary propaganda, rushed the British Concession at Hankow. Landing parties from the British gunboats and local volunteers had been ordered not to fire, so as to avoid 'incidents'. Shortly afterwards the British Concession at Kiukiang was rushed in the same way. Both these raids were directed by the Russian advisers of the Chinese Government at Hankow, who aimed at destroying British trade and prestige.

While these demonstrations of 'National Aspiration' were going on, various war lords were running a perplexing series of civil wars for private gain. These Tuchüns, as they were known, were military strong-men, sometimes bandits, who, by extortionate practices, were able to hire mercenaries or conscript workers to keep them in control of various sources of revenue.

General Pai Chung-hsi was fighting a private war in Chekiang, while the Hunanese Communist-controlled troops entered Nanking and began an attack on foreign residences, consulates, and business property. The killing, looting and destruction went on for several days, and the foreigners were saved only by the British cruiser *Emerald*, which put up a barrage round the area.

Chiang Kai-shek subsequently entered Nanking and established a Government there in opposition to the Nationalist Government at Hankow. During these operations the naval forces of the Hankow Government, represented by an obsolete cruiser and three gunboats, and the Nanking Government fleet, which consisted of two wooden sloops and a railway train ferry steamer with a battery of field guns lashed to its decks, carried out a long-range, intermittent duel, which lasted for two days. Although neither side managed to hit the other, they caused some anxiety to those of us who had to pass between the warring fleets. The Hankow Government Navy had not been paid for six months, and at the end of the action turned over to the Government of Nanking.

Feng Yu-hsiang in the north, lately returned from a visit to Moscow, was at the same time conducting an even larger and more active civil war with the south. Not to be outdone, the ex-bandit, Chang Tso-lin, now a war lord, joined in the so-called fighting by attacking both sides with complete impartiality.

All these invading bodies of unreliable troops, operating from widely diffused parts of the country, would sweep down on each other and, seemingly, converge on Hankow, where I was then stationed. Although these rabble armies did an incredible amount of damage, and killed numbers of innocent people, there was little actual fighting, and none at all when it was raining. Chinese soldiers are never very partial to fighting in the rain, and as to their lack of resistance to bandits and robbers, a clue to their attitude is to be found in one of the age-old Chinese adages, which says, 'Of the hundred methods of military strategy, to run away early is the best.' All the troops wore the same uniform, and were distinguished only by the arm-bands they wore. Whole army corps would transfer to an opposing war lord without notice during a battle, which was often exceedingly embarrassing for the staff officers concerned un-less, of course, the troops could be bribed to come back by promises of pay (which was always in arrears) or by being allowed to loot a town *en route*.

It was a common sight at that time in Hankow to see the invading troops, when not quite sure of their allegiance, wearing the arm-bands of both sides. This practice was always followed by the local police and civil servants, until the new army had established itself, when the arm-bands of the defeated army would be handed in. The vanquished general was always allowed to escape with his women, loot, and personal retainers.

So complicated did the situation become that even the Russian advisers, headed by one Borodin and his Communist associates, could not understand what was happening in the muddle they had themselves created. This was made even more difficult for them when they were receiving conflicting instructions from the Third International in Moscow, as the result of differences of opinion between Stalin and Trotsky. As if all this were not enough, the situation was further disturbed by internal squabbles within all parties, armies and governments.

Eventually, it became unsafe for a foreigner to walk in the streets of Hankow; and as the outlook was so unpromising, all the European women and children were evacuated. The handful of men who remained were concentrated in the Asiatic Petroleum Company's building.

From this pandemonium of Chinese events I was transferred to take charge of the Middle Yangtze District of the River Inspectorate. This was indeed out of the frying pan into the fire, for, in addition to the various unattached itinerant armies, the whole area was over-run by ruthless Communist bandits. The latter developed a con-siderable degree of organization, and blatantly opened an office in Hankow; that is to say, in the very midst of their enemies. All the Chinese launches paid them a toll before leaving the port, in return for a safe passage up-river. They also insured merchandise, and issued safe conduct passes, not always reliable, to individuals.

To protect themselves from these insatiable marauders, the local country people formed themselves into volunteer bands known as Red Spears. Unhappily, in a short time they became almost as great an anxiety as the bandits themselves; for they were very partial to a little looting and indulged in fights with rival gangs for a division of the spoil, in which burnings and killings were not ruled out.

The customs station at Cheng-ling-ki, my headquarters, was little more than a village, pleasantly situated on a red sandstone bluff close to the river bank. Our large and pleasant house stood on a hillock inside a large compound of about forty acres surrounded by a high wall. There were two entrances, one being at the gate-keeper's lodge and facing the river while the other was at the back of the stables on the land side. Almost from the beginning of history the town of Yochow-fu, about a mile away, has been a key position, for the possession of which rival or revolting armies, factions and lately war lords had struggled.

A small creek afforded shelter to the junks, while there was a fairly good anchorage in the harbour for the occasional steamer. Here there were no consulates or protecting gunboats. Even if there had been, we, foreign officials of the River Inspectorate, were working under the Chinese flag and could not, therefore, accept British gunboat protection. We were quite cut off from the outside world.

With three launches, capable of 'keeping the sea' for three weeks at a time, I had to see that a close watch was kept upon all channels in the district, and to maintain an adequate system of marking them with aids to navigation for the quite considerable river traffic. Any sign of channel change called for an accurate instrumental survey. I had with me Richard Harvey, the only foreign member of my staff, three Chinese officers in charge of the launches, as well as clerks and typists in the office and a considerable number of Repair Yard staff, Light-keepers and, of course, Mr Whong, my ever-faithful secretary, who had been with me for twenty-six years. I could tell a hundred stories about his loyalty, his simple-hearted devotion and his amazing courage. I will give only one.

My wife was very interested in painting Chinese types and had asked me to look out for a colourful, ultra-fashionable type of young girl who would be willing to sit for her.

Soon afterwards I passed in the street two women who seemed adequately to answer the requirements. Mr Whong was with me at the time and I sent him back to ask if the young ladies would be prepared (for a consideration of course) to pose for my wife in her studio. If so, he was to arrange a suitable occasion. I passed on my way and forgot all about the incident.

We had staying with us at the time a very prim missionary and his equally prudish wife, who were almost strangers to us and were on their way to the hill station at Kuling. That evening our guests suddenly left without giving any reason, and it was not for some time afterwards that we discovered the cause of their sudden departure.

It was this. Mr Whong had duly arranged for a meeting with the women and wrote me a note to this effect which he left on the hall table, where it was discovered by the house-boy. He took it to our missionary guests, who were sitting alone in the drawing-room, and asked if the note was for them. The communication, which was quite open, read as follows:

Dear Mr Worcester,

In accordance with your verbal instructions, I am sending two whores to your house tonight. Their honorarium will be five dollars.

Yours faithfully,

Whong-Tze-Yu

On the opposite side of the river the bandits had established a stronghold on the low hills, and there they managed to hold out for many years against the Government troops, who used to fire on them from the safety of the right bank. Our Light-vessel there, which was used to guide shipping into the reach, frequently came in for the attentions of both sides, for, when she hoisted her Chinese colours, she was fired on by the bandits; and when she was 'out of position' and displayed a red flag, she was fired on by the anti-Communist troops.

These bandits had a none too savoury reputation. Their normal and well-known practice was to capture worthwhile individuals and then make demands for huge sums of money as ransom. When this was not at once forthcoming, a finger of the captured person would be cut off and sent by registered post to the next of kin with a note to the effect that further fingers (or the head) would be sent by the next mail if their claims were not met within a reasonable period.

So that I might have as much warning as possible, I soon established friendly relations with the local General. I was able, concurrently, to be apprised of the activities of the bandits through some of my staff, who were recruited from active members of the various bandit organizations on the opposite side of the river. They received the highest pay I could give, and were accorded more than generous leave conditions, so that they might keep their hands in on their profession and at the same time bring back intelligence of the movements and activities of their colleagues.

Stories came in from time to time of their atrocities, but, as the months passed, we grew accustomed to their presence on the opposite bank. A friendly bullet would strike the Custom House from time to time, and red flags would be waved; but these we soon came to regard as in the nature of a desire to keep in touch with us rather than as acts of hostility.

My bandit spies came in to tell me that the gangs had 'retired to study the classics', a phrase then current to denote the end of active operations. Passing steamers were no longer being fired on, and my friend the General felt that the situation had so far improved that he was able to disband a number of his troops. He kept their uniforms, and his pay sheets showed the same number of men; when unfriendly superiors came down on visits of inspection, he borrowed (without my permission) many of my Repair Yard staff, and conscripted others temporarily to bring his forces up to strength.

After a few months of this halcyon calm, and the situation having likewise improved down-river, I thought it was sufficiently safe for my wife and David our son, then aged 7, to join me. They came up by river steamer, bringing with them my polo ponies and David's donkey. We rode each day on the plain, and friends came up to stay for the shooting; for here the whole countryside was teeming with bird life. Wildfowl in particular were abundant—geese, duck, teal, swans, pelican and cranes—also snipe and pheasants.

Although in all my experience of China I had never known such calm, I took the precaution of keeping one launch with steam at half an hour's notice, and a suit-case packed with necessities for immediate evacuation if need be.

Additionally, I devised many different forms of booby trap and burglar alarm. But wild cats, villagers and even I myself kept on setting them off, and that made us jumpy. One variety, however, was a great success. It consisted of various trip wires connected to a mouse trap. A hole was bored in the wooden base to receive a blank cartridge, and a striker was soldered on to the 'break back'. The cheese bait was dispensed with, and one end of the trip wire attached in its place. When, therefore, the trip wire was touched, it released the hook holding the 'break-back' spring and striker, which hit the base of the blank cartridge, and so finally ignited a series of Chinese crackers. Usually these crackers are used to frighten devils away, and I hoped they might have the same effect on any ill-disposed persons climbing the compound wall. The modern Chinese crackers are little cartridges of coarse paper filled with powder and damped clay. The smaller variety are threaded on strings, with a continuous fuse that explodes them one after another. To this Brock's Benefit I added a 'Double-strength noise' cracker, which consisted of a double chamber with double fuse. It explodes a second time high in the air, whence it has been hurled by the first fuse. Another harmless little joke consisted of a skeleton cut out of thick cardboard, threaded on black string, and treated with luminous paint, hung in the dark recess of my clothes cupboard. Above, and out of sight suspended chains were made to rattle by means of strings operated by the opening of the door.

There were small scares from time to time, but these only served to keep us on the alert, and provided exercises for evacuation in an emergency. A minor incident happened one night, when bullets started hitting our house in great profusion; some came through windows on opposite sides of the house. While my wife and the amah were dressing David, and assuring him that this was an ordinary occurrence, I went to the gate-keeper's lodge, now vacant, and gave the signal for evacuation. In quite a short time my assistant, the clerks, draughtsmen and others of my staff had assembled at the rendezvous, and with my wife and David were scurrying down the pathway to the jetty, alongside which lay the duty launch. The bullets were flying high and well above our heads, but by the time we had reached the safety of the launch the firing stopped as suddenly as it had begun. After a short interval we went to sleep on board with loaded rifles handy; but before daylight the amah came to me and said she could stand the strain no longer. All her valuables, she said, were in her room on shore, and she begged me to send someone back to our house to retrieve them. So insistent was she that I set out by myself. She warned me to be careful, as the contents were very fragile.

In the darkness I cautiously crept back to the house, taking cover as far as possible all the way; I scaled the garden wall and cautiously avoiding the trip wires, climbed into the amah's room through the

4

window. All was quiet, the house and village were completely deserted, and after a fairly careful reconnaissance I returned to the launch dragging the amah's heavy box after me.

The amah was delighted at seeing her trunk. 'Now,' I said, 'Amah, I would like to see your valuables, which I might have risked my life to save.' She opened the trunk, and there lay some two hundred ducks' eggs. 'Ducks' eggs?' I said with great annoyance. 'Yes,' she replied. 'I assumed we were going to Hankow, and I need them to give to my friends as presents; they are cheaper here.'

It was some years before I came to appreciate the humour of this.

The next morning we returned to the shore, and in due course the frightened villagers crept back. The cause of the excitement would have delighted the hearts of Messrs Gilbert and Sullivan, and certainly it could not be compared with anything possible outside China.

At this time the Opium Suppression Bureau was strenuously supporting the smugglers. Salt was a Government monopoly, and the Salt Bureau was in active opposition to the Salt Administration (not to be confused with the Salt Gabelle), for the highly profitable privilege of protecting the salt smugglers. The unofficial troops employed by these three powerful Government Departments had all been out on patrol that night, and had made contact with each other in the darkness. All sides thought that they had been attacked by bandits or Red Spears, and had run away at high speed, firing in all directions as they did so.

From a hydrographic point of view we did very well, that spring of 1930. We managed to complete the survey of the Siang River, and were well advanced in the triangulation of the Tung T'ing Lake, a vast undertaking. We looked forward to a wonderful year's work, for the bandits were quiet, the invading troops had disappeared, and even the various governments seemed to have undergone a change of heart. I decided that I could safely leave port on my annual tour of inspection of the District, and so about the end of June I left for up-river in the Customs launch, *Chiangping*.

And then, one wet day in July, without the slightest notice, an organized band of 2,000 Communist bandits entered the village about midday. My wife, Harvey and David were just sitting down to lunch, when my vigilant secretary, Mr Whong, at great personal risk to himself, ran up to the house to give warning. The danger was imminent. Hastily throwing a few necessities into a suitcase, they left the large, rambling grounds of the house through the front gate only a few minutes before the bandits came in over the wall near the stables. They hesitated for a moment in consequence of the 'Brock's Benefit' display alluded to above, which went off to perfection in spite of the rain and, according to my house-boy, added very much to the general confusion, panic and excitement.

Meanwhile the courageous, but by now thoroughly frightened Mr Whong had rushed into the village and into the open door of the first house. Hastily divesting himself of his smart clothes, he donned the garments of a coolie and, after smearing his face with mud, ran as fast as his legs would carry him to a junk banked in on the foreshore. Here he hid down the hold; but it was not long before a party of bandits searched the junk. He lay in the bilges as quiet as a mouse, when suddenly the hatches were removed and a voice said, 'Is anybody down there?' 'No!' replied Mr Whong, whereupon one of the bandits fired a round down the hold, the bullet passing through the bulkhead and missing his head by a few inches. 'Why on earth did you say "No"?' I said to him afterwards. 'Because,' he said, 'I did not want them to find me.' Which, I suppose, was a good enough reason.

After scaling the wall, about fifty bandits burst into the kitchen of our house, soaked to the skin, where they were met by our No. 1 Boy. He welcomed them in, said his mistress was out for a walk, and begged that they would take off their wet clothes, which he would dry in front of the fire. Meanwhile all the other servants were hurrying round providing tea and biscuits and in quite a short space of time a 'Mad Hatter's' tea-party was well in progress.

This delay saved the three foreigners, for it gave them just sufficient time to reach the waterfront. The 'stand-by' launch had been surveying in the harbour and had, unfortunately, grounded on a sandbank; so when the refugees arrived at the jetty it was only to find that in the whole wide harbour there was no craft of any sort to provide shelter or means of escape except one small motor-boat belonging to the Customs. The engine of this at first refused to start, but after ten minutes or so of cranking it suddenly burst forth and, with the three of them and the amah on board, made off down-river just as the bandits began to penetrate to the waterfront. They started firing on the motor-boat as it disappeared out of the harbour. There was no safety nearer than 200 miles, the motor-boat had sufficient petrol for only fifty miles, and it was pelting with rain.

But miracles do sometimes happen; for after they had proceeded little more than five miles a British gunboat, H.M.S. *Widgeon*, came in sight and picked up the refugees.

Meanwhile the bandits searched the house and commenced looting in earnest. I was told afterwards that the skeleton in my clothes cupboard, already referred to, had caused the greatest panic and had resulted in my clothes being saved—but not for long, for they were destroyed in the subsequent fire.

The gunboat continued on its voyage up-river and soon came under fire from the bandits. My wife and the amah were given the hospitality of the Captain's cabin beneath the bridge, and a stoker was told off to look after and amuse David. Soon the Captain's head appeared through the trunkway in the deckhead, 'Don't be alarmed,' he yelled, '*Widgeon* is going to reply to the bandits with her main armament,' and, as he spoke, the three-pounder on the deck above opened fire. David and his stoker escort had foolishly been looking through the scuttle when a bullet came through and lodged in the stoker's shoulder. Freed from supervision, David ran out on deck to retrieve some of the bullets hitting the outside of the deck-house.

For three hours the fusilade continued. When finally the action broke off, my wife saw some of our belongings being loaded on to my ponies; David's donkey 'Biddy' kicking to the last.

H.M.S. *Widgeon* carried on to Changsha; but at nightfall my wife, David and Harvey were put on board a passing river steamer bound for Hankow.

While all these events were happening, I was at Shasi on my way back to Cheng-ling-ki, and on my return I was more than astonished to find most of the village in ruins and deserted and my house in flames. My staff had fled with the villagers, and I could find no one to tell me where my wife and David had gone or what had happened to them. I therefore pushed on down to Hankow, steaming through the night, and found them staying with friends, none the worse for their narrow escape.

The bandits captured several of my light-keepers and held them to ransom. When, however, it was discovered that no money was forthcoming from the Customs they were released. My men brought back with them the report that had the bandits captured my wife they would have demanded $10,000 as ransom money. When my wife heard this she was very indignant. She said the amount was far too little for the same bandits had asked $15,000 for a missionary they had captured at Wuhu less than a month before.

There is a sequel to this story. On arrival at Changsha a ration of tinned sausages was served to all hands on board the gunboat. There was, however, one dissatisfied Mess, for a tin had gone bad. On investigation a bullet was found inside. This had penetrated the ship's side, entered the store-room, passing through a wooden case and into the tin of 'Bangers'.

The situation in Hankow was again tense; and, as we had lost our house and all our furniture and effects, and as I was due for home leave in October, my wife and David left China for England.

I opened an office in Hankow and lived in the Club and settled down to await developments, which were not long in coming. This time nature took a hand in my affairs.

We learn of numerous instances of extensive floods on the Yangtze, as far back as 922 B.C.; but not for hundreds of years has so destructive an inundation ravaged the central districts as that which occurred during the terrible summer of 1931, when 25 million people, inhabiting an area of 700,000 square miles, were affected in various ways by this, the greatest flood in the recorded history of China. Approximately 140,000 people were drowned, and a crop worth millions of pounds was lost. The streets of the Wu-han cities were flooded to a depth of nine feet, while the surrounding country was thirty feet under water.

In the circumstances it is not surprising that the inhabitants used any sort of conveyance that would float. At first the cyclist could negotiate the streets, motor-cars could dash through the flooded thoroughfares, putting up a huge bow wave, and the rickshaw could still make a rich harvest in carrying those unwilling to get their feet wet.

But still the water rose, and boats made their appearance in streets far from their true sphere. The 'Merchant Princes' used to go to their offices in boats, sitting in state in wicker arm-chairs. The police patrolled the streets in sampans fitted with an outboard motor, a machine-gun in the bows, and as many men in the stern sheets as possible. The street vendors used large, water-tight trays to carry their merchandise, which floated on the surface of the water, and propelled them by pushing with their noses when the water in the streets reached to their necks. Blocks of ice, used for cooling drinks and preserving food, had a hole bored in them to take a short rope, which was in turn attached to a larger rope, and these miniature pack-ice fields would be towed through the streets by half-submerged coolies. This was a great labour-saving device, for one coolie was capable of towing more than 100 blocks. Some of these pack-ice fields would cause serious traffic jams. When pedestrians started getting drowned in the streets, the dead bodies were towed through the town, secured to the tow rope by a small grapnel. It was a common sight to see dead bodies moored to a pillar box or lamp post, awaiting the arrival of a police boat.

The fire brigade boat was painted red, and carried a portable hand pump and many lengths of hose, while a bugler sat in the bows to blow a warning blast to the half-submerged carriages, rickshaws, boats, tubs and rafts of all kinds, that they might get out of the way in time. When called to a fire, the brigade would not start rescue work until the fee for their services had been paid in full.

Policemen on traffic duty stood on high stools or sat in trees. Overhead cables, some of them live wires, soon came within dangerous reach of the boathooks of cargo boats. There was a regular service of boats to the Race Club from the Bund at Hankow. The contractors charged a small fare, and did a roaring trade. A dice box was available in each boat, so that the members of the Club could while away the time in transit by shaking the dice to determine who should pay for all the passengers in the boat. Once out of the town the depth of the water increased alarmingly, as testified by the rule forbidding boats to make fast to the chimneys of the houses on Jardine's estate.

Even 50-ton lighters were used on the Bund, and with still rising water, junks came blundering up the flooded streets to remove cargo from the warehouses. The boatmen fastened their boathooks on to the nearest object, such as a telephone or electric light pole, some of which, with their bases undermined by the water, fell down.

One of the interesting features of these abnormal conditions was the variety of curious and ingenious substitutes for boats that were pressed into service. Anything that could float took to the water. Tubs, planks, dismantled doors, wooden bedsteads, caulked boxes and even coffins were to be seen being paddled about the streets. The Post Office rose to the occasion, and instituted a service of floating post offices housed in small junks. These patrolled the streets, collecting and delivering mail and selling stamps and postal orders. Floating post offices used a special cancellation on the stamps.

A Coffin comes in Useful

A junk, too, played a part in the culminating disaster. While the devastating flood waters continued to exercise a stranglehold on the city, and the horrors of famine and disease mounted daily, a conflagration, probably the most destructive and spectacular ever seen on the Yangtze, broke out on the 27th August, 1931, on the Texas Oil Company's property at Hankow. The fire originated in the cooking stove of a junk which was unloading benzine, which burst into flames. The burning spirit ran along the top of the water; it was carried by the current into the Texas Oil Company's warehouse, and, before anything could be done to avert the tragedy, a blaze was started which, in a few seconds, had reached alarming proportions. Smoke and flames from the burning oil rose up high into the sky, to the accompaniment of continuous explosions as heated steel drums of oil were shot up 100 feet into the air, there to burst with loud reports.

Although the floods did cause a great deal of inconvenience, it is surprising how little the essential services suffered. Indeed, in some cases they were made easier; for example, when the Chinese inhabitants needed water, all they had to do was to lower a bucket out of the window to obtain an unlimited supply, instead of having to take a long walk to the foreshore. Rubbish, too, had merely to be thrown out of the windows, whence it would float away or be dredged later by municipal boats with nets.

The cinemas never closed. As the water rose, boats would carry passengers to the jetty outside the entrance doors, and duck boards were built up in the aisles to the stalls. The audience would squat on the seats, and, as the water continued to rise, they sat on the backs of the seats. When later the seats were flooded, the dress circle only was used. The Club servants, who lived next door, hired the pit to harbour their ducks, the windows being closed to prevent them from swimming out.

Little by little the water filtered into all the houses. The greatest excitement prevailed when the cloakroom boy, at the entrance to the Hankow Club, announced that a fish had swum in. It was chased from room to room by members operating from duck boards, and was finally captured in the bar by methods which would not have been approved by Mr. Izaak Walton.

When finally the water in the houses rose too high even for duck boards, that is to say when the planks perched on barrels, or other supports, were too high to enable an entrance to be effected through the doors, the ground level had to be abandoned in favour of the first floor, the most usual approach being through the window by means of a ladder.

So that I might be completely independent of all transport worries, I designed and had made a canvas boat on the lines of an Eskimo kayak. This was a great success, and so envious were my friends of this method of transport that I had to keep it for greater safety in my room at the Club. When it was required for service, I would put it through the window and lower it into the water below by means of its painter. I would then get through the window myself, down the ladder, embark and paddle over the submerged six-foot wall and out of the Club grounds on my lawful occasions.

The flood at length receded, and I claim the honour, which was not disputed at the time, of being the first foreigner to set foot on dry land after three and a half months. Unpleasant as this long period was, it had one great advantage in that the Chinese, for a time at least, forgot all about Unequal Treaties, Self-Determination for National Minorities, Extraterritoriality, Democratic Government by the People, and the hundred and one other slogans which none of them understood, but which caused so much trouble.

It was now time for me to go on home leave to England. For the first part of it I stayed in Maidenhead. 'It's lucky you weren't here during the summer,' said a friend to me, 'we had a terrible flood here; there were six inches of water on the road one day near Maidenhead bridge.'

While I was in England, the Japanese invaded the lower Yangtze Valley – without declaring war, as was their custom. While passing a news-cinema in the Strand, I was attracted by a poster outside: 'LOOTING ON THE YANGTZE'. For a trifling sum we sat in a comfortable stall in the theatre and witnessed Japanese planes dropping bombs on the Customs godown at Kiukiang, where our newly-acquired furniture was stored. This was followed by a reel showing the Chinese subsequently looting the godown. So clear was the picture that I could almost read my name on the labels of the cases they were pilfering.

CHAPTER 4

Shops, Fortune Tellers and a Doctor

AT times one would feel disgusted to the point of nausea by the filth and smells of the narrow gutterways of streets teeming and steaming with unclean humanity. On such occasions fate often seemed maliciously to prepare unusually obnoxious objects to outrage one's senses. An execution in the streets, worse smells than usual, beggars with most revolting sores, the endless chatter of coolies and so on. More often, however, one would walk through the streets enthralled by this pageant of life in the raw, and the sound of the hawkers peddling their wares, when they emphasized their appeal with artificial aids, the tap-tapping of little drums, or the tinkle of two pieces of brass chiming together.

Each street would have its itinerant salesmen, who would take up their stands by the roadside: the cheap bookseller, who would have his flimsy volumes in a double line on a bamboo framework from which the paper-backed books were suspended by a string through the binding; the herb seller with his queer distorted roots, dried herbs, and jars of dried snakes; frogs and deer-horns constituted his stock-in-trade, laid out on a dirty sheet spread out on the ground. Then the barbers, each with a travelling basin and seat, busy over a shampoo, haircut or ear-clean. But best of all were the dignified old gentlemen who sat with tables before them on which were arranged writing materials—ready to indite a letter for the illiterate – and all the paraphernalia of fortune telling for the curious or uneasy: little numbered strips of bamboo to be selected at random from a jar, whereupon the prophecy to tally with the number would be read off. On the front of the table there would hang a notice admonishing the careless to be on the safe side and take occult advice before undertaking anything of importance.

One could not help feeling alive to the beauty of a curved roof, with a dolphin standing enchantingly on its head at each pointed corner, and the clear, soft sky behind. Romance would beckon at each street corner, colour spilled in reckless splendour in huge baskets of persimmons, more flaming than the oranges, which are usually green in this part of the country. For sheer variety of outline and colour China has no equal.

The noises of the Chinese street would be fused in a mixed clamour of voices, street cries, the monotonous song of the carrying coolies, barking of wonk dogs, and all the various clanging, clinking or drumming of the small instruments used by pedlars to call attention to their wares.

The shops, too, were always absurdly attractive. One would be full of all sizes of earthenware kongs, from vast tubs to small bowls, each splashed with warm reds and greens. The coffin shops with their smart black and red lacquer coffins, and the umbrella shops with green shining paper umbrellas hanging in rows from the roof, invariably caught one's eye. But perhaps the most interesting of all were the shops displaying firecrackers and funeral accessories. These dealt in all the paper articles which are burnt at funerals, and thus transported in smoke to the next world: houses, suits of clothes, chairs, boats, rickshaws and the hundred and one things required by the dead in the hereafter.

For many centuries the Chinese advocated that a dead man's soul should be given all the comforts that he enjoyed in this world. He should have a large staff of servants, houses, horses, rickshaws and so forth. With the invention of paper in the early Han Dynasty, B.C. 206, the 'joss' equipment began to be made of paper with split bamboo frames. They are more elaborate today.

Exploration of the dingy shelves of these shops often revealed a bizarre touch of realism in portraying the estimated needs of that army of silent clients who have lived long enough in this modern China to acquire a taste for the products of science. For in addition to sedan chairs and bowls of paper fruit were trunks, suitcases and such exotic articles as motor-cars, aeroplanes, steam engines, electric light fittings, gramophones, wireless sets whose backs open to disclose five paper valves, and telephones so cunningly contrived as to tempt one to make a long-distance call to Hades. There would be black and brown shoes, complete with laces and imitation rubber heels; cosmetic sets containing powder, cream, lipstick and scent; clocks to tell the time in an existence where one imagines all time stands still, even a neatly rolled umbrella to be burned by some confirmed pessimist who cannot picture the perfect climate of the Elysian Fields. For the latter too, no doubt, was designed an exact paper replica of a three-switch G.E.C. electric heater.

All this is an inexpensive way of ensuring that the soul will be able to meet all its liabilities in the next world, with something over for pocket money. It sometimes happens that an old man has no surviving children, and that his next of kin are already dead. As he will, therefore, have nobody to offer him a paper house after death, he anticipates the event and burns one for his own use, having taken care to forward it to one of his relatives in the nether world, begging him to keep it in store for him until the day when he shall come to enjoy it.

The same shops print banknotes for the use of the dead, as issued by 'The Bank of Hell'. It is interesting to observe that there is inflation even in the spirit world, for none is for a lesser amount than 200,000 dollars. The modern worshippers put this money into paper boxes made in the shape of fire-proof and burglar-proof safes. The Chinese are very far-seeing, whatever people may say to the contrary.

Once while undergoing Customs examination in Canada, on my way to England, I was asked if I had anything to declare, and when I replied that I had not the examining officer, pointing to one of my small trunks, asked me to open it up. It happened to contain my collection of these accessories. Very carefully I placed on the counter before him a radio, a wrist-watch studded with diamonds, an electric toaster, several boxes of cigars, bottles of brandy and scent, and bank notes to the value of many thousands of pounds.

When the Customs officer had somewhat recovered from the shock he said, 'I'm afraid, in addition to double the duty, you will be liable to a very heavy fine for attempting to smuggle these articles.' It was not until he had handled the 'contraband goods' that he would believe they were all made of paper.

Shop assistants in China are experts in wrapping up parcels. The paper used in the shops today is almost unchanged from that used hundreds of years ago. A piece of red paper is often inserted on one side of the parcel, giving the name of the commodity with ample adjectives, such as: 'White Swallow-nest soup powder, suitable for presentation to the Emperor.' These red labels are not only useful for identifying the contents, but also serve as good omens; for the Chinese always feel better when they receive a parcel with a red label. Red is the colour for happiness, and it also has great devil-dispelling qualities.

Large and heavy goods are wrapped in a very soft, coarse paper, made of hay and grass, which is much in favour for another purpose. Bottles of wine or soya-bean sauce are packed in light cane baskets, known as *Pu Pao*. These serve not only as a wrapping but as a convenient method of transport, and also prevent the bottles from being broken. When buying a ham or a couple of dozen 100-year-old eggs, such rush baskets are indispensable. But the attainments of these talented shopkeepers are best revealed in the shops specializing in 'Happy Parcels', that is to say those specially prepared for Chinese weddings.

When the Chinese exchange presents during the Dragon Boat Festival, the mid-Autumn Festival and the New Year, they send each other eatables of from two to ten different kinds. Each kind of 'ceremonial present' is known as a 'colour'. Usually each set of presents consists of four to six colours. To show your goodwill, one of the 'colours' should be a whole ham, for a ham shows the donor's affection and prestige. It is, moreover, the symbol of goodwill and respect, just as the olive branch stands for peace. In selecting a ham it is important to pick the left leg, for the meat from here is considered to be more tender. The present of a ham, however, is not supposed to be accepted; and many Chinese, practical as usual, often hire one for the occasion. There was in Shanghai a large modern store which was willing to accept a deposit for the hire of a ceremonial ham. When it was returned to the sender, it might be sent back to the firm with a coupon given against the deposit, and it was then possible to buy any other goods carried by the firm. In the unlikely event of the recipients ignorantly or impolitely accepting the ham, the buyer would have to pay the balance of the purchase price.

In all the fishing villages there are special shops to cater for the needs of the junk people. In the larger villages the main street is composed almost entirely of shops, all of them open to the street, and closed at night by shutter doors. At dawn the shutters are taken down, and family ablutions are performed in the street. There are shops which sell fish hooks, blocks and rope twine. The latter is made of coarse grass fibre and laid up by a primitive jenny. Rope walks are established in the streets and open spaces.

Some shops are devoted to the selling of idols, hand-carved on the spot, and gaily painted with gold and vivid colours. In the smaller shops there are vegetables, dried fish, eggs black with age, and other foods. Dentist's establishments are at once recognized by the long strings of extracted teeth which decorate their doors. And there are the petty dealers who take up their stand at the roadside. Among these the fortune teller must take pride of place.

This is a very ancient profession and is mentioned in Chinese history as far back as the second century B.C. The whole complicated theory and practice of geomancy, necromancy and fortune telling are vaguely founded on the *Pa Kua*, which forms the basis of the Book of Changes. Fortune tellers are divided into many different schools of thought, some specializing in astrology, some in physiognomy, some in telling the future from the date of birth, some by feeling the bones, by measuring the head, by eyelid vibration, by lines on the face or by fingers. From each of these seeming trivialities the fortune tellers claim to derive good or bad omens, and each claims his own as the best and most effective method of predicting the future.

While the extent to which such superstitions influence the daily life of the people varies greatly in different parts of the country, they are everywhere real and living factors in the minds of the masses. Even the movements of dogs, pigs and cats are considered omens in some provinces. The intrusion of a pig, it is claimed, is a prologue to poverty; for a pig cares only to enter dilapidated houses. The entry of a stray cat or dog on the other hand is held to denote financial success, for these animals are chiefly interested in going to prosperous families for the abundance of food and the superiority of the rats to be found there. The Chinese consider it a great misfortune when a cat gives birth to quadruplets, because the figure 'four' suggests the number of coffin bearers and the character for 'four' looks like a box or coffin.

A kitchen infested with cockroaches may be an indication of dirtiness, but it is a sign of prosperity according to the Chinese. A kitchen without cockroaches shows clearly, they affirm, that poverty is on the way. It may occasion no surprise then when one's good-natured cook transplants some of his cockroaches into one's clean kitchen to solicit the blessing of the god of wealth.

Shops selling the elaborate type of fan are fast dying out. One of the few requisites for comfort, according to Chinese ideas, is the fan. Fans are said to have originated in China many thousands of years ago, and a fan of pheasants' feathers is recorded as having been made by Kao Tsung of the Shang Dynasty. Originally they appear to have been introduced to keep off the dust raised by chariot wheels. Fans made of the feathers of rare birds were in great demand under the Ming Dynasty, for it was said that they not only produced a superior cooling effect but also had a magical influence, so that flies and mosquitoes dared not approach the holder.

Fans, it is said, betray the intelligence and personality of their users. It is not uncommon in the summer to see coolies, quite devoid of clothing, struggling to track a heavy junk up-river, vigorously fanning themselves meanwhile. Even beggars use fans; so do loafers and racketeers. Scholars and officials, however, use quite a different variety.

The way a fan is used, too, tells the character of the owner. A refined man, for example, would never wield his fan violently at a terrific speed; the correct way is to fan slowly, gently and delicately, concentrating a light breeze on the palm of the disengaged hand. The palms, it is said by serious students of the art, are related to the heart; and so, when one of the palms feels the breeze, the heart reacts to the drop in temperature, which in turn creates a psychological effect essential to the well-being of the user. When the action of the fan is slowed down, the heat, so it is said, is less acutely and keenly felt. A non-U man will not only be guilty of fanning his chest but, it is reported, even go so far as to create an artificial typhoon on the lower part of the body. This, of course, is considered most indelicate.

The professional painters and calligraphers of Hangchow, Canton, and Ningpo are world famous; Tang Po-fu, who lived under the Ming Dynasty, was probably the most successful fan artist. So famous was he that he never carried any money in his pocket. Whenever he was short of funds, he painted a few fans and sent them to the pawnshops, a method even simpler than the traveller's cheques of today.

There was a pharmacy, in fact there were two, within a stone's throw of my gate in Ichang, but though they were certainly of an old-fashioned type, they did not advertise the nature of their wares by any display of brilliant scarlet and azure liquids in enormous decanter-like bottles such as dazzled the eyes of my youth; indeed the uninitiated would pass them by without realizing that they were selling drugs at all, still less that a self-styled doctor presided over the sale of his own medicines at the more popular of the two.

These shops, which are portable, have the enormous advantage of having no overhead charges, or in fact anything overhead at all except the cool autumn sky of China; for all the drugs are laid out by the roadside on a once-white cloth measuring roughly eight feet by four, and behind them squats the doctor's assistant who officiates over the grinding stone, the knives, and the curious little guillotine used in the preparation of the medicines.

The 'doctor', unless absent at the bedside of a patient too ill to attend the clinic, lounged in a small bamboo chair, smilingly at the public service. For a consideration he would diagnose, and prescribe for, all the ills to which the flesh is heir, and in China that heritage is larger and more varied than the West would dream possible.

The doctor himself had been conceived along homeopathic lines like some of his medicines, for he stood three feet two inches high in his cloth shoes. He gained a little extra height from a large trilby hat, and a great deal of extra dignity by virtue of his black, spade-shaped beard, unusually full for one of his race. Surely a man so richly hirsute would possess a remedy for falling or fading hair? The endowment of health, too, so necessary a qualification for one of his profession, would appear to have been his, for despite his stunted stature he was robust and vigorous, without a trace of the malevolent discontent so often seen on the face of a dwarf. On the contrary, this little mannikin was as cheerful as Tom Thumb and, judging by the droll smirk on his broad face, just as successful in outwitting those larger than himself.

One day I saw him being interviewed by a policeman, probably over some formality regarding the hawker's licence necessary for all who peddle their wares in the street. The policeman, in order to discuss matters more amiably on the level, had seated himself on the little bamboo chair, and the doctor was standing before him, wringing his strangely-shaped square hands with their unnaturally short, thick fingers. He was exhibiting all the signs of great mental distress, but every now and then cocking a roguish eye at the arm of the law to see how his histrionics were going down.

Whenever I took my walks abroad, I paused beside this Lilliputian practitioner, round whom there were always a few loiterers, staring in open-mouthed curiosity at his odd selection of *materia medica*. These varied from genuinely curative herbs and simples to the most grotesquely futile or revoltingly noisome remedies. At first sight of them one might be forgiven for thinking that the contents of a dustbin had been carefully arranged according to shapes and sizes. On the right in bundles of about the same length lay three rows of roots, sticks and branches, all dried to a uniform state of colourless monotony, the only variation being in the occasional distorted or bulbous shapes reminiscent of Arthur Rackham's elfin trees. On the left, laid out with some attempt at window-dressing, would be a mixture of curious fragments vaguely suggestive of the ingredients of a Witches' Cauldron. Small pieces of what might be bone or stone strung together like loosely-knit vertebrae. Dried and battered pieces of moss whose virtue lies in the place whence they are taken, such as roofs, old wells, and the bottoms of boats. These are used to apply to sores and wounds. The pods and seeds of countless flowers, including all parts of the lotus, which is valued for tonics and aphrodisiacs. The globular rhizome of the water plantain, which if gathered in the Eighth Moon and taken for any length of time has the effect, so we are told in the 'Peng-Sao' of Chang Ping Cheng, that 'Eye and ear become acute, hunger is not felt, life is prolonged, visage becomes radiant, and body light, so that one can walk upon the water.' After

5

these extravagant claims, that of also alleviating difficult childbirth seems trifling. There would be small pieces of amber into which, when a tiger dies, his soul is transformed; hence the Chinese name, Hu P'o, 'Tiger's soul'. The medicinal value of this, as may be imagined, is exceptionally high, and smacks of the occult and trans-cendentalism, as does the use of tiger's bones. And there would be cardamon seeds, rape and cassia; the latter if combined with toad's brains is strongly recommended.

The ground and powdered leaves of the common mugwort rolled into pellets are used as a moxa for cauterizing, which is commonly employed for many ailments from itch to sterility. It is also used by Buddhist priests to burn the three rows of three, four or five scars on the heads of the neophytes at the ceremony of initiation. Sometimes this moxa is even used to brand one or more scars on the face of a three-days' old child to ensure its living through infancy, the usual places being between the brows, on each cheek a little below the eyes, at the root of the nose, or on the upper lip. The leaves of this same plant are often hung up together with the sword-like leaves of the acorus (the common flag) at the head of the principal room of the house on Dragon Festival, the Fifth Day of the Fifth Moon.

Flowers or slips of wood from the peach tree are efficacious in driving away devils. Alongside them would be dried centipedes whose crushed bodies yield arsenic, and spurious substitutes, mainly campanulaceous, for the rare and expensive Chinese medicine *par excellence*, the *Panax ginseng*, which is held to be a universal panacea. One of the sun-dried Aconitums (maybe *Datura*, or the *Hyoscyamus*) if moistened and applied two hours before, is said to produce numbness for any form of primitive operation. There are many species of Aconitum used medicinally. Some it is proper to pluck in the Eighth Moon, others should be dug up in the spring. In former days the tips of arrows were treated with poison made from this plant. All these varieties are carefully prepared with due regard to the Yin, or female, and Yang, or male principle of the plants and the conditions to be cured.

Various seeds such as those of the radish are recommended as expectorants. The large number of these makes one wonder why they should be necessary, for the whole nation seems to be suffering from an overdose of just such a stimulant. Dried seaweeds, which are regarded as having a cooling though rather debilitating effect on the system, are common, and various types of lichens, mushrooms and fungus. Of the latter, the most sinister is a large, dried disc, vaguely suggestive of some horny pachyderm, which owes its potency to the fact that it only grows inside coffins; while the most peculiar is the *Cordycaps sinensis*, said to be common in Southern Tibet, and in the province of Szechuan. This is described in its Chinese name, Hsia-ts'ao-Tung-Ch'ung, as being a plant in summer and an insect in winter, and is most appropriately classed among the drugs called Uncommon Things. It is used in the treatment of jaundice or phthisis, and if taken with duck its powers are said to be so increased as to make it nearly as sovereign a remedy as ginseng. This curious little fungus grows as a parasite on the head of the pupa of a caterpillar, and consists of a greyish-brown, spurred filament, rather twisted in form.

Other remarkable cures are various grasses, which like the mosses derive their value from whatever auspicious site they have been gathered in, such as the mouth of an old well, a hole in a tree, or the grave of a woman who has died in childbirth. These are mainly infantile remedies, and it is believed that if one of them be placed beneath a child's sleeping mat it will prevent its crying in the night, or else ensure the mother's deafness.

Cow's cud is prescribed for vomiting and cholera. Other odd ingredients are 'Rotten wood from the East side of the City'; wood from a tree struck by lightning (this will infuse courage into those who have been frightened by fire); ashes of wood from an old privy, as a remedy against effluvia; wood from an old coffin; wood, to be more romantic, from an 'East-extending branch of a pear tree'; and driftwood which, if placed in wine, is guaranteed to prevent intoxication.

The Chinese are fond of plasters, which are made from various substances soaked, as a rule, in a universal basis of castor oil, nux vomica, male hair and twigs. One of the commoner plasters is made of wood oil and resin. One of the most startling, a cure for ringworm, includes among other ingredients 300 day lilies and some

charcoal dust mixed with pulverized brick from a city wall in Shansi, the whole to be sealed with yellow wax in a porcelain jar, and
buried in the ground for twenty-one days.

The Chinese gift for ingenious and poetical nomenclature is
displayed at its floweriest and most fantastic in the names of various
popular pills. These, the commonest form of medicine, are chewed
and not, as in the West, swallowed whole. To quote a few of these
intriguing names, who would not gamble a few cents on a pill so
promising as 'Hundred Felicities', or the 'Fairy Flat Peach'? What
elixirs of youth are suggested by the titles, 'Everlasting Spring',
'The Beating-Age Pills', and 'Returning Youth'? The 'Plum Flower
Lozenge' sounds fragrant and ethereal, until we learn that the harmless bean flowers and olibanum which go to its make-up are mixed
with woman's milk and toad's spittle. 'Myriad Harmonies' and
'Helping the Yin and Bringing back the Soul', sound too good to
miss. More robust and dashing are the masculine labels such as 'The
Tartar General resumes the Battle', or the 'Five Tigers'. The latter
is composed of aconite, ginger juice, dragon's blood, wild sesamum
seeds, flowers of sulphur, and the skin of the scaly ant-eater. Then
there are the 'Man Red', made of pulverized tapeworm washed in
child's urine and mixed with other drugs which after that seem
immaterial; 'Rhinoceros Pills', which include, among other powdered drugs, musk-ox brain and rhinoceros skin boiled in honey;
and finally, most superlative of all, the 'Pill of the Seven Precious
Handsome Whiskers'.

Once when I noticed a larger crowd than usual clustered round the
site of this chemist's stall, I found, by peering over the shoulders of
the gaping spectators, that the clinic was in full swing with an out-
patient undergoing treatment. The sufferer, with a fine air of non-
chalance which, whether real or assumed, did him credit, was
seated on a low stool with one leg stretched out in front of him on
which the little doctor was exercising his skill with the maximum
amount of advertisement and flourish. With his curious gait, which
was neither a strut nor a toddle, he rolled rapidly between patient
and rugs, selecting nostrums for preparation by his assistant.

The only outward sign of trouble in the limb was a slight thicken-
ing of the ankle, and the doctor, on being shown the seat of the pain,

applied thereto a small metal cylinder inside which he had first inserted a piece of lighted brown paper, presumably to produce a
vacuum. Whether this caused any unpleasant sensation it was impossible to judge, for the patient continued puffing at his long pipe
with the same air of complete detachment. The reaction amongst
the onlookers was, however, good, for they pressed still nearer in
the hope of more interesting developments. The doctor moved the
little metal tube and surveyed the spot with professional gravity,
pressing the flesh, and drawing the attention of both patient and
bystanders to the improvement already supposed to be apparent.
With surprising agility the little man skipped to and fro, collecting
a new kind of paper to be ignited in the cylinder, or a minute portion of this or that drug for incorporation in the particularly black
and sticky-looking plaster being prepared by his assistant. This,
when it was ready, he warmed and clapped briskly on to the ankle.

The consultation was finished, the play was over, the crowd
began to disperse. The patient rose, still showing no signs of either
satisfaction or doubt. Groping in the recesses of his clothing, he produced a dirty paper note worth rather less than $1\frac{1}{2}$d., with which he
liquidated his debt for 'Professional Services' and then moved off.

Though his charges were small this pocket Aesculapius, albeit a
quack, thrived at his trade. I was told he had a wife and children of
normal size, and he certainly looked happy, as well as important
and prosperous. Always with an eye to the main chance, he was not
above casual pickings of a less reputable type. Once in a way our
sequestered town was invaded by foreign tourists. On one occasion
I met a small party of them strolling down the street in the aimless
way of the sightseer. To my astonishment I saw the little active
figure of the doctor pursuing the strangers, palm-upturned, uttering
the whining, servile plaints of the experienced beggar – and uttering
them to such good purpose that two of them, with amused smiles
at his comical aspect, threw him enough to keep a genuine beggar
in funds for a week.

Not in front of the strangers (that would have involved too grave
a loss of face) but after a decent interval, my wife, with whom I
witnessed this bare-faced imposture, accosted the doctor.

'I saw you,' she said. 'How can you, a respectable, indeed a professional man, reconcile it with your dignity to beg from the foreign devils?'

His teeth gleamed whitely above his beard in a disarming smile.

'Pride will not fill the rice bowl,' he murmured apologetically, 'and "No man can be sure of avoiding prison or the beggar's bag".'

CHAPTER 5

Formosa

I HAVE travelled in many different ways in China, but seldom have I travelled so uncomfortably as when I went to Formosa in 1947 by the luxury liner, *Chi Wah*, the *Queen Mary* of China. She had been given to China at the end of the war under Lease-Lend or one or other of the U.N.R.R.A. variants.

In normal times she carried the rich of New York on short cruises, and so was fitted with every comfort known to man; but under the Chinese nothing would work. Nobody bothered about the inconvenience, and in any case the Government had not the dollar exchange to enable them to buy spare parts for the various gadgets, which were therefore allowed to wear out or rust away.

Among other luxuries, each cabin had its own w.c. Mine refused to flush except at quite unpredictable times, when it half-flooded the cabin. Another trying invention was the port, which refused to stay closed. It was supposed to be electrically controlled from the bunk, and from other strategic positions in the cabin; it also controlled the light. But all the mechanisms refused to function. It was so modern that it was expected almost to anticipate one's wishes, but all it did for me was to fly open wide, let in a howling gale from outside, and switch off the light. This would happen at irregular intervals and completely without warning. Nothing would induce it to remain closed for more than a few minutes at a time. It was at its best when I was warm in my bunk. Immediately it would open with the noise of an express train, let in the elements and switch off the light. When I turned out, switched on the light, and attempted to fill the cavity with raincoats and suitcases, it would just as suddenly close, jamming the coats and switching off the light. When I got back into my bunk it would again open and permit all the raincoats and suitcases to fall with a splash into the water which had accumulated from the automatically flooding w.c. and from the gale outside, and then switch off the light. The water flooded the electric log fire, and, as the vessel rolled, travelled across the cabin and swamped the mechanical grandfather clock. My suitcase crossed and recrossed the floor on the crest of this wave with monotonous regularity.

The public rooms had once provided American millionaires with super luxury; under democratic China the music and smoke-rooms, and various saloons, were invaded by the deck passengers. In order to provide more space, sofas and arm-chairs were passed out on deck, and the deck passengers built houses out of the furniture. Enormous pots of palms found their way on deck and were used as foundations for small forts, which the deck passengers built for their families. Some of these buildings were most ingenious, being constructed out of suitcases, blankets, carpets, mats and indeed everything moveable. Inside these impregnable zarebas, cooking would be carried out and the whole life of a busy town enacted. The furniture which could not be moved out on deck was also well used. The grand piano, for instance, provided accommodation for three people on top and six beneath, while several giggling girls banged on the keyboard. The crossing was extremely rough, and those deck passengers who could not get under cover or borrow sofas suffered considerably.

The only place clear of the thrusting deck passengers was the Dining Saloon. Here everything was done 'foreign fashion'. The Chief Steward and Head Waiter were loaded down with gold lace; the Chief Engineer looked like the Port Admiral. Here was the Captain's table, the Purser's table, and so forth. Some passengers came down in foreign pyjamas, some in their underpants.

Anxious to be attentive, my steward brought a spittoon of enormous proportions, almost the size of an umbrella stand, and placed it close to me. So attractive was this spittoon that during the meal passengers would make long voyages from various parts of the saloon to unburden themselves into it. They spat as only a Chinese can spit; some were so skilful that they may well have spat for China at the Olympic Games.

On reaching Formosa we went alongside the wharf at Keelung. The town is situated on the northern extremity of the island and is backed by a range of high mountains. It forms the starting-point of the railway, and is the main entrance to the island. Needless to say I lost no time in getting on shore.

The island of Formosa is one of the largest in the eastern sea, and is separated by a channel 100 miles wide from the mainland of China. The name 'Formosa', or 'Beautiful Island', was given it by the Portuguese, who first visited it. The Chinese themselves call it T'ai-Wan. It is roughly 210 miles long by about 70 miles wide. The eastern half of the island is extremely mountainous, while the western half is a fertile plain.

The history of Formosa is obscure. It appears first in Chinese annals when two expeditions were sent there in the time of the Sui Dynasty, A.D. 605. Being unable to conquer the island, the Chinese, rather typically, considered Formosa unworthy of being included in the Celestial Empire;* thereafter the curtain falls until 1430, the date when the eunuch Wan san Ho was driven there in a storm. The island was subsequently occupied in turn by the Japanese, Spaniards and Dutch. The rest is modern history. In 1887 it became a separate province of China; but at the close of the Sino-Japanese War, in 1895, it was ceded to Japan. At the end of the last war it again reverted to China, and later became the headquarters of General Chiang Kai-shek.

The inhabitants of the island can be divided into three main classes. First, the uncivilized aborigines, that is to say those unsubdued tribes who originally occupied the island, but who in more than 300 years of ceaseless warfare have been driven up into the mountains. Secondly, the civilized aborigines or tribes who have submitted to the Chinese and adopted many of their habits and customs. And finally the Chinese, who at various times have crossed the Formosa Channel and settled among the aborigines of the island.

The aborigines appear to belong to Malay or Polynesian stock. This view is strengthened by the fact that in 1886 a cast-away canoe was picked up off Formosa in which were three men and two

* There is a tradition on the island that the Chinese Emperor, wishing to conquer the island without recourse to sending troops, gave orders that the largest and fiercest man-eating tiger should be captured and sent to Formosa and there liberated so as to terrify the inhabitants into submission. Later a representative of the Emperor visited the island to see the results of the campaign, only to be met by a chieftain wearing the animal's skin.

women. They had come from Luzon, and had been blown out to sea in a gale.

It seems reasonable to suppose that from time to time, in years gone by, Malays have been driven thus to Formosa and, unable to return to their own country, have settled down and inter-married with whatever race was in occupation. Certainly the prevailing winds and currents in this part of the world would greatly assist such voyages. This supposition, if correct, would explain why many of the craft of Formosa show signs of outside influences in decoration and construction.

The rivers of Formosa are few in number; their mouths are almost invariably choked with silt, and they are very shallow and winding. The harbours on the eastern side are not numerous, and not very accessible. They, too, are subject to a constant accumulation of silt and mud, which renders them shallow and cramped. Those of the west coast are, in most cases, mere roadsteads, while the sea coast, except in the extreme north, is a succession of sandbanks, reefs and shoals. It is a navigator's nightmare.

In early 1948 it was extremely difficult to get into Formosa unless one was an U.N.R.R.A. official, and even then the Immigration authorities liked to be assured of some adequate cash grants or equipment beforehand. So I felt relieved when I was passed by the examining authorities. The Chinese officials were at this time busy consolidating their position in the island. Although the local inhabitants did not like the Japanese, they soon came to the conclusion that the Chinese were infinitely worse. 'The Japanese were lucky,' said one man to me, 'they got the atomic bomb; we got the Chinese.'

It always seems to rain in Keelung, I was told, and the day I arrived was no exception. I spent my first day in Formosa in what had been a Japanese hotel. It was quite charming except that the man in the next room to mine shared his apartment with about twenty turkeys. I lay awake half the night listening to these restless and irrepressible birds clearing their throats. The pandemonium which they occasioned is hard to imagine; yet the Chinese occupier of the room on the other side informed me the next morning that he had not heard them. The explanation, of course, is that a Chinese has no nerves at all, and in any case would not particularly care whether twenty turkeys gobbled singly, simultaneously or not at all.

I took the 5 a.m. train next day for the south. Accompanied by my secretary, I went in due course into the dining-car and called for two breakfasts. Soon afterwards we each received a plate containing six eggs and bacon. 'Do you always,' I said to the half-Japanese waitress, 'serve six eggs?' 'No,' she replied, 'we don't, but when you ordered two breakfasts I naturally assumed that you each wanted two breakfasts.'

I had always wished to study the boats of the head-hunters of Formosa, but when I went to the island everybody I met told me they had no boats, because they lived far up in the mountains. I found this unconvincing. It had always been my experience that boats, sometimes quite interesting ones, have a habit of turning up in all sorts of unlikely places – and so why not on mountains? My only difficulty was to know how to get there.

The train arrived at Tai Chung at noon, just missing the connexion on to the south, which meant a delay of twelve hours. Sorrowfully I went up the main street of the dirty little town and sat down in a tea house to think. When finally the tea-boy arrived, I said to him, 'What are the boats like in the mountains?' He looked at me with profound suspicion, and then said, 'The boats there are merely hollowed-out logs of wood. I don't advise you to go near them for they are built by the head-hunters, and they are as dangerous as smuggled salt.'

As I shall explain in a later chapter, there are no dug-outs in China; and so, when the tea-boy made this remark, I nearly jumped out of my skin with excitement. I don't think I ever before experienced such a thrill of discovery. Archimedes in his bath was nothing to this.

With a voice quivering with emotion I said at once, 'I will give you five dollars immediately if you will find a sure way of getting me up into the mountains this night.' In quite a short time he was back. He brought with him the tickets, and a list of people he had bribed to get them.

Briefly, I took a train along the branch line to Shushu, and then found myself and a light handbag (containing my note and sketch books, a toothbrush and a razor) precariously perched on the curved bamboo roof of a very rickety bus. I shared my commanding position with a basket of enormous proportions containing ducks. This basket was well lashed to the roof, and, as soon as the bus started to take the road, I was able to obtain great support from it; but, while the interminable number of hair-pin bends were being negotiated, all my knowledge of horsemanship was required to keep me in position.

At each stopping point a man would place a short ladder against the roof and, through a large door in the basket, remove some of the ducks. When the basket was half-empty it occurred to me that I would be not only safer, but more comfortable, if I joined the few remaining ducks in the basket. This change of position turned out to be a great success.

We passed through most wonderful scenery. It took six hours to reach 4,000 feet above the sea; and then, just before dark, after a short run on a perfectly flat road, the bus suddenly stopped outside one of the most magical hotels I have ever seen. It had been Japanese, and had not been long enough in Chinese hands to be spoilt. The culture of Nippon still lingered in the neat planning of the approach, the exact width and direction of the paths, and the dainty dwarf landscape gardening.

When travelling in the interior of China, all the traveller can reasonably expect for a meal is a fish head and a bowl of congee; but here, in the remote mountains of Formosa, an almost luxury hotel was to be found. Each resident has a small flat. The guests sleep on the padded floor on a thick quilt, with another exactly the same placed over it, rather like a sandwich. At 5.30 p.m. the half-Japanese maid comes in and, kneeling beside the minute table, cooks the evening meal on the floor. At 7 p.m. she brings in a huge mosquito net in the form of a tent, which takes up most of the room. With great modesty, bowing low, she asks the guest if she should remain for the night. If she is not required, she hands the guest a piece of paper and a pencil, on which is to be written the time of calling in the morning.

In China the only hope of a bath is the village bath house, which has been known to offend sensitive minds. But here bathing at all times was encouraged, and I was determined to take advantage of it. The amah san reported that she had prepared my bath and conducted me by the hand into a semi-darkened room, at the end of a long corridor. When left to my own devices I could find no electric light switches; but, peering through the darkness and setting what appeared to be a prudent course for the centre of the room, I tripped over two bath tubs in rapid succession, the last being full of very hot water. Disregarding these minor misfortunes, I pressed on with praiseworthy zeal, until my attention was directed to what appeared from the feel to be a tiled bath. It was about the right temperature, perhaps cooler than I had been led to hope for, but I felt relieved to have reached my objective. With my toe I tested the depth, which was satisfactory; and, having removed the kimono provided by the management, I slipped in. I was somewhat astonished to find so much soap about, but, in the part of China I came from, soap was hard to come by, and I certainly did not grumble at this *embarras de richesse*. Having had a good wallow up to the chin, I returned to my room. Later I imparted the news of my important discovery to a passing Chinese guest, and advised him to follow my example. He stopped, however, only long enough to tell me that I had entered the tank containing dirty water from all the bath-tubs.

The next day I was to witness the Japanese style ceremonial bath parade of all the guests in the hotel. The bather, after having deposited his bedroom slippers at the entrance door, at once disrobes and places all his garments in an allotted locker. He then secures a tub filled with water and kneels down beside it, lathering himself all over. While this is going on, he is probably in deep conversation with his neighbours, men or women, for both sexes bathe together with perfect order and good nature. It is a most cheery party; no introductions are needed, and all the men, women and children laugh and chat over their tubs and exchange greetings with various friends. If this amicable arrangement should be introduced into English life, it would, I feel, brighten what is after all a dull routine.

High up on the range of great rugged mountains, which rise 12,000 feet above the sea, live tribes of primitive people, who possessed some of the elements of civilization long before the Chinese invasion of Formosa. The origin of these aborigines, who are re-

ported in some places to be cannibals, has so far never been satisfac-
torily settled; but, as previously stated, they are said somewhat to
resemble the Malays and the inhabitants of Polynesia.

The Chinese from the first steadily pushed the Che Huan or Un-
ripe Barbarians back into the low hills fringing the mountains, so
robbing them of their fruitful plains. In consequence, the aborigines
have always entertained a deadly hatred of all intruders, which they
evinced by putting to death all those unfortunate enough to fall into
their hands. In their mountain fastness they remained fiercely independent, defiant and inscrutable, living a happy, care-free life by
lawless, predatory practices – which did not exclude head-hunting.

Such was the position until the Japanese became possessed of the
island in 1896. Even they never completely succeeded in subduing
these unsociable, hardy and warlike people, though it is said that
they tried all known methods. On one occasion they surrounded the
area with electrified wire. The head-hunters experimented for a
while and then felled trees across the wire, over which they crossed
in triumph in search of Japanese heads.

It was not only hatred and natural suspicion which inspired their
head-hunting; it was the custom for a member of the tribe to take a
head to prove his manhood before he could get married. The eligible
women certainly believed that 'two heads were better than one'.

Head-hunting is also said to be useful in cases of litigation. When
a dispute took place between two members of the tribe, it was often
settled by awarding the decision to the man who first brought back
a head. If one of them brought in the head of his opponent, a great
deal of time and trouble was saved.

The aborigines are divided into several tribes, mutually hostile
and differing from one another in customs and language. The only
tribe of interest from a nautical research point of view is one known
locally as the Vonum group, the most active and progressive of the
head-hunting tribes. They live in the central range of mountains.
Until quite recently they have had little contact with civilized
peoples, and are consequently said still to retain many of their de-
plorable characteristics. The local missionaries report that they
quarrel and fight on the slightest provocation, that they are great
drunkards and, in secret, still head-hunters. Perhaps the local mis-

sionaries expect too high a standard. My own experience, after a stay of several weeks in one of the lake-side villages and up in the mountains, was that they were a most hospitable and kindly people. My hosts did not appear to cast any longing glances at my skull.

High in the central mountains is a fine lake four miles long by two miles broad, called Tsui-sia-hai, or Lake of the Water Savages. This was later renamed by the Japanese, Jitsugetsutan, or Lake of the Sun and Moon. Within the last few years, a number of the Vonum tribe have settled, comfortably and contentedly, on the banks of this lake.

With the advent of the Americans and the refining influences of U.N.R.R.A., these one-time savage and inhuman people have become kind, gentle and law-abiding members of society, supporting themselves by agriculture, fishing, and by posing for photographs. In addition to these virtues, they are now said to be both ungrasping and simple. There is a local story, which may well have a background of truth, concerning two aborigines who became the happy possessors of five American dollars, but could not find a satisfactory way of dividing them equally. They both took two dollars, but still there remained another; indeed, each time they transferred the odd dollar, one or other became possessed of more than his fellow. They sat down by the wayside and tried to figure it out, but with no success whatever, until a passing Chinese offered to settle the problem for them. The Chinese gave each aborigine one dollar, and the remaining three dollars he put in his own pocket. The savages were delighted with the clever way in which the Chinese had solved what had previously seemed an insoluble problem.

The type of boat used on the lake consists of a dug-out of the most primitive kind, hollowed out from a single log. The typical dug-out conforms in outline to the tree trunk from which it was made. The bottom is nearly flat; the bow and stern, which are slightly up-turned, are interchangeable and have a certain amount of over-hang. They sometimes run to narrow extremities. The boats are generally propelled by one man, occasionally by two, using crude lanceolate paddles. Sometimes a short mast with a triangular sail is used.

The method of hollowing out the log is by cutting a shallow groove six inches or more in width, the length of the logs. The boat is then hollowed out through this groove to a uniform thickness by means of crude adzes.

Shrimp fishing is carried out to a considerable extent on the lake. In each dug-out will be two men, one of whom paddles the boat, while the other stands in the bow and lowers into the water several small, narrow basket traps, all attached to the same rope at intervals of two feet. The traps, which are of uniform size, measure ten inches deep with a width of three and a half inches. Each basket is baited.

When the traps have remained in the water a sufficient time they are drawn up, and the captured shrimps are emptied through a trap-door into the creel. Sometimes they are kept alive by the fishermen, since many epicures prefer eating live shrimps. They are served for the table in a vessel which contains yellow wine, strong vinegar and sesame oil. The shrimps, while under the influence of alcohol, leap about in an extraordinary manner, which it is said gives them a finer flavour.

CHAPTER 6

About Some Boats of Kwangtung

KWANGTUNG, with an area of 100,000 square miles and a population of 32 million inhabitants, is the most southerly of the provinces of China. For the most part it is a mountainous region, except in the delta area, and here it has unparalleled facilities for inland navigation by means of its three remarkable rivers and their feeders. These converge, and pour their waters into the sea through countless channels in the alluvial plain, at the head of which stands Canton, the capital. Kwangtung has, moreover, a deeply indented coastline, 800 miles long, and of all the provinces in China it is the best provided with excellent bays and ports. These happy navigational benefits have bred a hardy type of seaman, whose knowledge is the outcome of generations of experience.

The delta of the Si Kiang is very fertile, and its products include matting, sugar cane, bamboo, inlaid ware, wheat, tea, ivory carvings, tobacco, groundnuts, silk, ginger and oranges. There are extensive coal-fields, and the delta is at the heart of the rice country.

As a means of transportation the Si Kiang is navigable by junks all the way to the borders of Yunnan. Except for rice, fish and sweet potatoes, most of the products pass Wuchow on the way to other ports of China or abroad. Such valuable minerals as tungsten, manganese, tin, antimony and bismuth are carried down-river, while large lumber rafts float along the various waterways, to be used in Canton or Hong Kong.

There is a saying that 'everything new originates in Kwangtung'. This is largely true. It is also a fact that the province is probably the most conservative in the whole of China. There are, for example, numerous instances of local manners and customs, each connecting present-day life with that of centuries ago. In respect of its boats, too, this province is a curious and most interesting mixture of old and new.

★   ★   ★

Hong Kong is, of course, a British colony and strictly speaking does not therefore count as a part of Kwangtung. Its boats, however, are so interesting, having in no small way influenced some of those in Kwangtung proper, that a short reference must be made to it and them.

The beautiful island of Hong Kong, which I visited in 1948, lies off the coast of Kwangtung and is some forty miles east of Macao and ninety miles south of Canton. It belongs to the Ladrone group of islands. The Chinese characters of its name are of doubtful meaning, but 'Fragrant Harbours' is the most generally accepted translation.

Formerly the island was part of China, and it was nothing more than a pirates' lair. It was ceded to Great Britain in 1841, and the transfer was confirmed by the Treaty of Nanking in the following year. From these humble beginnings the Crown Colony has grown to be one of the most prosperous ports in the Far East. The population, which numbers well over a million, is very cosmopolitan, and includes people from all parts of Malaya, India, Europe and America, as well as 800,000 or more from neighbouring Communist China.

Of all the sections of Chinese in the colony, the most interesting is the maritime population. They are by far the least affected by foreign influence, and their mode of life and manner of work are today much the same as they were hundreds of years ago. Their junks are not only a means of providing them with a living, but are their permanent homes. The fishermen work in clans, and the whole family shares in the work.

Although foreign influences have made little impression on the junkmen, the same cannot be said of their junks and sampans. The present design of the big fishing junks of Hong Kong, which combine characteristics of Chinese and European craft, can be traced back about one hundred years and is not to be seen in any other part of the world. The high stern, the horizontal rails, the fenestrated rudder and its ingenious trunkway, the cut of the sails and many other features are not found in any fishing craft except those of Hong Kong. Moreover these junks are, as a general rule, built of imported wood, such as teak and hardwood from Singapore and Manilla.

Some junks are built for sea-going trawling, while others are con-

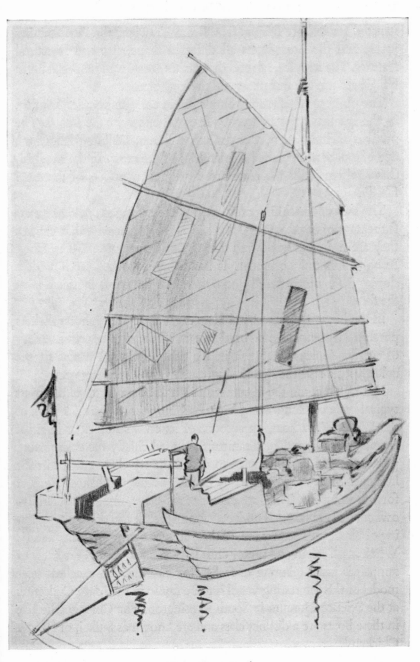

Hong Kong Junk

structed for inshore fishing. The Beam Trawlers, the Purse-seining junks, and the Long-liners all differ in shape, size and structural features. The nets, ice, salt and the catches are stowed in special holds lying between the mainmast and the high stern.

The number of fishermen employed in each junk varies from six in the smaller types to twenty-five and more in the larger. The number includes men, women and children. Children below the age of 15 are not counted as members of the crew. In the small inshore fishing junks the crew are usually all members of the same family.

The sails of the fishing craft are, for the most part, made of mats for reasons of economy, and also because, being heavier than canvas, they are more easily dowsed during fishing operations. The Hong Kong sail is unique in cut. It has a hump-backed leech with a sloping luff, which stands out well before the mast, particularly at the foot.

In the bays of Yaumati and Shaukwan there are typhoon shelters protected by sea-walls and breakwaters. Here are to be seen a variety of smaller junks. These fish in the more sheltered waters of the colony. As a rule they work singly, with small trawling gear.

Last of all come the innumerable small boats. Perhaps the most typical craft of Hong Kong is the harbour ferry sampan, known as the Walla-Walla boat, on account of its crew's notorious habit of arguing over fares. These sampans are used chiefly for transporting passengers and their baggage to and from vessels at anchor in the harbour. They are found solely in Hong Kong and show signs of foreign influence. They are excellent sea-boats, are usually family-owned, and are handled with consummate skill and daring by grasping old ladies assisted by one of the younger members of the family. When small steam and motor craft have run for shelter, the harbour sampan is just beginning to feel in her element. An excellent scale model of this interesting vessel is to be found in the Maze Collection at the Science Museum in South Kensington. The Chinese who live in these boats are a distinct class and are known as Suikai, or 'Water Chickens'.

There are also countless bum-boats of various types and sizes. These boats are regularly licensed by the Government. Actually everything is licensed by the Government. A story is told how one of the senior officials of the Health Department became convinced that rats were being brought into the Colony by the fishing junks. Consequently a reward of twenty cents per rat's tail was offered in an attempt to stamp out the scourge. The result was disastrous, and the reward had to be abolished, because all the fishermen were too busy working on their rat farms to have time to go to sea. This story may be apocryphal; but, whether true or false, the Fisheries Department of the Colony must be given full credit for the wonderful work that is being done to improve the lot of the fishermen, and the state of the industry as a whole.

The primary objective is to ensure that the fishermen receive a fair price for their catch, and that the profits go to the fishermen as producers, not to the middlemen. Each fishing village has its own co-operative syndicate, which collects and sells the fish. Moreover, the syndicates sell rice and flour, salt and ice to the fishermen at the lowest price possible. They also operate a welfare centre and schools for the children, and believe it or not, for the fishermen themselves. There is free medical treatment, and a maternity home for the wives. All these services are provided by the syndicates out of the profits.

There is also a compulsory saving scheme. Two per cent is deducted from the fish sales and is banked in the name of the fishermen, who can draw it out once a year. Lastly, loans are made to fishermen of repute by the Government to enable them to build new junks or to repair old ones. The Government encourages the junkmen to build their own junks – the type they have been accustomed to operate.

*   *   *

From Hong Kong I went to Macao in a dirty little steamer. Two curious men sat at my table, to the right and left of the Captain, the place of honour in the saloon. They had long, beaky noses, and they spoke English with a curious accent. I wondered if their enormous self-content was innate or bought at the bar.

One of them started off with would-be airy persiflage, and then turning to me asked why I was going to Macao. When I said I was going there to study Chinese junks they both burst out laughing, and with a sly wink one of them said, 'That's all right, we're smugglers too.'

Macao is situated on a rocky peninsula, and has been occupied by the Portuguese since 1557. It has a long and splendid history, in which both trade and religious missions have played a leading part. With the rise of Hong Kong its importance declined, and it became famous for its Fan T'an gambling houses. It was at one time one of the wickedest places in the world, but comparatively recently it has become very moral. This I'm afraid was not due to a change of heart, or to the good influence of the missionaries, but simply because everybody was so busy smuggling that they had no time for vice.

The Chinese have developed the art of smuggling to a science, and whole volumes could be devoted to their skill and industry in this highly-organized profession. It was in Macao, many years earlier, that I started my career in the Chinese Maritime Customs, where I served for some years in the revenue cutters of the Preventive Service. Here I saw plenty of active service and thoroughly enjoyed myself, until the Great War broke out and I was called up to serve in the Royal Naval Reserve.

It is a very easy and comfortable run by river steamer from Macao to Canton, and it can be accomplished in a very short time. In the harbour of Canton are to be seen boats of every possible description. Boats abound for scavengers, for thieves, for honest traders, for ladies of the town, for barbers, for marriages, for feasting, for theatricals, for smuggling, for lepers and for ferries. The junks and sampans that navigate these waters and the crews that man them are a source of never-ending interest.

After I had settled in at Canton, one of the first boats I looked for were the pig-boats of the Pearl River. When I had known them in my early days they were almost world-famous, but now I found they had completely disappeared. When I asked a junkman how pigs travelled to Hong Kong, I was told that they went by land. This is what had happened.

According to Kwantung Customs regulations, farmers exporting livestock to Hong Kong received an import licence entitling them

Kwangtung Junk

to bring back into China foreign goods to the value of the livestock they exported. The farmers, whose favourite article of export was pigs, had been in the habit of selling the permit to professional importers for a price usually about half the value of the pigs. In an effort to increase their earnings the farmers, after passing their pigs through the border check stations, began to drive them back again into China at unchecked points, in due course appearing again with the same pigs and so receiving another import permit.

Round and round went the pigs, until in an attempt to halt the practice the authorities moved the check stations a mile inside the border, thus making it more difficult for the farmers to circle round again. This move failed to produce effective results, for the pigs were carried round. The Customs, therefore, began marking 'passed pigs' by cutting off their tails as they went through the check stations. However, the farmers beat this one too. There are quite a few pigs raised in the Hong Kong area, so the Kwangtung farmers traded their tailless pigs for pigs with tails, sold their import licences and took the Hong Kong pigs across the border and then, by bringing them back, secured another import licence.

*　　*　　*

When the first paddle steamer to reach China, the *Forbes,* arrived at Macao in 1830, the local Chinese pilot betrayed no astonishment whatever. 'These have been in use in China for hundreds of years,' he said. He was right. Although the Chinese do not claim to have invented steamers, they can with justice claim to have invented paddle-wheels. The first use of them is attributed to a skilful general named Li Kao, who lived in the sixth century. Of him it is recorded that he built fighting ships with 'two wheels on both sides, so that the boats ran as fast as horses'.

Later, in the Sung Dynasty, a rebel general named Yang Yao used paddle wheels in the Tung T'ing Lake; but without much success, it would appear, for he was up against the clever General Yo Fei who threw down bamboo mats ahead of the paddlers and brought them to a standstill.

The traffic between Canton and the various towns and villages within the delta has been carried on from time immemorial mainly by means of a class of vessel known as 'passenger boats', the Chinese substitutes for railways and stage-coaches. According to Customs records, about the year 1882, a new type, fitted with a paddle wheel, and known as the wheel boat, made its appearance. At first four boats were employed between Canton and Fatshan. So popular did the service become, however, on account of its speed and economy, that it was not long before 100 of these wheel boats were operating in the passenger-carrying trade between Canton and the surrounding districts of the delta.

The average size of a wheel boat of this sort used to be about forty feet long with a beam of about eight feet. It was constructed of China fir planks and hardwood frames and bulkheads, about twenty or so of the former and seven of the latter. Forty to fifty or even more passengers would be the normal complement, divided into three classes. The first class were accommodated in the spacious house, which occupied most of the boat. There was very little head room, and so the passengers had to lie down or squat. The second-class passengers would occupy the upper deck of the house. The most interesting part of the craft was its motive power, which was provided by from six to twenty men in relays, working three rollers in the form of a treadmill, the pedals of which were irregularly spaced in order to prevent their keeping step. The treadmill was connected by iron rods to a paddle wheel situated at the stern. The third-class passengers worked their passage on this treadmill, and the owners thus received a considerable amount of manual propulsion free of charge. The framework of the wheels and the simple machinery for driving them were roughly (but strongly) made of iron, and the floats of hardwood. A Chinese type of lug-sail was set when the wind was fair; and under ideal conditions, with the treadmill fully manned by experts wishing to reach their destination quickly, the boat could attain a speed of perhaps six knots.

Formerly these boats covered a wide area, but of late years their routes were confined to short distances only, and they have now, unhappily, together with other interesting craft, passed into the limbo of forgotten things.

* * *

Probably the earliest record of China's culinary art is contained in the Book of Rites associated with the name of Confucius, who has been revered for centuries as the fountain of wisdom and virtue. The great teacher, who lived from 551 B.C. to 479 B.C., laid down the traditions of the festive board. He ruled that a banquet should consist of seven delicacies, namely: cake with gravy, rice cake with roast pork, roast mutton, pickles, duck, giblets and finally what Confucian scholars term 'miscellany'. Later, however, gastronomic demands became more advanced. The frugal 'Seven Delicacies' developed into a more imposing menu, which included Dragon's Liver, Phoenix Marrow, Hare's Lung, Leopard's Gall, Gorilla's Lips and Creamed Cicada. Nowadays, alas, the secrets of preparing these masterpieces have been lost; but perhaps it is just as well. To-day the gourmet has to be content with varnished duck. This variety of duck is as popular today as it was in the days of old; indeed there are special boats devoted entirely to catering for the needs of the gourmets of China.

Canton without its duck boats would not be Canton. Farmers for forty centuries, the Chinese have invented many practical methods for producing food, and not the least of these is the rearing of ducks. In the vicinity of Canton there are fifteen Chinese incubators which hatch an average of 2,800 ducks a day from March to October. Canton alone consumes five million ducks a year. Wuchow, on the West River, is probably the largest duck-producing area in the province. Customs returns show that that city exported regularly at least 3 million birds a year to Hong Kong and Macao alone.

There is no recognized breed of duck in South China. The white Peking duck, weighing three to five pounds, has become established throughout the country as the most popular variety.*

The process of incubation is typically Chinese. It is extremely novel and simple, but requires considerable skill and experience. The eggs are placed in rattan baskets, containing rice husks, in a room heated with charcoal stoves, the baskets being moved nearer or further from the stoves in order to obtain a uniform heat. Finally, the eggs are placed on shelves. In course of time thousands of ducklings emerge and, when a day old, are sold to farms situated on the banks of creeks and canals. Here they are intensively fed on boiled rice and fish scales. Later they are put on a diet of chaff, mixed with maggots from cesspools. After twenty days they are ready to go afloat and are sold to the duck boat owners.

The duck boat of Canton is a craft of some twenty-three feet in length and ten feet beam. There is a low house amidships for the accommodation of the ducks, while the duck-herds live in the afterpart, which is slightly higher. The ducks are accommodated in pens formed by a number of very long stout bamboos, running fore and after as well as athwartships across the junk, so as to form a widely-spaced framework. Upon this structure a light flooring of square framed gratings made of split bamboos is lashed. Along the outer edges a light rail is erected, and to this grating two gangways capable of being hoisted are secured at the fore end of the junk.

These boats each carry a complement of 1,000 to 1,500 ducks. They move from place to place and they bank in, so as to enable the ducks to land, by running down the drawbridge-gangways provided, and pick up snails and other delicacies in the paddy fields. The ducks are extremely tame, and it used to be one of the sights of Canton to witness the almost military precision with which they

* It was introduced into England in 1873, the occasion being the reception of the Foreign Ministers by the Emperor T'ung Chih.

marched down the gangways to the grazing fields. It is said that some of the ducks are trained to look after the flocks and prevent them from straying, much like sheepdogs. This, if true, may account for the strict discipline which seems to prevail, and the alacrity with which they march back at a signal from the duck-herd, who bangs a gong and administers summary chastisement to any laggard.

After a hundred days afloat their nautical life is over. They are killed, soaked in a solution of brine called Laolu and hung up to dry for three months. At the end of this period they are varnished and are ready for the table.

The projecting bamboo pens and top hamper make the duck boats very top heavy; and, when a storm approaches, they may be seen in large numbers scudding for shelter under bare poles. Should an unexpected squall strike the vessel, or should she be pooped, the lee platform strikes the water and in so doing often frees the birds. Accidents of this sort not infrequently happen, and the river for miles around becomes carpeted with ducks.

*   *   *

There is a Chinese adage which says, 'to live in agony is better than to die in comfort'; nevertheless, except in the case of the death of a parent, which is a calamity, every Chinese loves a funeral. There is wine and music and plenty to eat.

Most Chinese start saving up for their funeral when they are quite young, and the men of the old school used to take their coffins with them wherever they went. 'Never mind how you live; get buried well' is another Chinese saying, and enormous sums are spent on funerals in China. A son will not hesitate to spend a year's income for his father's coffin, and the poorer people often cripple themselves financially for years in paying back what they have borrowed for a funeral in the family. The dead must never be neglected. Not only is it wrong to do so; it is positively dangerous, for the departed spirits, instead of watching over the household, may become 'hungry ghosts' endowed with terrible powers of revenge.

Religious services are held day and night for periods of three, seven or as many as forty-nine days consecutively. On each third and seventh day period a special ceremony has to be performed seven times. The chief mourners must display the most lamentable misery, and expense is no object, as this shows not only the financial position of the deceased but the virtue of the chief mourners. The latter always obtain vocal assistance from professional mourners, usually women, who, even as amateurs, are able to wail better than men. A good professional able to sob in a hair-raising and heart-rending manner can command a large income.

The funeral procession is most important. In the old days wealthy Chinese always kept a white horse, to be ridden when attending funerals, because white is the mourning colour. Although perhaps permissible for ordinary rides, it would be considered very bad taste to ride a white horse to a wedding.

Although the funeral ceremonies can be held at any time, the same cannot be said of the burial. The essential thing to a Chinese is that, no matter what his station in life, he must be buried where his ancestors were buried, near his ancestral home. But for many reasons the body of a Chinese who dies in another district cannot always be sent back at once. Floods, civil wars, bandits and so on may delay the passage home. In any case the geomancers, if the person is rich, take a long time to settle the exact site of the grave. If the man is poor, the matter can be put through very speedily; but, the richer the family, the longer does it take the priests to make up their minds.

And so, while waiting for passage, the coffin goes into a mortuary. Those of Shanghai and Canton are world-famous, and here may be seen literally hundreds of coffins in row upon row, all waiting to go back to their ancestral homes.

China being so well served with waterways, the coffins usually go by water. In other parts of China the craft used for this melancholy duty are not specially built for the task, but in aesthetic Canton that is not the case. Here is to be found a special type of junk used for the coffin-carrying trade only.* It is constructed on slender lines, and built of soft wood with hard wood frames. There are four

---

* These boats are not to be seen except during the summer, for the Chinese believe that it is unlucky to move a coffin during the winter. To an occidental this seems inexplicable, for there is nothing lucky in being dead or in a coffin; but to a Chinese it appears the most natural thing in the world.

Coffin Boat

bulkheads and ten frames. The planks of the fore-deck are removable, to permit the coffin to be lowered into the hold. The midship compartment consists of a comfortable cabin, where the relatives of the deceased may be housed during the voyage. The boat is propelled by a crew of six oarsmen. It is not clear how the Fy Teng, or quick boat, got its name. The junkmen affirm that it was originally designed as a high-speed craft and was, therefore, much in demand for carrying sick people to hospital. When, however, the motor came into general use in Canton, and the means of transport improved, the boats' mission changed from that of carrying the nearly dead to transporting the remains of those already departed.

*   *   *

Some hundred years ago in the Sung Dynasty there lived an Emperor who made war on his enemies. He went to the battlefield himself and left behind two of his most trusted ministers to take care of the country during his absence.

It is sad to have to relate that these two ministers so far forgot their duty as to intrigue with the enemy. When, victorious, the Emperor returned, he was perfectly furious, and passed a law that from that time onwards and for all time the two ministers with their families, relatives, their wives and children, their servants and their descendants, together with all their animals and livestock should be sent to the boats and never again be allowed to live on land. Moreover, they were not permitted to compete in the Imperial Examinations, and were unable to hold any official positions or to own land.

That is the legend of the origin of the 'Floating Population' of Fukien and Kwangtung. Their descendants now live in more or less similar conditions in certain districts in South China. They are a class apart; and, although the law has been somewhat modified (indeed in 1730 the Emperor Yung Cheng allowed them to settle in the immediate neighbourhood of certain parts of the river), they do not appear to have taken full advantage of the concession. They apparently prefer still to live afloat with their livestock and belongings.

The 'floating population' of Canton depend upon each other for their wives. As a general rule they do not marry girls whose families live on shore; indeed until quite recently they were not allowed to do so by law, and to this day they still observe, by habit, the disabilities imposed upon their forebears. Up till comparatively recent times it was the custom for a man who wanted a wife to place a platter of straw on the end of his oar, and a woman who accepted the offer did the same with a basket of flowers.

No inconsiderable part of the huge multitude which composes the population of Canton lives in boats. A conservative guess would put it at 200,000. Formerly there were officers appointed by the Government to regulate and control this portion of the inhabitants of the city. The whole of the Canton waterfront bristles with boats of every sort, the floating homes of this vast population, who are born, live their entire lives, and die afloat.

Parents and children, uncles and aunts and grandparents, are all crowded together in a form of floating house, and all live in comparative harmony. Even the smallest variety of boat or floating dwelling seems elastic enough to accommodate at least two families totalling eight or nine persons, and a troop of children. By European standards it would be considered overcrowding, but to the Chinese overcrowding is the normal condition and they are in no way inconvenienced by it. In the complex and compact life led by these simple people, their unbounded ability to sleep in any position and place, with every sort of noise going on around them, is a great advantage. Chinese children, moreover, are wonderfully suited to

Canton Floating House

the cramped life of the boats. Instead of squirming and wriggling, as our children begin to do almost as soon as they are born, they lie impassive where they are put. It is also noteworthy that at a more advanced age, when Western children would enter into competition with the wildest monkey, Chinese children will stand, sit or squat for hours at a time.

Chinese children too big for a cradle, when not strapped to their mother's back, are usually kept in a form of truncated barrel, open at the top or upper end. The barrel has a moveable false bottom or platform, on which the child stands with its head and arms outside. This platform is kept at the desired height by pegs. As the child grows, so the false bottom is moved down, peg by peg, until it finally reaches the true bottom, when the child is considered to be sufficiently responsible to look after itself on deck.★

However many children there are, they all seem wanted, for the parents fit them into a sort of life-belt made from bamboo or wood, which is attached to any convenient hold-fast by a short piece of rope. So that, if the child falls overboard, it can be readily hauled back. Some parents add a bell to the life-saving device, which accelerates salvage operations considerably. At the age of four the child begins to handle an oar, and is quite safe on deck.

Naturally parsimonious, the Chinese spend the minimum on their food. They are content with a monotonous repetition of inferior rice, served with cabbage or some other inexpensive vegetable fried in oil. Each fills his bowl from the great rice-pot boiling on the galley fire, and with this as a basis, deftly, with his chopsticks or with a porcelain, short-handled spoon, helps himself into the same bowl from the smaller dishes, which are placed in a circle on the deck.

Dogs, cats and hens add congestion to the small available space. Dogs are very popular in all the boats, most of them being named, according to custom, Lai Lu, which means Come Wealth, while some are called Lai Fu, or Come Happiness, their owners believing this to be a good omen. Here they say is a case of Wealth and Happiness that can be at your command. White is the colour for mourning, and so white dogs or those with white tails are *personae non gratae* in Chinese families; for the same reason white cats are not much in evidence.

Cats held official rank in China during the Ming Dynasty. They were given high-sounding names, such as Black Whirlwind, and some wore golden ear-rings; others wore necklaces. The Emperor's favourite cats were not expected to catch rats; this menial duty was attended to by cats of inferior rank. Doubtless they would be called Non-U or working-class cats today. They were all looked after by

---

★ The Junk women of the Upper Yangtze have solved the double problem of safety and transport by carrying their babies in bamboo baskets slung on their backs. These baskets are known as Pai Tze. They have a small shelf-seat inside for the comfort of the passenger.

Only boy children are valuable enough to be buoyed. Note the bell; as long as it tinkles the child can be accounted for, when it is silent he is probably overboard. The child in the picture is wearing a padlock on his left ankle to prevent his being stolen by evil spirits

eunuchs of varying rank according to the official status of the cats. Unhappily, today, cats are kept solely for the purpose of catching rats and mice.

Hens are always held in high esteem in China not only for their egg-laying propensities, but because of their habit of cackling and so announcing to their friends the discovery of interesting food. For this reason they are regarded as the symbol of Loyalty to Companions. In most cases ducks and even pigs live on board. The pigs often go ashore in search of food and variety by day and return home at night when called to their quarters afloat.

The boats are all moored in regular rows or streets,* the perfection of neatness, packed tightly together; and a brisk trade is carried on in these narrow water roads, which form the thoroughfares in the floating town of boats. From a Chinese point of view they enjoy comparative comfort. Nor do the occupants need to go ashore. Small craft laden with every form of commodity supply the needs of their customers, from an earring to a silk dress. Barbers, priests, beggars and others all call at the door. There are also floating shops which call for orders.

In recent years the well-known slipper boats have come to be used as floating dwellings by the more prosperous class of river worker. Each morning the wage earner goes off in a small boat to pursue his daily avocation on lighter or wharf or even in fishing, leaving his wife in charge of the floating tenement. During the day the boat, manned by the womenfolk, is used for ferrying passengers or carrying cargo about the harbour or across the river. The family then live in the after end, the cargo is carried amidships, and the passengers are in the fore-part. The cleanliness of the boats is quite remarkable. The smaller children are kept out of harm's way by being strapped to their mother's back, as she leaps from boat to boat, in a two-knot current, or swings to and fro at the *yuloh*.

No matter whether it is day or night, whether the tides are helpful or adverse, whether the wind is fair or foul, life in the small boats and floating houses of Canton goes on month after month, year

---

* The washing in these boats is always kept low. The junk people believe that washing hung high displeases the spirits, because such obstacles interfere with their flight through the air.

after year. This happy care-free life has many advantages: the taxes are insignificant, water problems do not exist for an unlimited supply can be obtained from over the side, and social rows with neighbours can be solved by moving to another street of boats. It seems a matter for regret that so little attention has been given to these people, who have found, even in these primitive conditions, sufficient for all their wants.

I stayed long enough in Canton to make plans of some of the small craft; and, while I was working on board one of the junks, I suddenly noticed a passing small sampan of a most strange design. In the first place the fisherman in the stern was using a paddle, which is not the usual method of propulsion; secondly, the form of each end of the boat was most peculiar, for the keel continued into a ram-like structure projecting fully two feet beyond the hull at each end. When I saw this I nearly jumped out of my skin with excitement, for this form of construction is what the nautical research experts term 'Bifid'. According to Hornell, certain forms of this bifid arrangement date from the Bronze Age; it was well-known in the ancient Greek and Roman ships and exists even today in craft of Alaska, in the Aleutians and among the island people of the Western Pacific. But I had no idea that this form of bow and stern existed nearer to China than the Philippines. I dropped the work I was engaged upon, and set off down the foreshore in pursuit. The boat banked in a mile further down river and, breathless from my run and the excitement of my discovery, I asked the man why his boat was so constructed.

One of the most annoying traits of the Chinese is their seeming inability to give a direct answer to a question, however simple. 'What is the time?' you ask your cook. He stares vacantly and then says, 'Now?' You ask an educated Chinese, 'What is the date?' to which he replies, 'Today?' My experience, in nautical research matters at least, is that there is a reason for most of the unusual features which so constantly crop up; the difficulty is to find it.

I repeated my question, 'Why is your boat so constructed?' 'That boat?' he said, staring at me with a bewildered look. 'Yes,' I returned, 'that boat.' After an appreciable interval he said, 'Because my father built it like that.' 'But,' I persisted, 'why did your father build it like that?' 'My father?' he replied. 'Yes,' I said, 'your father.' He looked at me as if I had taken leave of my senses. 'For no particular reason,' he returned. So it went on; I could find no adequate reason for this novel form of construction, but he permitted me to make a sketch of the boat, which is here reproduced.

Patiently the fisherman and his son waited, and, when at last I had finished, the father said, 'Well! it's time we ate rice.' They turned the boat bottom up, and using the projecting ends as a carrying pole walked away. I watched them spell-bound, as they travelled over

the high dykes, winding their way through the narrow streets of the village and out across the paddy fields, until they were lost to view on the skyline. It was then that I realized the function of the bifid bow and stern as used in China.

It is a commonplace to say that the junks and sampans are doomed. Doomed they may be, but they will die hard and slowly in Kwangtung, where what seems to be an endless variety of craft still carries on business on the river roads of China.

CHAPTER 7

Games and Pastimes

FOR thousands of years the Chinese have taken no interest in any kind of sport requiring vigorous exertion. For countless centuries it was considered bad manners to run – unless running away from a tiger. Indeed, rapid movement of any kind was considered unbecoming and, even today, it is a physiological fact that exercise is superfluous to the educated Chinese. There is a well-known story of a Chinese watching a game of tennis. 'How much,' he said, 'are they paid for doing that?' When told 'nothing' he refused to believe it, for it seemed to him quite incomprehensible that people of good social position, abundantly able to hire coolies to do it for them, should thus rush about in the sun.

True, polo is said to have originated in China during the T'ang Dynasty, but owing to the strenuous nature of the game it soon came to an untimely end. Football, too, was played in China long before it came to Europe, albeit in a much more refined manner. Instead of playing to score a goal, the players formed a circle and passed round an inflated pig's bladder. The player missing a kick lost a point.

It is, therefore, easily understood that to the Chinese of the old school, games calling for any sort of violent action were considered with both condescension and contempt; instead the official classes, at any rate, were expected to be able to play the Chin, the Five-string Harp, to play chess, and to be able to appreciate the subtleties of calligraphy.

*   *   *

The Chinese pride themselves on being the most literary nation in the world. Pens, paper, ink and ink-slabs are called the 'Four Precious Things'. To be a good calligraphist, therefore, is one of the essential qualifications of the Chinese scholar. It was especially so in the old days when the quality of penmanship was one of the main factors in deciding rank in the Imperial Examinations.

It is difficult to define good calligraphy, and to the occidental it is almost impossible to understand the subtleties of an art to which some calligraphists would devote a life-time of study. There is, of course, much more to it than the ability to write the characters neatly and squarely; the refined calligraphist must be able to convey an intimate expression of his own nature. These characteristics of brush writing, it is affirmed, naturally require great concentration, mental exertion, and most laborious care. Many Chinese scholars of old resorted to various ways of learning to write beautiful characters. One of them is reputed to have suspended his wrist with a rope from the ceiling in order that he might not feel the strain in practising penmanship night and day.

There are, moreover, accepted styles which modern Chinese seek to imitate. Broadly speaking, some favour what may be described as the rough and tough variety, in which the strokes are forceful and strong. Then there are the slender and neat strokes of the refined school, while a different kind of execution is to be found in the light and delicate, almost feminine type of writing. The size of the work, that is to say the actual size of the characters, varies considerably, and is usually governed by the artist's approach to his subject. Recently a Chinese calligrapher of the modern school in Shanghai distinguished himself by using a mop to write life-sized characters. Instead of an ink slab he used a bucket filled with ink. The paper was laid on the floor, and the calligraphist, after removing his shoes, proceeded to walk up and down as he executed a stroke. This method is not advocated; it is far from being refined, and probably owes something to foreign influences.

Calligraphists make a living by selling their work to temples or collectors, while some hire themselves out to write scrolls for auspicious occasions. A story is told of an old lady who wished to do honour to her sixtieth birthday, which is considered to be the most important of all birthdays. She sent for a calligraphist and instructed him to write a scroll praising her achievements and hoping she would live a long life. She naturally assumed that he would inscribe it with felicitous phrases such as 'Happiness as great as the sea', 'Old

Age green as the perpetual pines', with perhaps an allusion in smaller characters to the fact that she had attained 'Six decades of Felicity'.

In course of time, however, she received a scroll reading as follows:

> The aged Mrs Whong is not a human being.
> Her son and daughter are not human beings
> The Boy and Girl are both thieves
> In future none of them will have rice to eat.

Mrs Whong was naturally furious and, accompanied by her irate children, went to see the calligrapher. Forgetful of the Chinese teachings of the Five Constant Virtues – Benevolence, Justice, Propriety, Wisdom and Confidence – she demanded an explanation.

'Why are you so angry?' asked the calligraphist. 'I have not finished it yet.' Whereupon he added a sentence after each of the slanderous statements he had previously penned. This is a translation of the final composition:

The aged Mrs Whong is not a human being. SHE IS JUST LIKE THE GODDESS OF MERCY.

Her son and daughter are not human beings. THEY ARE RESPECTIVELY SHAN T'SAI AND NUNG NIU (ATTENDANTS OF THE GODDESS).

The boy and girl are both thieves. THEY STOLE THE PEACHES OF PARADISE AND GAVE THEM TO THEIR MOTHER.

In future none of them will have rice to eat. THEY WILL LIVE ON THE FOUNTAIN OF LONGEVITY.

The seventh moon is the Festival of the Hungry Ghosts, and directly it is over it is considered chic to be seen walking about with a little cage made of bamboo tucked away in one's sleeve. To most of us a cricket is a cricket, an insect that makes a rather irritating noise. To the Chinese, however, it is a little pocket Caruso. They keep crickets for their song, and they know exactly when one is singing out of tune. Large sums are paid for an insect which will sing well on the note. The song of the cricket is also a reminder to the housewife that winter is approaching and that the family clothes should be taken out of pawn. Moreover it is an excellent antidote

The Cricket immediately escaped

against evil spirits, for no evil spirit can stand a cricket. There are, however, other types of cricket to be noted, such as the fighting cricket, the most important of all.

The Chinese have a great literature on the subject of crickets. They seem first to have come into favour in the Sung Dynasty, A.D. 960–1280, a period which covered the second era in Chinese history, when the country was completely at the mercy of the barbarians. At this time, it seems, the Chinese began to keep crickets in cages for their song. So popular did the practice become that, according to historians, the Emperor and his officials at Court neglected affairs of state in order to listen to cricket concerts. It is said that the influential Prime Minister, Kia se-Tao went so far as to promote his subordinates on the strength of the quality of the crickets they presented to him. This resulted in one of the greatest quests for crickets in history. In some districts magistrates, in order to win favour, accepted the best grade of cricket in payment of taxes.

One of the most dramatic stories concerning crickets is recorded in the Liao Chai. Once an official found a valuable cricket for sale. In order to acquire this treasure he had to exchange his best horse for it. So that he might win rapid promotion, he resolved to present it to the Emperor. He placed it in a box and took it home. Unfortunately, during his absence his wife, anxious to see the insect which had been bought so dearly, opened the box. The cricket immediately escaped, and was eaten by a passing hen. The wife, frightened by the consequences of her act, strangled herself. On his return the official, on hearing of his double loss, committed suicide.

On another occasion, and this is a happier story, a magistrate acquired a cricket which on being set to fight, displayed the most remarkable powers. Then one day the magistrate's son opened the box containing the cricket, which instantly escaped. The boy made a grab at it and pulled off one of its legs. The wife turned pale when she heard what had happened, and the boy ran away. The parents went in search of their child, who was eventually found at the bottom of a well. When they were preparing to bury him they found he was still breathing. Later he recovered, but he was out of his mind.

Meanwhile the father heard an indistinct chirp outside the house. He opened the door, and in limped a lame cricket. Looking carefully round, the little creature lovingly hopped into his sleeve. With a leg missing of course, he seemed worthless as a fighter but, believe it or not, he won every bout in the ring; indeed he was such a wonderfully aggressive performer that the magistrate sent him to the Emperor in a golden cage. The cricket became a great favourite at Court, for in addition to his prowess as a duellist he could dance in time to music. The Emperor, in turn, gave him the name of Dew of Immortality and heaped magnificent gifts of horses and silks on him, and instructed the Literary Chancellor to pass him to the first degree. The Magistrate was also rewarded and the crowning joy of all was that the son recovered his reason.

Singing crickets are as popular today as they were hundreds of years ago. Each autumn, millions of dollars change hands in the cricket chirping industry. Special hunters go to the fields to capture the insects, bringing them to market and selling them to wholesale dealers, who in turn dispose of them to the public. Many people keep hundreds of crickets in their homes, stacked in jars. The rich employ experts to look after theirs.

A cricket fancier's house is continually pervaded by a deafening noise. This the Chinese like very much, for as a general rule they do not object to noise. Quiet to their mind suggests gloom, and in order to break the tranquillity they even carry crickets about with them in cages about four inches high. Some have double cages for two crickets and thus achieve what is known as Shuang Li Yin or 'Double strength noise'. Some insect lovers who do not wish to miss any of the chirping carry them in their pockets or up their sleeves when travelling to the office. Others like to be sung to sleep, and put the cases under their pillows with the insects going full blast.

Ever since the Sung Dynasty cricket fighting has been the chief national game, and one of the most popular pastimes in China. In the course of many generations the Chinese, through long experience and practice, have accomplished a natural selection of fighting crickets. The strongest, bravest and most ferocious come from Kwangtung in South China.

Many textbooks, both contemporary and classical, have been written on the subject of keeping fighting crickets. The best fighting crickets are believed to be the incarnations of great popular heroes of the past. Books give elaborate rules for the proper feeding of crickets. Opinions seem to differ as to what is the best food to ensure a fierce and strong approach to an opponent. They must be fed on a varied diet. Some give them a dish of rice, cucumber, lotus-seeds or shrimps. Others declare that the best food is a hard-boiled egg. Still others say that they fight more eagerly and willingly if fed on a diet of minced cricket-legs obtained from past opponents.

If crickets fall ill from over-eating, they should be given a *bouillon* made from a certain butterfly's wings. If they catch cold they should immediately be put on a diet of mosquitoes. If they run a temperature, roots of the wild pea will restore them, while in the case of difficult breathing a dose of pounded centipedes should be administered.

Good fighters command large prices, indeed they can cost as much as a racing stable, and many men have ruined themselves by investing in large studs of these insects. There are heavy, middle and light-weight champions; the fighters are matched on equal terms according to size, weight and colour, and are carefully weighed on a pair of miniature scales.

Owners of famous fighting crickets travel long distances to meet

their competitors. Fights usually take place in an earthen jar. First
the umpire, called the 'Director of Battle', recites the history of their
past achievements and the prizes they have won. The transfer of an
insect fighter from one jar to another is done by means of 'the house'.
This is an earthen box with two openings and a lid on the top. The
fighter is pushed in through the top and both the side openings are
covered with the thumb and finger. The house is then put into the
enemy jar and the fighters are lured out to face each other. When the
adversaries first meet, their natural instinct is to escape; but they are
stirred into action and manœuvred to meet each other by the umpire,

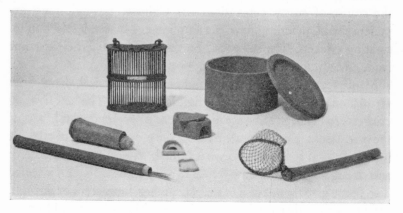

*Cricket Appurtenances: 'Double-strength' cage for singing crickets:
the House; the Fighting Arena; the Carrying Cage; Food Plates;
the Tickler (in case); the Catching Net*

who tickles first their heads and then their tails with a rat's whisker
inserted in a reed holder. It is not long before the insects fly at each
other with their characteristic chirp, and the battle begins. Their
owners are never allowed to touch the fighters once they have entered the ring. They can only sit near the arena and watch the fight
with elation or disappointment as the tide of battle may flow.

The engagement may last for thirty minutes or three seconds. Off
goes a leg here and an antenna there, and so the fight goes on until
one or the other gets his head bitten clean off. Sometimes a cricket
gets 'punch-drunk', or attempts to escape by climbing up the sides

of the arena. In such an event he is given a final test. If he cannot stage a come-back, he is thrown away.

Chinese cricket-lovers take the greatest care of their insects, particularly if they are in the championship class. Despite every precaution, few crickets survive the winter. When a good fighting cricket dies he is buried in a silver coffin, with the hope that more good fighting crickets, attracted by the honourable funeral, will be found near the grave next year.

When I was in Chungking I was invited to a cricket contest on board one of the junks. The whole of the fore-deck was matted-in. The laodah's* wife was there, and her mother; and several of the mother's uncles, with their daughters, nieces and many others. Other old friends of mine, Chang, Wong and Sung, with their relations and friends turned up in great force. It was quite a party. There were heavy-weights as well as light- and middle-weight crickets to fight that night.

The umpire called out the names of the belligerents, and recited their achievements. Bright Moon on the Water had won a roll of silk at Wanhsien. Flower of the Four Seasons had won a roast pig at Ichang. Conquest of the Five Poisonous Plants had distinguished himself at Fuchow and so on, for there was a long and distinguished list of fighters. Next they were matched according to size, weight and colour. The principles of the handicapping are quite beyond the comprehension of the occidental, and to me – though not to the audience – all the crickets seemed to possess the same qualifications.

So that I might have practical experience on the subject of crickets I bought a pair of fighting insects (their Chinese names were Progenitor of Tempest and Black Fury) and all the gear connected with them: the loose boxes for transport, the catching net, the ticklers, the 'house', the drinking bowls and the plates and dishes. I looked after them myself, and I can truthfully say that no baby was tended with more care and devotion than my two crickets. I fed them in strict accordance with the rules, and I gave them their morning bath in the manner prescribed by the book.

When I thought they had reached a physical state of perfection, and were able to do themselves justice, I invited a few friends to

* Laodah; literally, 'Old Great'. The shipmaster.

dinner and announced that my crickets, now named Mills and Dempsey, would give an exhibition bout. Unfortunately, they had got out of their separated houses, and when I removed the lid they lay peacefully sleeping in each other's arms. I had been cheated again. Freddy Mills was a lady.

Shuttlecock is probably one of the most popular games in China today. It is played all over the country, but by nobody so skilfully as by the children. Its origin can be traced back to the first century, when it was supposed to have been played by the Court ladies. Today it is played in a great variety of ways. The players kick the shuttlecock and keep on counting. The player who misses 3, 6 and 9, or any number having these figures in it loses a point. A good player can perform a great number of trick shots. The easiest is probably to kick the shuttlecock in the air so that it falls on the forehead, and then with a nod the player lets it fall on his knee. By stretching out a leg it then falls on the toe. Children make their own shuttlecocks. A short quill is cut into four at one end, and sewn to a piece of cloth, a coin, to give weight, is sewn into the cloth, and the shuttle-cock is ready for service.

Flea-catching cannot, strictly speaking, be said to be one of the official sports of the Chinese. But it does play a large part in the life of the average coolie, and the flea-trap of Chungking is so peculiarly Chinese that it must be briefly mentioned.

In a newspaper there once appeared the following advertisement:

GUARANTEED: Send Postal Order for 2s. to the address given below and you will receive by return of post a device which will instantly kill every kind of insect. MONEY RETURNED IF NOT STRICTLY TRUE.

The sender of the postal order was rewarded by receiving two small pieces of wood, on one of which was marked a cross. The instructions directed that the insect to be destroyed should be placed on the spot marked X, and the other board placed on top, both boards being pressed firmly together with the insect between.

The Chungking flea-trap, while it cannot be said to carry the same guarantee, serves much the same purpose, for it is capable of dealing with any insect foolish enough to be caught. Its greatest success, however, seems to be with fleas, which for this reason are associated by name with this well-known contraption. In writing of it, however, I find myself in some difficulty, for this interesting device has been completely ignored by all the authorities I have consulted. Naturalists have pried into all possible details concerning the flea; volumes have been written about its habits, fortunes have been spent in compiling data about its private life, and no less a person than Lord Rothschild has made a life study of it. Yet nothing apparently has been written about the flea-trap, which used to play such an important part in the daily life of the Szechuanese.

Essentially this trap consists of a small section of bamboo with a series of longitudinal slits cut in its sides, or outer walls. Through this cylinder runs a wooden rod, which is charged with bird-lime or other adhesive substance. The flea, bounding brightly and innocently into space, knocks its head against one of the slats and, stunned, falls through the apertures into the trap, where it immediately adheres to the rod.

There are two varieties of trap on the market, the small, or what may be termed the Portable Trap, which is stowed in the coat sleeve, and that used in bed, which is of considerable size measuring sometimes as much as six inches. Fleas, like human beings and other insects, have heads and hides of varying thickness, and a blow which may stun or disable a fragile or delicate young flea may hardly affect another. Much, too, depends upon their recuperative powers, and whether they can sufficiently recover consciousness after striking the outer bars to exercise their gymnastic powers in jumping clear of the deadly rod. Unfortunately no statistics are available to show the percentage of fleas which avoid this lingering death, either by some lucky bound or by passing scatheless right through the trap.

There are many references to fishing as a sport in the Chinese classics. The best known, which dates from 1132 B.C., concerns the famous Prime Minister Lü Shang. This good and wise man used to fish with a straight hook, so that no fish need be caught against its will, while the fish self-sacrificingly vied with one another to attach themselves to the line, so as to supply the sage with food. Lu Kuei

Meng is the Izaak Walton of China. In his book, written in the ninth century, spearing with a four-pronged weapon, shooting with bow and arrow, and diving into shallow water with a wooden rattle are all referred to in some detail. But in spite of their undoubted skill as professional fishermen, there are few amateur exponents of the art.

The flying of kites is a very ancient Chinese sport, indeed there is evidence that it originated during the former Han Dynasty (206 B.C. to A.D. 25), if not before. History records an engagement in which kites saved the life of an Emperor. Trapped inside a city, and threatened with certain annihilation, it looked as if he were likely to lose his army, his throne and his life. Suddenly, however, one of his faithful followers thought of a brilliant and ingenious method of frightening the enemy. Several large, sturdy kites were constructed, fitted with bamboo whistles, each of which had a different tone, and when these were high up in the air they made curious sounds. During the night the enemy was suddenly aroused from sleep by sounds, coming apparently from the sky, which seemed to say, 'Beware Han'. Thinking them to be their guardian angels warning them of danger, they fled in panic and the Emperor made good his escape.

Kites were again used in battle during the days of the T'ai P'ing Rebellion of 1851. A distinguished General named Pao Chao found himself completely surrounded by the rebels. His forces were out-numbered, and unless reinforcements could be rushed to him he faced annihilation. The General sent for his Chief of Staff. 'Write a note,' he commanded, 'to Tseng Kuo-fan and tell him of the alarm-ing situation here.' Accordingly the Chief of Staff went to his desk and wrote down the many titles of his superior officer, and then gave an accurate appreciation of the position. The general was furious: he seized the pen from the Chief of Staff, and wrote one character on a piece of paper. Around it he drew several circles. The character he wrote was 'Pao', his surname. The kite experts were instructed to attach this message to a kite, and when it was high in the air, to cut the string.

Receiving the note, Tseng correctly interpreted the message as meaning 'Pao is surrounded', and they pushed on with renewed vigour. The General was duly rescued, but it had been a hair's-breadth escape. This is probably the first recorded occasion in China of a message being sent in code.

The ninth day of the ninth moon is the Têng Kao, or Mounting the Heights Festival, and marks the opening of the kite-flying season. The shops at this time are full of kites of every sort, made in designs of huge birds, pretty girls, eagles, motor cars, giant insects and other objects. Most kite enthusiasts, however, prefer to build their own kites to original designs. The Guilds, too, are especially interested in the festival, and every spring they hire skilled workers to make elaborate kites. These are of enormous proportions, sometimes twenty feet in length, and may require four or five men to keep them under control. The sky is full of colossal centipedes, dragons, frogs and butterflies, which are made to roll their eyes. At the end of the day knives are fitted to the cords, and the Guilds and private individuals stage battles in the air. Gigantic frogs and mythical animals strive for aerial supremacy, and after dark the surviving kites are fitted with small coloured lights. The fights continue well into the night.

In the matter of wine-drinking, it is difficult to generalize about the Chinese. It cannot be said that there are no great drinkers among them, nor is it true to say that they are conspicuously noted for temperance. The most famous of all Chinese drinkers was, of course, Li Po, usually accepted as the greatest of all Chinese poets. He died about a thousand years ago by jumping into the water, after a heavy bout of indulgence, in pursuit of the reflection of the moon.

Another interesting poet-drinker was Liu Ling, who lived in the third century A.D., one of a group of hard-drinking scholars who formed a club called the Bamboo Grove. Liu Ling appears to have been the greatest drinker among the group, if not the best scholar. He always went about with wine, and had a servant accompanying him carrying a spade; this man had orders to bury him where he lay should he fall dead from excessive drinking.

A Chinese wine party is always a noisy affair. This is for two reasons. First, it is the unwritten law that the host should force his guests to drink beyond their capacity. The second is the popularity of the Chinese wine game of finger-guessing. In this, two persons put out a certain number of fingers at each other, at the same time shouting out what each guesses to be the total number of fingers put up.

Wine drinking, however, only forms part of a wine party or feast, for food is almost as important. There are two schools of thought on the subject. Some think that there is wine at a feast because the food is too good to be eaten without wine, while others think the food is there because the wine is too good to be drunk without food.

It is said that the difference between a lamb and a Chinese is that whereas a lamb likes to gambol on the grass, a Chinese will gamble on absolutely anything. Singing birds perhaps come next to crickets in providing a popular game of chance. The rules are exceedingly complex, and an added attraction from the Chinese point of view is that little exertion is required.

In almost every Chinese city is to be found a gathering of bird-lovers, each carrying one or more bamboo cages equipped with curtains, so that the birds will not be disturbed while making their daily trip to the rendezvous. Here there will be hundreds of cages hanging from trees, while their owners or trainers stand for hours listening critically to the chorus of highly-trained birds.

The hobby is shared by both aristocracy and proletariat. Indeed, the Empress Dowager was well known to be an ardent lover of singing birds; she even had a room in the Palace decorated like a landscape in order that the caged birds should feel perfectly at home.

Puppet shows in China can be dated back as far as the close of the Han Dynasty, 221 A.D. This period is generally known as that of the Three Kingdoms and is regarded as the most romantic in Chinese history and stands first in popular interest. The wars of this fantastic period are full of hair's-breadth escapes and astonishing adventures. A commander-in-chief in those days had to be able to deal with many different adversaries, including fairies, dragons, devils and evil spirits. He had, moreover, to take account of miracles, and had to have a good working knowledge of astrology and divination.

One of the famous generals of the period, Chen Ping, in the course of a retreat found himself surrounded by his enemies in a town with

Bird Competition

a high encircling wall. He had only a handful of troops left, food was running short and the situation was, to put it mildly, critical in the extreme. He was, however, able to save the day by resorting to a ruse that won the admiration of his countrymen. As the enemy drew close in pursuit, they were both amazed and delighted to see a group of beautiful girls dancing on the city walls, to the accompaniment of exquisite music. The general was called, and he too was held spellbound by this wonderful exhibition of choreography. He could issue no orders for fresh offensives; he cancelled military conferences; he almost forgot the meals his wife had prepared for him. Every day he would sit watching the dancing on the walls, and he was even tempted to go nearer to get a close-up of the elegant women.

The general's wife, however, was a jealous shrew and at length brought pressure to bear on her husband. She persuaded him to abandon the siege and to withdraw his forces. As a result, the besieged general and his resourceful troops were saved from capture or worse. The cream of the story is in its climax. The beautiful dancing girls proved to be puppets, and this famous incident is said to have been the origin of the puppet shows which are so popular in China today.

8

Shanghai — Chungking

MY last experience of Shanghai, which was in 1939, was rich in comedy. I went down to the S.S. *King Yuan*, to see my heavy luggage delivered on board. The last piece to arrive was my cherished new toy, a ten-valve Philips wireless, which I had sent to the Agent for expert packing. The packing case was deposited on deck, and the coolies departed. About an hour later the second officer said to me, 'I have practically been sitting on your radio to prevent it being carried on shore again by a coolie, who seems determined to take it away.' I tried to placate the coolie with a 'cumshaw' and to persuade him that, now all was well, he could go; but the man protested that he must take the box away. On being questioned he said that the thing was no good as it was and that we had better let him remove it. I asked why. Had the radio been broken in transit? 'Oh, no!' But it certainly would not 'talkee'. On further pressure he disclosed the fact that the box was entirely empty. I rushed ashore to the nearest telephone box and rang up the Agent, who merely exclaimed, 'There! I knew this would happen. The radio was all overhauled and packed, only they forgot to put it in the case before nailing it down; send it back, and we will really put it in this time.'

We were sorry to leave Shanghai, for it meant parting with our faithful cook-boy, who had been with us for many years. We could not take him with us, for the journey was far too expensive, but I promised to re-engage him if our paths should meet again.

The journey to Haiphong in the coasting steamer took thirteen days and was uneventful, in spite of our calling at Amoy during the Japanese blockade. We landed in Indo-China on the 5th July, 1939. I was changing money in the bank when a man came up and introduced himself as the British Consul. 'I see and hear you are British,' he said, 'will you, therefore, carry a bag of confidential mail to the

In Indo-China even the sentries appreciate the necessity of the siesta

Minister in Chungking?' I rather demurred at this, but finally agreed
to act as unofficial King's Messenger on the understanding that I
should be allowed to keep the bag. Accordingly I called at the Con-
sulate and took delivery; had I known the nuisance this bag was to
be I should have stood out against carrying it at all costs. I dared not
leave it about, and so had to find a place for it in my already bursting
suitcases.

In Indo-China the most immediately noticeable difference from
the China I knew was the change from ubiquitous blue clothing to

all shades of brown and rusty reds. There are, of course, many other differences: the startling black teeth of the women, making their mouths a gaping cavern; their attractive chignons, with the long, thick hair gathered to one side behind the right ear and inserted into a white or black tubular-shaped cloth, which is wound round the head like a halo; their free, swinging walk, so different from that of their languid, slinky cousins; the small, shapely build of both sexes, and their rounder, neater-featured faces.

Haiphong is a typical little France on colonial soil, with cafés, shady boulevards and lots of red wine. Subira Frères, the Customs Agents, took charge of all our luggage and promised to send it to the Hotel du Commerce by 3 p.m. However, it never turned up at all that day, and we had to make shift for the night as best we could. It was typical of Indo-China that the hotel manager registered no surprise at our occupying his best bedroom with no luggage except a basket of sketching materials and a sealed bag of confidential mail. The next day I dashed to the Customs, for the Agents had said the Customs needed my keys. When I arrived there, however, the Customs official said he did not want the keys and nonchalantly scratched his chalk hieroglyphics over the luggage, releasing it at once.

From being a sleepy little port at the entrance to the Red River, Haiphong had leaped into prominence as one of the three important back-door entrances into China; and there was so much merchandise coming in, particularly arms and ammunition, and so many lorries standing about, that there was no one to take delivery and no means of keeping pace with arrivals. Everything was hopelessly blocked. No one could find anything, and even locomotives had vanished without trace.

After two days spent in worrying the Agents we left by the 1 p.m. express, that is to say the slow train for Hanoi, with complimentary first-class tickets. We were ushered into a second-class carriage, and when this was pointed out to the guard, with the explanation that we did really want a first-class compartment, he pasted a piece of paper over the second roman 'one' and honour was satisfied. The wireless in its small nailed case came with us, also a fair amount of hand luggage, and of course the important sealed bag of confidential mail. One official boarded the carriage later and expressed deep concern at the amount of luggage, especially the case containing the wireless. I pleaded wistfully with him that it was 'très, très delicat'; he shook his head, spread out his hands, shrugged his shoulders and let it pass.

The train reached Hanoi about 5 p.m. and we went in a rickshaw to the Metropole Hotel, which we found very comfortable, with excellent food. The luxurious private bathroom suffered from bizarre plumbing, and was something of a whited sepulchre; for it developed practical joke propensities. The water ran into the bath most reluctantly and, once in, utterly refused to leave it by 'the usual channels'. When I complained to the *caisse* they sent up an army of plumbers, who burst into the bathroom. They spent the whole day there, making extensive excavations in the cement floor and covering everything with mud and dirt to such effect that the next day, when I emptied the waste water from the hand basin, it ran into the bath.

Hanoi, the capital of Tonkin and the seat of the Government of Indo-China, is a charming town with broad, long boulevards, good shops, cafés in the streets, French-looking villas, each in a garden, two very picturesque lakes, and interesting temples. The transport problem is easily solved by the superior 'pousses-pousses', for the rickshaws here are pedal tricycles resembling luxury prams. The disadvantage from the passenger's point of view and the advantage from the driver's is that, when a collision takes place, it is the passenger who suffers. Nowhere is it possible to sleep except under a fan, and yet the temperatures are not excessive; but the limp air is exceedingly trying except between 6 and 8 a.m. The local silver and tortoiseshell ware is enchanting.

The train left the next morning at 7 a.m. and we were at the station well ahead of time so as to be able to repeat the success of the previous day and get all our small gear, and especially the wireless, into the railway carriage with us. This had all been very comfortably arranged fifteen minutes before the train started when an official came along and said that the carriage we were in had broken an axle. All our gear had to be taken out and parked on the platform, while the engine fussed round and brought a new carriage. All the 'Walla

Walla' and the wrestling of the tiny *porteurs* with the luggage, particularly with the awkward-shaped wireless, all the endless tipping had to be done again. In the end we were only settled in just before the train started.

At first the country was mainly paddy, but after a while we passed through tropical jungle, with dense undergrowth and bananas and lianas everywhere. The bananas with their curious startling red flower hung down in a ragged way; the lianas formed a dense blanket of green over the trees, though the acacias seemed able to shake themselves free. There were small banyan trees, but nothing like those in Hanoi.

The train stopped that night at a rest house or bungalow. The engine driver and his assistant banked the fires, and we all left the train for the night. As usual I carried the sealed bag of confidential mail with me, and slept with it under my pillow. The first-class passengers spent the night in a fairly comfortable bungalow; the remainder went to a mat shed rest house. French was still the most useful language.

The next morning at 6 a.m. the engine driver pulled the whistle lanyard and made it fast to the rail, and for some twenty minutes we were subjected to a deafening noise. This did not stop until all the passengers and their children and belongings had climbed back on to the train. The train made a very slow start, which was understandable considering the amount of steam which had been expended; and then, after crossing the Red River, we waited an hour on the Chinese border for passport and Customs formalities.

Soon after our start we began to climb, still more or less following the Red River, which from being a sluggish, broad stream became a mountain torrent; but the thick, soupy water remained the same curious pinky-red colour. The railway line circled mountain after mountain, crossing great chasms on trestle bridges. Once the train emerged from one tunnel on to a dizzy cantilever bridge, and vanished into another tunnel on the opposite side of the mountain.*

---

* The Japanese raided this line. On one occasion a single plane dropped, apparently by accident, an incendiary bomb just as a train crossed this bridge from one tunnel to another. The bomb landed on the last carriage and was carried into the tunnel before it exploded. It set the train alight and killed all but a few passengers.

The gradient was usually so steep that the train made very slow progress, the ancient engine simply puffing its heart out, and the long line of carriages whining and groaning and leaning over with a screeching of brakes as they wound round sharp curves above steep precipices. There are over 180 tunnels, totalling fifteen miles in length. The railway is an astonishing engineering feat, and took eleven years to complete.

The next night the train stopped at Kai Yuen. The same procedure as before was followed, and the sealed bag of confidential mail again came along with me. At 5 a.m. a start was made on the last lap of the journey. After a long climb the train emerged on the heights looking down on the great rice plains of Mengtze, the whole plateau encircled by mountains. Down we went to the plain, itself 5,000 or more feet above sea level, and then up on a new climb before finally descending to the plains of Yunnan Fu at an altitude of nearly 6,000 feet. Here the air is cool and fresh. It is never too hot in summer, although it rains intermittently from May to October; it is never too cold in winter, although it then blows incessantly and dust storms are frequent.

We stayed at the Hotel du Lac, which is under French management. It is a large adapted temple standing in the middle of a small 'Hallowed Lake', full of tame fish. The Manageress was a queer, fierce old French lady. She chased the boys, who quailed before her shrill commands and shrieks for 'Jacques', the head boy. She daily dispensed stores with a pomp and ceremony which would not have disgraced the Brigade of Guards, and she was followed by a Pekinese dog named Pom-Pom and a nondescript dog named Babette.

Two days after our arrival was the 14th July, and after dinner this elderly Lady of the Lake, all dressed up in black silk and accompanied by the younger manager in his 'smoking', departed to celebrate, with the entire French community, the Fall of the Bastille. During the absence of authority someone broke into the laundry and stole nearly all the dirty linen belonging to the hotel and its guests. This made me even more anxious about the bag of confidential mail, and so it was carried about with me wherever I went.

Yunnan Fu was full of Chinese troops who were very quiet, well-dressed and well behaved, all of which was most unusual. Guests were coming and going all the time in the hotel, which was doing a roaring trade now that this had become such an important centre. Groups congregated, and one heard endless conversations on the same subjects: cars, lorries, the state of the roads, 'special' areas, bombed regions. All sorts of nationalities seemed to have drifted here, all wishing to sell something to the Chinese, chiefly munitions.

The Confucian temple, just off the main street, had been a place of great beauty, but now displayed a mixture of squalor, neglect and decay, despite the ineffaceable elegance of the buildings. A pitiful sort of zoological garden had been arranged for the amusement of the Chinese crowds, and these, their hands in their sleeves and idly gazing, strolled aimlessly about the once-sequestered courtyards. In the entrance court was a battered mass which had once been a Japanese plane. The beautiful white egrets had adopted the trees as their permanent quarters, and continually swooped down on the topmost branches, their long legs neatly and gracefully streamlined beneath them.

The dingy, ill-kept cages housing the few animals displayed, did not seem to have been cleaned, painted or repaired for decades. A large, lonely pelican reclined on the beaten earth of his prison, with a foul, green puddle of water before him. I have never before seen a bird lean back on his tail with his legs out in front of him as if quite exhausted, and his melancholy eye and drooping attitude filled my heart with pity. Two foxes seemed happy enough in a cage which they shared with a small bear. The monkeys were miserable, huddled up together on a perch, and below them a magnificent peacock looked like a faded beauty, with his plumage broken and dishevelled. In the same cage with him was a gorgeous golden pheasant, whose breast gleamed rosy-orange in the sun's rays. Depressed by these poor captives, I passed on to explore the buildings.

No trace of Buddhas or tablets remained. The central pavilions were used to lounge in, or in one case as a tea house. The flanking buildings had at one time been laid out with various exhibits for the education and edification of the masses. One had medical charts and diagrams of the human body, diseased and well; another had a few moth-eaten, stuffed fauna – a wolf with glassy eyes, a lustreless peacock, a giant lizard and an even larger turtle. The paper windows had been popped and torn in a thousand places by inquisitive fingers, dust lay over everything in a thick pall. The final degradation of these noble precincts was the display on each pavilion, at eye level, of hundreds of the crudest war posters, showing the Japanese performing every form of torture and atrocity on the Chinese and the latter ejecting them from the Middle Kingdom with more pictorial vigour than, alas, truth. I penetrated into a side court where pines, cryptomerias and acacias made a welcome shade against the red sandstone walls, and the sun gleamed on the rich tiles of the lordly, tilted roofs. Here a tangled plot of garden gave an illusion of the repose once natural to it, brightened by a few roses and oleanders.

Yunnan, 'South of the Clouds' or, to give it its new name, Kunming, is a very picturesque town with narrow lanes and houses with charming, curly roofs. The province is larger than Great Britain and Ireland. The country people are extremely interesting, particularly the remote tribes-people in for marketing. The women alone are highly distinctive, wearing much shorter trousers with a deep-coloured or ornamental border and the same pattern on their short, wide sleeves and round the curved neck-line. The coat is often red and sometimes embroidered, and they wear a short blue apron with coloured or mitred ends tied behind. They all have big feet, that is to say unbound feet, and their shoes have upturned toes and a broad red patch vertically up the back of the heel. Their straw hats are finely woven, often with a black pattern underneath and they wear them high off their heads on a sort of small, stiff red turban. Silver or white metal ornaments cross the turban and hang in chains down each side of the face. Over their hair, which has flowers, jade or beads in it, they wear a dark blue handkerchief, square always, under the turban and hat. They look strong, healthy, cheerful creatures, swinging along under the heavy basket loads which nearly all of them carry on their backs. A dahlia stuck under the hats gives the women a very jaunty look. Some of the men wear a sort of half-wooden cangue round their necks, cut in a semi-circle, and sling the weight of their burdens from it.

In spite of quantities of streets and endless shops, mostly supremely unattractive, one could buy nothing one really wanted in Kunming, and the prices were grotesque. The provincial tax is a great nuisance to the small traders. The tax collectors picket the railway station and harry all the country people who come in by train, lifting twenty cents or more off each as tax on the few vegetables or packages they carry. Doubtless more than half of this sticks to the bottom of the green collecting bag that each petty official carries slung from his shoulder.

After thirteen days in Kunming we left at last by plane. I had planned to make the last part of the journey to Chungking by truck; but at the last moment, when the negotiations were practically finished, the National dollar suddenly crashed, and at the same time the Government introduced a ban on all foreign imports. This, of course, upset all prices including that of petrol, which became virtually a Government monopoly. In arriving at the decision to fly I was also influenced by the fact that I was still anxiously carrying the bag of confidential mail.

Even our air passage was uncertain, and was postponed for several days owing to the fact that the Chungking aerodrome, situated in midstream on a small island, was completely flooded. The plane in which we finally left was grossly overloaded, and two attempts to get it airborne were dismal failures. On investigation it was found that one of the passengers, a Chinese general, had bribed an airport official to allow him to bring with him a tombstone for his aged mother who lived in Chungking. The tombstone had been hidden in the nose of the machine.

The flight to Chungking, which took from 10 a.m. until 2 p.m., was not very interesting. We flew fairly high, at about 11,000 feet, and most of the time there was nothing but a bowl of fleecy clouds beneath us, between which, now and then, we caught glimpses of green mountains, winding streams and scattered farms. Both on taking off and landing all curtains were drawn over the windows for security reasons – for China was at war with Japan. When we got out of the plane we were officiously hurried across the aerodrome through knee-deep grass and we were not even allowed to look back. After a delay in a mat shelter near the river, while we filled in useless details (such as the age of one's father) on various forms, we were escorted to a launch lying alongside the bank.

The launch took four hours getting up against the strong cur-

We lived in Golden Duck Lane

rents, and it was growing dusk when we finally reached the hulk on the south bank. There to meet us stood Whang-Tai-Fu, our faithful cook-boy. He had made the journey of 1,400 miles from Shanghai, by every form of transport, and had got through the Japanese lines by buying a packet of Japanese cigarettes, one of which he presented to each Japanese sentry who stopped him.

One of the first things I did on arrival in Chungking was to visit the British Embassy and deliver that infernal bag of confidential mail. I pointed out that according to the terms of the agreement the bag was to become my property, whereupon the junior assistant broke the impressive seal and, after removing a number of old news-papers and some private letters, together with a form showing, as far as I can remember, 'The return of Unserviceable Aircraft in Peru', handed me the bag.

The housing situation in Chungking at this time was acute, but the Customs had managed to rent a house for me. Our new abode was No. 1 Gin Yah Hang, or Golden Duck Lane, so named because in it people's voices were said to sound like the quacking of a duck. No one had ever *seen* the duck, and so a mystery grew up round it and it was promoted to be a golden duck. A later legend had it that after the arrival of the foreigners in Chungking the echo was said to be so noticeably fainter that it was thought that they had stolen the golden duck.

The house was two-storied and high for its width and was there-fore known as the Shoe Box. It had been constructed forty years before, at the cost of what was then £20. The house was built by the method known as *pisé de terre*, that is to say of rammed earth on a stone foundation, an art which according to tradition was practised by the Chinese as far back as 1324 B.C. It contained two small bed-rooms, 12 feet by 12 feet, a reasonable-sized kitchen, a bathroom, and a living-room measuring 12 feet by 18 feet. Upstairs, on the side of the house facing the river, there was a narrow veranda which seemed to hang perched above space. It was as precarious as it looked too, for when we had inspected the tall, bunding foundations on which we were pinnacled we were no more reassured by this scrutiny than we were by the flimsy nature of the inner walls, one of which had a magnificent meandering crack, through which a good

view of the harbour could be obtained, and of which the cook re-
marked graphically, 'every day he catchy more big'.

The entrance from the street of steps outside was through a huge
double-doored gate in a very high wall. Opposite the gate there was
a low wall or screen to prevent the entry of malignant spirits, for
spirits cannot move out of a straight line. Inside there was a courtyard.

Water coolies used to carry large buckets of water up from the
river, some 200 feet below, and empty them into big earthenware
kongs which stood outside the kitchen. A bamboo stick with a
small piece of alum inside was used to stir the water and settle the
mud. This was our drinking water. Not only had this practice become expensive, but the splashings made a great mess, so I asked the
cook why we did not use water from the handsome well in the
courtyard? He replied in effect that while I was at perfect liberty to
drink the well water, nothing would induce him or the other servants to do so. He said it was 'unfit to drink'. This reason he would
give every time I raised the question.

To set him a good example I gave orders that nothing but water
from the well was to be served to me, and after a month I told the
cook that I had been drinking the water regularly without any ill-
effects and suggested, if only in the interests of economy, that he
and the other servants should follow my example. Still he protested,
this time more strongly than ever. 'Please excuse our stupidity', he
would say, 'the water is unfit to drink', and that was the only reason
he would give. Finally I became quite angry and demanded an explanation. At that he made various gestures which seemed to have a
deep significance. He pointed with his finger to the gate leading in
from the street, then at the ground, and lastly down the well, all
without speaking a word. Then, when I failed to grasp the meaning
of this mime, he came closer to me and holding up two fingers of
one hand, at the same time lowering his voice to a mysterious
whisper, said, 'Master, three months ago they threw two dead
soldiers down that well.'

A balustrade ran along one side of the courtyard and overlooked
far below, at a very steep angle, the roofs of a pig-casing factory.
It took several months to get accustomed to the smells which rose

from this factory, and as it played such a large part in our lives in Chungking I feel I must digress a little to describe it.

In ancient days the intestines of animals were used in China for making bow strings, but after the introduction of firearms, archery went out of fashion and there was no market for the intestines. Early this century, however, an enterprising foreign merchant hit upon the brilliant idea of preserving this waste product and shipping it to Europe, chiefly Germany, to be used as casings for sausages. This quickly became a thriving industry, for apparently the Szechuan pig is better equipped in this respect than his opposite number in the West.

Admirers of the sausage will, perhaps, be interested to learn how the casings are prepared for export. The intestines are first soaked in water for twenty-four hours, and after rinsing several times are again left in water for a further day, when they turn pink in colour. Three pieces are then fastened together, making about thirteen yards in length, and sprinkled with salt. The following day they are pressed to remove the water. Finally they are packed in wooden barrels, the insides of which are coated with wax and lined with cloth.

Before the days of nylon this factory also dealt in pigs' bristles. The best toothbrushes in Europe came from China, and the most superior quality came from Chungking. It may seem surprising that it should be profitable to carry this seemingly common product to a market 12,000 miles away. The answer is simple: the Chinese are industrious enough to take the trouble to collect, sort, clean and classify the bristles.

A saunter, if one can be said to saunter on steps, up and down our street during the busy morning hours afforded an interesting picture of Chinese life in the far interior. Here in Chungking there are a good many variations from other parts of China. The physique of the people, known as 'Szechuan rats', is small and wiry when healthy, though one used to see a large number of pitiful specimens who were tubercular. The river folk and junkmen looked muscular, and they are masters of their craft. The chair coolies must be a lot tougher than they look, for two men will carry a man of any weight at a good swinging gait through the steep, winding streets, and up hills for an indefinite distance, with only one man as a relief, and sometimes without him. It is quite an alarming experience to be carried at a rapid pace up almost perpendicular flights of steps, round corners so abrupt that one's shrinking body overhangs the most noisome ravines, and then down the other side in a sharp, forward tilt which forces far more of one's weight than is pleasant on to the precarious stirrup supporting one's feet.

The only other method of locomotion is by the sturdy little Szechuan pony. These animals are kept in excellent condition by their owners. They are almost without exception well-groomed and well-fed, and are as sure-footed as cats. These strong little beasts carry men and women of all sizes at a trot or canter down the steps and paths, and the clatter of their hoofs and the jingle of their harness bells is a distinctive feature of the place. It is quite disconcerting to round a corner of a narrow street and be confronted with one or two cantering ponies, who appear completely out of control. Their riders, with wildly-waving legs and arms, hang on by some miracle as their mounts swerve and graze past the apparently indifferent pedestrians, who scarcely bother to step aside.

Enormous clumsy buffaloes also use our steps, and are specially shod for the occasion in straw sandals. It used to be rather overwhelming to meet a convoy of three or four of these vast beasts, ponderously descending the narrow street, waving their great horned heads from side to side, and sniffing the air in an arrogant way.

The picker-up of unconsidered trifles haunts all the roads and by-ways, dexterously lifting cigarette stubs, scraps of paper, or any bit of refuse he thinks a use can be found for, with a long, pronged stick, and flicking it over his shoulder into the deep basket slung on his back.

The umbrella mender is a quaint figure. He carries all his crude and paltry paraphernalia slung on his back, and above his head nod an assortment of old, crooked handles, forlorn, naked umbrella sticks with protruding spokes, and one or two primitive tools for repair work. Now and then a Taoist priest passes, looking with his long rat-tails of locks done up in a bun on the top of his head like some eldritch figure. Sometimes the locks of hair that escape and fall down his neck are black and greasy, sometimes grey and scanty.

Often a sparse bead adorns his chin. A high, round, black cap, with the middle portion of the crown cut out, accommodates his bun, which is skewered into place with a jade or brownstone pin. Occasionally a vast hat surmounts the whole, covered with a coarse blue cloth and tied on with strings, beads, or silver chains under the chin. The high hats of the Buddhist priests are just as picturesque.

If one likes things Chinese, there is always something interesting to be seen on the narrow steps of Golden Duck Lane.

CHAPTER 9

Chungking

CHUNGKING, 750 feet above sea level, and 1,400 miles from the sea, stands a grey, close-huddled city, sprawling over two hills which rise about three hundred feet sheer from the water at the point of a rugged peninsula which runs like a tongue down between the two rivers. Despite the red sandstone nature of the rocky promontory, it presents the same uniform grey aspect as the buildings upon it, an aspect due as much to the atmospheric effect of constant mists and cloudy, lowering skies as to the nondescript walls and slate roofs of the houses.

The origin of Chungking is as indeterminate as that of any of the older Chinese cities. It has certainly stood on the site for a period computed by the Chinese historians to be about four thousand years, and it is therefore older than Rome. The earliest classical references link it to the semi-legendary Hsia Dynasty of 2,200 B.C. In 375 B.C. it was incorporated in the Kingdom of Pa, the capital being situated about thirty miles away.

Soon after this it must have gained in importance and been recognized as a town, under the name of Chiangchow, or River Prefecture, for the first wall was built around it. The town has had a change of name sixteen times, thirteen of its names making use of the word Pa. The name of Pahsien, which is still sometimes used as an alternative title, was adopted in the fifth or sixth century A.D., while the present name of Chungking, or Repeated Good Luck, dates back to 1188 in the Sung Dynasty.

The city wall, which has been built and rebuilt during its long history, was described by a famous warrior, Chang Fei, in 230 A.D., as being $4\frac{1}{2}$ miles long and made of mud. A stone wall was said to have been built in the fourteenth century and was pierced by 17 gates, 9 open and 8 closed, symbols of the Pa Kua. It has been extended from time to time, notably in 1664, soon after the city was declared the administrative centre of the provincial Government. Eight of the nine gates afford communication with the Yangtze or Kialing Rivers; and the ninth, the land gate, leads to the main road, where, at a fork named Liang lu K'ou, or Two Roads Mouth, one branch goes to Chengtu and the other to the north. This gate, and much of the wall, was destroyed in the seventeenth century when the ruthless rebel leader, Chang Hsien Chung, entered Chungking at the fall of the Ming Dynasty. This man was a scourge to Szechuan, and by his cruelties considerably reduced the population. He was finally defeated and killed in 1644, at the battle of Hsi Ch'ung. The present walls, with crenellated top, were last thoroughly repaired in 1761. They measure five miles in circumference (or would if they were still uninterruptedly standing) and undulate over the rocky eminence, the lowest level being at that point where the rivers join.

Of the several city gates which lead down to the river's edge by long, broad flights of steps, worn by the passage of countless feet, the chief is the Gate of Peace. Two hundred and forty steps, fully twenty feet broad, lead up to the main street. The results of bombing and street planning have served to clear and widen this famous flight of steps, but formerly it was closely bordered by houses, and shops of the meaner sort, and it provided one of the most typical and most photographed scenes in Chungking.

In 1934 a quite inadequate water supply was inaugurated for the town. Before this, all the water for the city was carried up the century-old steps, through all the different gates, by poorly-paid coolies who would earn four or five cash – then about a farthing – for a load of two heavy wooden buckets of tawny Yangtze water.

These streets of steps, filthy at the lower end, and continually wet from the droppings of the water carriers, were then, as now, thronged with life. Something or other is always being carried up or down; buying and selling goes on in the open-fronted shops, which are little more than stalls, and the inhabitants live out their meagre lives within sight and sound of the street, where most of their toilet and the daily routine of their lives is carried on in the public eye, with an almost complete lack of privacy. In the light of this fact the modest bearing and, in the main, neat and clean appearance of the Chinese women, with small means of existence, is most

Chungking: an impression of the Gate of Peace

praiseworthy. Slatterns, of course, are to be seen, as in all countries, but considering that it costs money to be clean and tidy, an amazing proportion of these people, who live on the edge of starvation, are neat and approximately clean, with hair well-oiled and smoothed into the old-fashioned, intricate coils, or kept short and trim in the new fashion. Any small access of prosperity will result in a crop of the heavy black curls produced by an incredibly cheap permanent wave.

Outside the walls, and overlooking the river, haphazard dwellings cling to the cliff-sides of the promontory, precariously supported one above the other and at all levels on stilts of varying length and uneven distribution, and approached by crazy stairways. These houses on piles are as notable a feature of Chungking as the winding streets of steps.

Below the steps of the various gates the falling water levels of autumn and winter disclose an extensive foreshore, sometimes of rock but mostly of shelving mud. On both banks of the river flimsy matshed houses spring up, until quite a village forms, with streets and shops; yet with rising water the little town is pulled down in an unbelievably short time, and the whole community migrates to a higher level.

The better classes live in the upper city, and to the west and south. The movement towards modernization, which started with an electric light plant and telephone system in 1913, continued with a street-widening programme in 1929, when a motor road was built from the land gate to the village of Tseng chia yen. This new road was laid over the grave-covered hills, which so impressed Somerset Maugham that he described them as 'pressing in upon the living as though they would force them into the turbid swirling river'. In the following year the motor road was extended into the city and cut ruthlessly through the old-fashioned, narrow, crowded lanes. Since then others have been made.

The streets run though the town along the length of the peninsula, as it were in terraces. Motors are now to be seen everywhere in the city which, until 1927, had had no kind of wheeled traffic in its steep and crowded streets, constantly interrupted by flights of steps. The new broad roads in the town still keep most of the old names. Some

of these are strictly utilitarian and self-explanatory, such as the
Copper Beaters' Street, Oil Market Street, Lower Water Street,
Stone Slab Street and Long Level Street. Others preserve an air of
romance or fantasy.

A legend concerns the slaughtering and marauding rebel chieftain, Chang Hsien Chung, who apparently, like other men of blood,
had his softer moments. One day he passed a woman with two small
children, the larger of whom she carried, while the smaller one she
led by the hand. Curious to know the reason for this, Chang stopped
to ask her and was enchanted with her answer, which was that the
larger child belonged to a friend while the little one was her own.
As a reward for this excessive courtesy, Chang told her to hang a
willow branch over her doorway if she should ever find herself en-
dangered by his troops. The street in which she lived was therefore
known as Willow Street.

Du yu Kai was in former days the site of the residence of the Du
Yu, or Official in charge of Government letters. Nien Hwa Kai likewise housed an official, a man with so great a love for flowers that
all the flower hawkers collected outside his door, until the street was
like a flower market. As his favourite was the lotus, the street became the Lotus Flower Street. A love of flowering trees also prompted the titles of Plum Blossom Street and Laurel Tree Street; Shansi
Kai with its numerous banks and wealthy shops received its name
from the merchant settlers from that northern province, who
opened silver, gold and pawn shops in that street.

The name White Elephant Street, with its implication of super-
fluity, has a ridiculous ring to Western ears, but it seems that in
ancient Chinese classical literature elephants and lions were as
naturally linked as lions and unicorns in England. White Elephant
Street in Chungking is balanced by the Shih Dsi Shan, or Stone
Lion Mountain on the south bank across the river, which, with
Lung Men Hai, or Dragon's Mouth, forms a symmetrical trio.

Progress, of course, brings better living conditions for the patient
millions, but one can spare a sigh for the romance of the past. The
old skyline of Chungking showed clustering thousands of grey-tiled
roofs, enchantingly tilted at the corners, and varied here and there
by an airy pavilion, or the brilliant green or orange glazed tiles of a

temple roof. The narrow streets of open-fronted shops, the lanes with high, blank, secretive walls, were thronged with old China. Through these would be carried the green sedan chairs of the high officials of the Yamen, or the blue ones of those of lower rank. The runners who went before them were distinguished by red hats, and they cleared the streets with rawhide whips.

Of the countless interesting old temples of Chungking, many were demolished in the new town planning scheme, and others are used for quite other purposes. Only two properly function as temples. One, the Loh Han Ssu, contains 500 Buddhas. Three-hundred-year-old records of repairs done to this temple point to its being of some antiquity. The other, the Tsang Gan Ssu on Dah Tieh Kai, is said to date back 1,500 years, to the T'ang Dynasty. It contains an interesting old stone tablet, and houses a Lamasery school.

One of the very few remaining landmarks of the past is the grave of General Pah, near the main land gate. He lived during the Chow Dynasty, 1122 to 255 B.C., when the territory around bore the same name as he did – Pah Kuei. There are two stories of this patriot, and in both versions he performed the valiant, and seemingly nearly impossible deed, of cutting off his own head. Both stories, too, concern the unremitting warfare that was a feature of those old, restless days. In one case, when the District of which Pah was Governor was threatened by rebel troops, he asked for assistance from the Kingdom of Chu, and promised to yield up three cities as payment. The sought-for help was rendered, but when order was restored and a Commissioner came to claim the three cities as the price of peace, the General said they were too valuable and he sent his own head instead. The King, touched by such devotion, buried the head with full honours, and chivalrously announced that he would have valued the General alive more than the three cities. The other version is more curt and less flowery. It merely records that, as General Pah stood on the city wall directing the fight he realized the day was lost, and in humiliation and desperation cut off his own head, which fell down to the foot of the wall and was apparently lost, for his body was finally buried with a wooden head. In both cases the people under his rule mourned him deeply, and buried him with great honour. The grave is situated in a little tea garden. The two stone tablets recounting the story of his death have been lost and found several times since the ancient tragedy was first enacted. Now there is only a plain headstone, bearing a record of the repair work done in the twelfth year of the Republic.

One other relic of feudal times is to be found everywhere in Szechuan – the white turban, which is more in the nature of a scarf or kerchief, and which the inhabitants wear tied round their heads in perpetual memory of, and mourning for, that favourite of all Chinese heroes of the period of the Three Kingdoms, Chu Ko Liang. He it was who, by his skill and cunning, set Liu Pei on the throne of Shu, as the Kingdom of Szechuan was then called, and advised and aided him in his endless struggle against his enemies.

Szechuan has produced its quota of famous men. China's foremost poet, Li Po, was born in the province, and a famous contemporary, Tu Fu, lived much of his life there. Despite its isolation and distance from the Imperial Court, block printing was here first carried out 500 years before it appeared in Europe. Szechuan was always fertile ground for insurrection; in its provincial capital of Chengtu, resentment of the alien Manchu rule flared out in October, 1911, with the open rebellion which, under the leadership of Dr Sun Yat Sen, became the revolution that within a year had overthrown the Manchu dynasty for ever.

The soil of Szechuan, fertile for rebellion, is even more productive agriculturally, and there are hidden sources of untapped wealth in the minerals below the rich red earth. The climate, so trying and depressing to all who are not accustomed to it, causes all vegetation to flourish furiously. The hot, steamy summer encourages this growth, which is scarcely checked by the winter, for despite daily fog and a raw, chilly atmosphere, it is never really very cold. Spring and autumn may be said hardly to exist, so sudden is the transition of the seasons. The prevailing wind, save for the southerly breezes of June and July, is north or north-west.

This semi-tropical climate and the fecund soil have made of Szechuan the garden of China, with a rich and varied flora. Fruit and vegetables succeed each other in rotation. Cherries in late April are followed first by apricots and then by peaches, water melons, litchis and tangerine oranges. Pears, of a more indifferent quality, grapes and persimmons fill in the gap until the autumn season ushers in the citrus fruits, two kinds of delicious oranges, and the pumalo which, together with walnuts, lasts well into the spring. The golden heaps of oranges sold everywhere in the grey streets of the town are an unforgettable sight.

The flower stalls provide another rare note of colour in this rather drab city, for the province is as prolific in flowers as in other forms of vegetation, and they blossom freely throughout the year, both earlier and later than elsewhere. For a comparatively small sum you can buy armfuls of lotus, mimosa, tuberoses, tea roses, narcissus, chrysanthemums, iris, cosmos and many varieties of spring fruit blossoms. Orchids, primulas and maidenhair ferns grow wild in the hills on the south bank, together with many other flowers, including the azalea which grows with profusion among the cliffs and mountains, one of its Chinese names being the 'red that glows along the hill-sides'. The azalea is peculiarly fitted to represent Chungking, or more generally the province of Szechuan, to which it is linked in a legend concerning the cuckoo and the most ancient of the Rulers of Shu. It is said that this King very reluctantly gave up the ghost at the time the cuckoo's call was heard, and ever after it was believed that his spirit had entered the cuckoo, and that its cry of, 'Would that I were back' expresses his longing to return to earth. The bird, in its role of the unhappy king, is said to have spat out blood, which fell upon the azalea blossoms and dyed them red.

There are several centres near Chungking where there are natural hot springs, some with geysers rising thirty feet into the air. The northern hot springs can be reached by bus, or else by launch up the Kialing River, a tour which includes the passage through the three gorges of the Pa Mountain Ranges. Each gorge is about ten miles long. They are known as the Goddess of Mercy Gorge, the Hot Spring Gorge, and the Dripping Nose Gorge, the latter after several caves shaped like human noses, which drip continually with moisture from the cliffs.

Chungking was opened to foreign commerce in 1891, by an additional article to the Chefoo Agreement of 1876. The real pioneer of foreign trade in China's far west was Mr Archibald Little. As early as 1898 he attempted steam navigation of the rapids in his seven-ton *Leechuan*. She safely negotiated the passage up from Ichang during the low-water season of that year, but it was necessary to employ trackers to haul her over some of the rapids. In 1900 he sent up a steamer, well named the *Pioneer*, and from these determined beginnings came the great change which was to result in making Chungking the modern commercial capital of Western China. Every form of transport, old and new, can be found here. The old-fashioned sedan chairs and buses, taxis or luxury limousines dash past. High-powered motor vessels and speed boats jostle with the age-old junks still built after the plan of Lu Pan or some other honoured worthy.

Upon the river below the town lies the airport, an island with a stone runway, which uncovers with falling water. From here passengers may travel by plane to Chengtu in an hour or less. To appreciate what a revolutionary change this involves, it should be mentioned that formerly it took ten days by chair, or a month by river.

With the Sino-Japanese hostilities the first great migrations to the further unoccupied provinces had time to settle down in new surroundings. Whole universities, as well as factories, industries, engineering plants and handicraft works were bodily transported a thousand miles into the west. New districts have been opened up, new industries started and, above all, a new feeling of national interest and unity has arisen. All the chief cities of Szechuan, Kweichow and Yunnan have doubled, trebled and in some cases quadrupled their populations. Even when the stimulus of war has been withdrawn, the forward movement in these areas must continue.

There is communication with Kweichow, Yunnan and the south by means of a high road, starting on the south bank at the suburb of Hai Tang Chi, so named after a kind of plum that grows in the nearby hills. A constant ferry service unites Chungking with its prosperous south bank extensions. The most important of the ferry termini is at the straggling village of Lung Men Hao, and it connects with an ancient highway, which rises in steps from the foreshore. This winding lane of steps, made from heavy stone slabs, is a busy thoroughfare, and traffic is continuous up and down it. An endless stream of coolies carried merchandise up and down; long-distance mule and pony trains with bells jingling and led by wild and hardy-looking tribesmen get inextricably entangled with the ordinary traffic: riders, foreign or Chinese, pass at a quick pace up or down the steps, which present no difficulties to the sure-footed Szechuan ponies: priests and beggars, hawkers with wooden clappers and parchment drum, announce their presence and their wares. Occasionally the traffic melts away, so that huge water buffaloes may pass. The old roadway leads out through the narrow and dirty village, along an area of what might be called ribbon development, and then climbs the mountain behind, known as the second and third ranges, some 2,000 feet above sea level. These ranges are divided by a wide, flat valley, green and smiling, and rapidly becoming overgrown with villas and bungalows built to accommodate the rising tide of refugees and newcomers.

The village of Lung Men Hao, named after the lagoon which lies off the south bank, is sheltered from the force of the current by long rocky ledges. The upper entrance between two of these high jagged rocks is known as Upper Dragon Gate. On the highest point of one of the rocks is a shrine to Shui Kuan Yin, the Goddess of Mercy, who saves one from watery perils. Two more shrines mark the lower section of rocky ledges, one to Buddha and the other to the same Shui Kuan Yin. These shrines are protected by wooden grilles and are freshly gilded and painted when they appear above the river's surface each low-water season, for though they stand some twenty feet above the river in the winter months, they vanish completely under the yellow summer floods. The ordinary rise of the river is 70 feet, though it has been known to be over 100 feet. When the river is at its height it is quite dangerous to cross, and there have been innumerable accidents to sampans, particularly at dusk, after dark, or during a fog.

The history of progress in Chungking is linked with the history of steam navigation on stormy and previously forbidden waters. Only by means of the modern marine engine has the truth been removed from the old Chinese proverb, 'it is more difficult to ascend to Szechuan than to ascend to heaven'.

CHAPTER 10

The Upper Yangtze

As nearly all the junks I was now studying are designed to navigate almost impassable rapids of some sort, it will be necessary to give a brief, general description of the Upper Yangtze and some of its more famous rapids.

The eastern portion of Szechuan is steeply mountainous, and sparsely populated by people of a totally different type, and in some cases speaking a different dialect. It presents a great contrast to the western half of the province, known as the Red Basin, which will be described later.

Ichang marks the boundary between the divisions of the river known as the Middle and Upper Yangtze, and is moreover the gateway between the vast Hupeh Plain and the rich and rugged grandeur of Szechuan. It is some 1,000 miles from the sea, and lies on the left bank of the river. On the right bank there is mountainous country right to the river's edge. The climate here is one of the most equable on the Yangtze, being dry and pleasant and warmer than in most other ports in winter, and favoured in summer by welcome breezes. The vegetation is temperate and sub-tropical and shows a wide range from cotton, winter wheat, barley, peas and beans to rice, poppies and tung oil. Nevertheless there is no local trade and the place derives its undoubted importance solely from its geographical position. It is an ideal point for the transhipment of cargo from junks or steamers built for the leisurely navigation of the Lower or Middle River, into other craft specially constructed to negotiate the hazards of the Upper River.

The hills on the right bank take the form of a series of pyramids rising sheer from the water's edge, connected by ridges and ravines, and merging finally into the extensive ranges that lie behind. The triangular-shaped hill exactly facing Ichang is called by foreigners 'The Pyramid', though to the Chinese it is known more poetically as the Mountain of Lonely Evening. It rises to a height of 572 feet and, when viewed from some miles up-river, has exactly the appearance of the great pyramid of Cheops at Cairo. A small temple built at its base used to house an ingenious priest who acquired alms with the minimum of trouble by extending to passing Chinese junks a long bamboo with a small basket hanging from its tip. The peculiar position and form of this hill were believed by the local geomancers to have a malevolent effect on the prosperity of Ichang, and to these evil influences were attributed the ill success of the Ichang candidates at the triennial examinations. The local trading community likewise suffered from a tendency to hand the profits of their business over to strangers. A subscription of ten thousand dollars was accordingly raised to build a Buddhist temple and monastery on the high hill behind the town, equal in height to, and thus able to oppose, the baneful influence of the pyramid across the river. Even so, there were those who maintained that either the site was on the wrong hill or that the spacious three-storied pavilion was not high enough to achieve the best results.

*   *   *

Here, one thousand miles from the sea, the Yangtze leaves the vast alluvial plain and enters the mountainous area, where its course is confined sometimes to little more than a ravine. The river is tortuous, and these defiles can be as narrow as 150 yards, the greatest breadth being 673 yards.

When the great freshets come down, due to the melting of the snow in Tibet, and at the same time the rainy season sets in, conditions alter rapidly. Vast volumes of water come pouring down, raising the level by leaps and bounds. In its struggle to fight its way through the bottlenecks formed by the gorges, the river becomes a gyrating mass of turbulent waters.

The 350-mile stretch between Ichang and Chungking is hazardous in the extreme, containing over seventy rapids and probably more navigational risks to the mile than any other place in the world. The rapids, however, do not all run at the same time.

Some only exist at summer levels, others at mid level, and others again only in the low-water season.

In addition to these hazards, the curving course of the river contains innumerable other perils. Isolated pinnacles, hidden shelves, rocky points, steep-to and shelving banks follow each other in bewildering succession. Had the position of these hidden dangers been selected by an experienced wrecker, they could not have been placed in a more diabolically clever manner.

The junkmen of the old school will tell you that rapids are formed by a submerged dragon, long, sinuous and dangerous, lashing its tail. They also affirm that rice thrown over the bow of the junk will do much to appease the intruder. Both assertions are fallacious.

Rapids, generally speaking, are caused where the river, running down a steep gradient, meets with some obstacle, and becomes a seething inferno of tumbling, tossing water, whirlpools, eddies and backwaters. Unless one also produces the tremendous roar of the water it is impossible to convey anything like an adequate impression of an Upper Yangtze rapid.

They differ greatly in their natural characteristics owing to the different conditions which affect them, such as a ledge across the stream, ledges projecting from both banks; a boulder, bank or rock extending from one side of the river; an obstruction in the middle of the stream; or where the river is contracted by a narrow gorge. Most rapids are formed by a combination of these obstructions and each presents its own problems and since there is an infinite variety of obstructions there is also an infinite variety of rapids. Then again rapids are periodical, that is to say they disappear, or at least lose their violence, at certain times of the year, and with the varying levels of the river. The sketch on page 142 is of an imaginary rapid.

It is not generally appreciated that the greatest strength of a rapid is almost invariably at its head; the maximum velocity where the water runs down an inclined plane is usually little more than a few hundred feet at most.

That portion of the Upper Yangtze known as the Gorges covers a distance of ninety miles from Ichang to Wanhsien, the general direction being westerly, and the number of gorges themselves five.

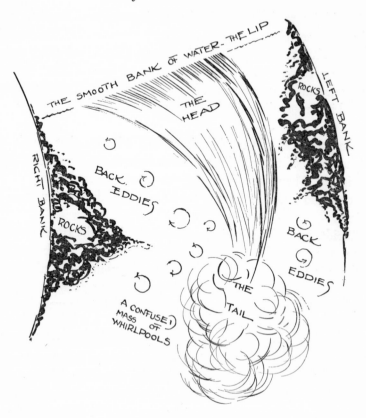

In this confined area, the river is at its narrowest and the strongest rapids occur.

The curving course of the river contains numerous other hazards such as isolated pinnacles, deadly projecting shelves, rocky points and steep and shelving banks. The rise and fall of the water in the gorge is, as may be expected, considerable. It is lowest in February and highest towards early August. Flood levels due to freshets show violent fluctuations. The whirlpools, caused by the ragged nature of the banks which deflect the water at an angle, are to be seen in the vicinity of the rapids, and also with rising water, when they attain their maximum violence. A dangerous variation of this feature is the running whirlpool, or Pao Hsuan which, while rapidly revolving at the same time, moves across the stream. This, if of any size and strength, constitutes a menace to all shipping. Another phenomenon

Above: *An upbound junk being tracked up the lower end of a rapid*

Below: *A downbound junk entering the tail of a rapid*

is the Chinese Fa-shui, or 'Boil' of water, which occurs at intervals at many of the rapids and races at mid or high level. The water will at a particular spot suddenly become very swift and angry. This activity is immediately followed by a sort of quiet miniature tidal wave, succeeded by slack water, or sometimes by an eddy or back-water. After a measured space of time when the rapid returns to normal, the whole performance is regularly repeated. Another odd characteristic of these waters is of rarer occurrence, fortunately, for it presents an alarming form of hazard. This consists of a strange, globular up-rising of water, like a vast air bubble rising to the sur-face, which after forming, collapses as if it had been sucked down by a vacuum pump, leaving a deep cavity into which the surrounding water crashes with a rushing sound. When one of these breaks loose the terror cannot be conveyed by any description whatever. Yet one more unpleasant feature is the formation of quicksands, or Sha-shui, meaning 'Sand Water', which owe their origin to huge silt deposits during high water when some form of check blocks a free exit for the channel. These too are infrequent and mainly occur in the autumn.

Running at a speed of from seven to nine knots and more as they do, it can be readily understood that the rapids cannot be sur-mounted by junks without much additional help to the ordinary crews.

A gang of trackers is usually hired through a form of labour ex-change which is to be found in the various riverside towns. The trackers are either casual or professional. The former are men who leave their normal work of farming or fishing for short spells to engage in tracking. The latter are, as it were, a class apart – a sort of low caste of individual, formerly opium smokers and of no great intelligence. These professional trackers are colourful characters, as no doubt they were thousands of years ago, but their life is by no means all picturesqueness but one of incessant toil and danger.

When tracking they attach themselves fanwise to the bamboo tracking line by a simple but practical form of harness, consisting of a loop of rope, or more often white cloth, passed over one shoulder and round the body, joined to a short length of light rope which takes into a bone, or wooden button, terminating through it in a wale-knot. A half-hitch is made with this round the bamboo rope, which bears against the button when the strain is on but loosens directly the tension relaxes, forming a safety device whereby the tracker can easily release himself in an emergency. Once harnessed to the junk the men display perfect discipline and team work and are controlled by the rhythmic beat of the drum from the junk, the note being varied from the signal 'Stop' denoted by a short, sharp beat; 'Slow' indicated by a slow and even rhythm, and 'Full speed' denoted by a rapid, constant drumming. The sound of the throb of the drum is a marked characteristic of the Upper Yangtze waters.

Before attempting a difficult rapid the junk is lightened as much as possible by the removal of some of her heavy cargo, and sometimes hours are spent laying out warps. One leads straight up the rapid, and two other 'preventers' are made fast ashore, so that if the main rope parts the junk would surge back to the place from which she started provided, of course, she did not come in contact with one or more of the vicious-looking rocks in the process.

Ascending a rapid in a large junk is an operation that requires the nicest skill and judgement and the most prompt and ready obedience to the smallest signal given by the lowdah or pilot. The slightest error or delay would often be fatal.

At a rapid all hands go ashore except the two or three men at the bow sweep, used to shoot her out into the current so as to clear rocks which the helmsman unaided would be unable to avoid, and two men to attend to the paying-out and hauling-in of the tracking line or to pole off rocks.

The ascending junks lie banked-in, below the rapid awaiting their turn to be hauled up. During this waiting period every man ashore and afloat has a different idea about how the operation should be carried out and proclaims it as loudly as possible. The noise of the hundreds of trackers can be heard from one end of the gorge to the other even above the roar of the torrent. Finally at a given signal on the drum from the junk, the tow rope is stretched, the breast rope to the shore is cast off, and the huge bow sweep sheers the junk out into the broken water. The order is given to the hundred or more trackers to move and the perilous ascent of the rapid has now begun.

From this moment except, of course, for the deafening noise of the rapid, there is silence and only one guiding spirit, the pilot, and until the junk is over the rapid everything is left to his judgement.

The water boils and foams about the junk but steadily, inch by inch, she ascends, the trackers under their headman, or ganger, attending carefully to the signals given on the drum. Sometimes it takes an hour or more to pass the 200 feet into calm water. The headman in charge of the trackers is armed with a stick and it is his duty by shouting and gesticulating to excite and encourage the men. He rushes about from one to the other. Sometimes he raises his stick high in the air over one of these as if he were going to thrash him, but bringing it down gently, taps his shoulder. At other times, when some particular exertion is required, he goes down on his knees and kotows. His actions are half-clowning and half-instructions to the trackers. The greater the exertion, the louder become the headman's shouts and antics, and the pilot in a frenzy hammers on the drum as if to beat a hole in it. Meanwhile the trackers move forward harnessed to the tracking rope, swaying their bodies and arms from side to side chanting a low, monotonous cry to keep in time. Arrived at the end of their beat each in turn casts himself off from the tracking rope, and running back to the end of the rope fastens himself on again.

Descending a rapid requires just as much skill and courage. A down-bound junk on entering the broken water almost disappears from view, but in a minute or so reappears in calm water below the rapid. Although the art is not obvious actually a tremendous amount of skill in the pilot is required to keep the junk in the axis of the current.

What happens to the old tracker? One could wish that some provision could be made so that after living in childhood in the fury of great waters in the face of an infinite number of difficulties and dangers they would pass the last part of their earthly voyage in a modicum of ease and comfort. And afterwards? May Yang Yeh, the River Guarding god, rest their souls in some true Junkmen's paradise where they can be free to enjoy their well-earned leisure, and where even the defaulters may be mercifully treated and not condemned for ever to track some ghostly junk up some never-ending rapid.

The Hsin T'an, or New Rapid, is one of the most dangerous in the river. It is situated 153 miles above Ichang.

This rapid is at its worst in the low-water season, and consists of three distinct steps; the Tou T'an or Head Rapid; the Erh T'an or Second Rapid; and the San T'an or Third Rapid. At the Head Rapid the fall of masses of rock into the stream has formed a series of dams. Through the gaps between, the river rushes as through sluice gates, the largest being close to the right bank, 70 yards in width and at dead low water about 150 yards in length with a drop of 6 feet. When the river rises the rapid disappears.

During the low-water season local pilots are engaged to navigate Chinese craft through this danger and it is a unique and awe-inspiring sight to see a junk descending. The junk is eased down the right bank into a little bay, above the head of the rapid, and when certain marks are on she is slipped, and heads as far as possible for the left bank, though she often travels, with accumulating velocity, broadside on, or even stern first, over the head of the rushing, foaming rapid, until by a combination of skill and good fortune she comes to the slack water below. Should she fail to reach the centre of the axis of the current, she may get shot out into a whirlpool or eddy, and as likely as not turn aimlessly in all directions despite the efforts of the men on the huge bow sweep. This is by no means an uncommon occurrence, and need not necessarily spell disaster. For piloting a junk through these three incredibly dangerous steps of the Hsin T'an at dead low water the local pilot risks his life for a couple of dollars a trip and if business is good he makes about ten trips a day. With luck, the upward trip passage should be accomplished in 1½ hours with the aid of 100 or more trackers.

It was near this rapid that a prosperous merchant, Li yun K'uei, lived. He was the father of the Chinese Life Boat Service. In 1854 he conceived the idea of collecting subscriptions from the traders whose junks had to face the dreaded Hsin T'an. With this money he built craft on the lines of fishing sampans, but exclusively used for life-saving work. The organization started with three boats, admirably designed for the work, and by 1901 there were forty-four of these boats in commission. To distinguish them they are painted red, from which their general name of red boats, Hung-Ch'uan, origin-

The Hsin T'an.

On left: *Looking down-river in the high water season.* Below: *Looking up-river in low water season*

ated, though these particular ones were known as Kan-Ssu-Tang, the Dare to Die Service.

Some years later the great statesman Li Hung-Chang, on his return down river from a mission in Szechuan, was so impressed with the splendid work done by these boats that he took the merchant down to Ichang and there obtained for him additional subscriptions. Three boats were built.

Li fell on evil days; his fields were flooded and funds became insufficient to maintain the boats, two of which were dispensed with.

Happily, however, in 1875, Ting Pao-Cheng, after personally experiencing the hazards of the rapids subscribed Tls. 4,000 to augment the numbers of the lifeboats.

Eight years later a high official of Hunan, Tai Pao-Ch'ao, was wrecked in a junk near Kweichow, and received valuable help from the red boats, though unfortunately his son was drowned. In recognition of their excellent work he petitioned the Emperor that the number of red boats might be increased and that they might become a regular institution. This was granted and a Life Saving Office was opened in Ichang, and the service was fully established.

The Life Boat Service was admirably organized, the river was divided into districts, each patrolled by small guard-boats under an official. These acted as river police and supervised the work. The boats stationed on the rapids constantly cruised up the eddies and down the rapids, keenly on the watch for accidents or for the cry of 'Chiu-Ming' (Save life), when a junk capsized.

As the rapids varied in danger according to the level of the river, so the patrol areas of the red boats changed. Every up-bound junk being tracked through a rapid had its attendant red boat. Down-bound craft, having less to fear, were not so attended unless they were seen to be standing into danger. When a wreck occurred, a gun was fired to summon all boats to help. This wonderful service lasted until 1940, and then quite suddenly disappeared.

Ten miles above Yunyang is the Hsin Lung T'an, or New Dragon Rapid. This dangerous low-level rapid is due to the immense landslide which occurred on the 30th September, 1896, when after forty days of incessant rain, a large portion of the hill on the north bank slid 150 yards forward into the bay and built up a projecting spit composed of the clay and rock debris. In one night the river was thus narrowed from 400 to 150 yards, the high spit converted a quiet reach into a boiling rapid, with a fall of nearly a dozen feet in 100 yards and with vicious whirlpools below the rapid. Many junks and junkmen are lost here.

The important town of Wanhsien, 1,000 miles from the sea, and about midway between Ichang and Chungking is most picturesque, backed by hills. The river that runs down from the mountains is bridged by a semi-circular arch topped by an ornamental pavilion.

One feature of the landscape deserves notice and that is the number of 'Refuge Cities' which crown the mountain tops round the city. For countless centuries the province of Szechuan has been in a constant state of turmoil in one form or another. Most rich families, therefore, have built fortified houses on their own particular mountain top.

During periods of commotion each family retires to its mountain fastness, raises the drawbridge, locks the door and waits for the trouble to die down. One such, behind the city, is situated on an unusual rock formation rising for 1,200 feet and reached by stone steps cut out of the cliff. The plateau at the top, which is said to cover about thirty acres, is fortified with battlements and walls enclosing a small refuge named the Celestial City.

The Fêng Shui★ of the town is said to be almost perfect, for a distant range affords protection from the evil influences of the Yin, or Darkness; a lower range on the opposite bank of the river screens it from south, yet being low enough to allow the benign influence of the Yang, or Light, to penetrate. Finally, a smooth point of rock juts out into the harbour just above the city, this providing the indispensable Lung, or Dragon.

The town is celebrated as a junk-building centre, as the Pei Mu, or cypress trees, grow in profusion round about. It is also famous for its bamboo paper and its pretty girls – the latter are not so apparent.

After a rambling course and a westward turn of the river, a re-

★ Fêng Shui, literally Wind and Water, the intricate system employed by Priests, geomancers, necromancers and the whole tribe of Fêng Shui experts, to fix the position of graves, temples, towns, dwellings, roads and so on in order that the dead, the gods and the living may be located under the auspicious influence of nature – whatever that may mean.

markable rock formation appears on the left bank twenty-two miles above the Fu T'an. This is the rock temple and pagoda or Shih pao chi, or Precious Stone Castle, sometimes translated as the House of the Precious Stones.

It consists of a yellowish, detached mass of rock of irregular rectangular shape and about sixty-five feet in height, which is itself set upon a 200-foot platform of rock, the whole towering some 300 feet above the village at the river's edge. A nine-storied pagoda which, it is claimed, is 1,500 years old, is built up against the east side of the cliff, and encloses a staircase which leads up to the temple and monastery buildings on the summit, which measures about 50 yards by 30 yards across. Beyond these buildings lies a small city of refuge reached by a bridge.

There are many legends connected with the Precious Stone Castle, one concerning a miraculous supply of rice. The scene was laid in the top storey of the monastery.

Authorities differ as to the details, but it would appear that if a priest put a handful of rice into a hole in the floor all of the inmates of the monastery were able to take out as much as they could eat, regardless of the number of the holy men who partook of it.

The rest of the story is soon told. In the time of Chia Ching, 1796–1821, a wicked and avaricious monk was appointed to the temple. Some say that he sold the heaven-sent food, others that he enlarged the hole so as to increase the dole. Whichever his crime the result was the same for the offended deities immediately stopped the supply. The truth of the story is proved to the satisfaction of the local people by the fact that although the hole remains there is a complete lack of supply of rice therefrom.

Just above this spot there is said to be a place where, for many years, no efforts of the industrious Chinese have availed to produce rice, but on the cessation of the miracle in the monastery just mentioned the gods compensated the country by fructifying this unfertile spot, since when rice has always been produced there.

The myth that Fengtu is on, or near, the site of the entrance to hell probably owes its origin to the presence of large caverns which penetrate some miles into the heart of the mountain. Another contributing factor to this belief is the report of 'Fire Wells' nearby, that

is to say of escapes of natural gas which, when ignited, will burn
continually.

In accordance with the tolerant Chinese custom various shrines,
both Buddhist and Taoist, have been raised to other deities. The ever-
popular Kuan Yin, the goddess of Mercy, is here represented with
1,000 heads and eyes. The temple is topped with a pavilion containing
images of two Taoist worthies who lived 2,000 years ago in the days
of the Han Dynasty. These are Wang Fan Pin and Yin Chang Sen
playing their favourite game of chess.

Two miles above Fengtu the left bank opens out into a bay called
Peishato. Above this a head of Buddha and three Chinese characters
are so carved on a spur of the rock as to face westwards. The characters signify Ta Fu Mien, or Buddha Face Reef, and there is a high
level rapid of the same name. This and a rapid just beyond are
caused by two big rocky shelves extending from the left bank, while
another reef and a bluff on the opposite side narrow the fairway
down to less than a cable's width. With an increase in water the
violence of these rapids, with a speed of ten knots and wave six feet
deep, becomes dangerous, particularly as the actual Fu mien T'an
rapid sets obliquely on to the Buddha Face Reef.

It is said that when the water rises over its mouth the Buddha can
see but can no longer voice a warning and when the river rises still
further so as to cover his head, he can neither see nor warn the junkmen who must proceed at their own risk. There is no junkman of
the old school who does not believe that it is the reappearance of the
Buddha which again stills the rapid.

The first steamer ever to attempt a passage up-river at flood level
met trouble at this spot. It was the steamer *Shutung*, which was
whirled round in the turbulent eddies and cast up on to the top of
the reef where she remained curiously poised for nearly six weeks
almost on top of the Buddha's head. Oddly enough she was very
little damaged and, with some difficulty, was finally launched again
from her perch, about thirty feet above the falling level of the
river.

The second rapid, immediately above the Fumien T'an, is the
Kuan Yin T'an, or Goddess of Mercy Rapid, which also only exists
at high water, when it is dangerous enough to justify the junkmen's

prayers to Kuan Yin, that most gentle and attractive of all the Chinese heavenly hierarchy.

Off Fuchow, usually in shallow water off the left bank of the river, the famous paddle wheel mill junks are to be seen. The un-initiated are always told that these are a new type of junk paddling their way to Chungking. Actually they are floating mills fitted into an old junk on which is built a house with a mat roof. Two or even as many as three, paddles which can be raised at will are, once the junk is moored, lowered so that they can be revolved by the swift current, and so operate the milling machinery.

A few miles below Chungking the river closes in again to a width of only 250 yards, and runs for a mile or more through a defile known as Tung lo hsia, or Brass Gong Gorge. The hills on either side rise in tiers from 800 feet to nearly double that height, and the cedars and bamboos add to the attraction of the scene.

In an open pavilion facing the river, and up a flight of steps, is an enormous gilded Buddha, often locally referred to as the Harbour Master. It was formerly the custom for junks to anchor here while the lowdah went ashore to pay his respects and offer thanks for the blessing of a safe voyage.

From here Chungking can be seen below it on the left bank, its suburbs of Kiang Pei, or north of the river, situated at the junction of the Yangtze, and one of its largest tributaries, the Kialing.

Despite the red sandstone nature of the rocky promontory it presents the same uniform grey aspect as the buildings upon it, an aspect largely due to the atmospheric effect of constant mists and cloudy, lowering skies as much as to the nondescript walls and slate roofs of the houses.

CHAPTER 11

Air Raids, 1939

WITH the advent of the invading Japanese forces the Central National Government of China withdrew from Nanking to Chungking, which became the war-time capital. In six months the city's population grew from a quarter of a million to more than two millions.

Our first week in Chungking was astonishingly cool and free from air raids; but then the heat started to stoke up, and the moon-lit nights brought the bombers, which had been held off for three months by mist and fog. We had six raids in five days. On the 12th July there was a memorably bad raid; and on the 19th and 20th August the Japanese dropped incendiary bombs with devastating effect. The first fire burned for two days, and the blackened walls stood up against the skyline in grotesque shapes as a monument to their work.

The raid on the 20th was exactly opposite our house, in the Wan Lung Men area. The miserable little colony of mat sheds which runs right down to the water's edge was ablaze almost instantly, and panic spread as rapidly as the fires. We could see men falling or jumping out of their windows into the inferno of flames. Probably some of them had gone back to try to collect a few cherished possessions. One man with a grim, set face, could be seen calmly and carefully wrapping the body of some loved one with a blanket, amidst the confused mass of wreckage surrounding him. The fire raged up the hill behind, and many people were trapped in the dug-outs, which opened into the affected area. The Custom House was the last to catch fire, and like everything else it was gutted. The little business section contained by the narrow White Elephant Lane was completely burned out.

This fire, or rather chain of fires, did not continue burning for quite so long as that of the day before; but it did a good deal more damage. The scope and intensity of the havoc, and the astonishing caprice of the flames, which here and there left a house or row of shops practically untouched, was amazing.

Gradually, as the summer wore on, the air raids increased in frequency and intensity. After each raid the troops were called out, and worked well clearing a passage through the streets, which were very soon opened to traffic. The Chinese quickly became well drilled in A.R.P. The First Alarm would go off with a prolonged blast on the city sirens, together with the banging of gongs and ringing of bells, accompanied by much shouting of 'Chin Pu', literally 'urgent news'. Old temple bells were pressed into service and placed at central points. The police station at the top of our street of steps, housed picturesquely in a curly-roofed temple, had one of these huge old bells outside the gateway, and it added its rather cracked and clanging voice to the general clamour.

The inhabitants living on the north bank of the river firmly believed that they would be safer from attack on the south bank, while those living on the south bank were convinced that they would be in less danger on the north, with the result that there was a vast traffic crossing the river when the first alarm was given. My friends the boatmen took full advantage of this. When the first alarm was sounded, thousands of boats would suddenly appear as if from nowhere, and the fees for crossing the harbour would be immediately doubled: these would increase steadily until the urgent signal was given, when all available boats would lie off the beach, and the boatmen auctioned the seats in them.

Accompanied by the cook, and carrying our few treasures, we would toil up the long street of steps to a neighbour's dug-out. The street would be alive with people going up or down to their nearest refuge: old women with small bound feet hobbling with their goat-footed gait and clutching a bundle of poor little belongings; younger women carrying babies on their backs, with children trailing after them; youngsters pressed into service to carry anything considered worth saving; old men fanning themselves in the still, hot, breathless atmosphere: all of them doubtless wondering if, when they returned to their miserable little shacks, they would still find them standing. Chinese ingenuity displays itself in unforeseen directions.

During the air raids the local thieves had added house breaking as a side-line to their normal activities. In order to make their work as hard as possible we had formed the habit of locking the bedroom door when we left for the dug-out. The key would be concealed by the cook, who invariably chose a slightly different place in which to hide it. His best effort was so successful that we turned the whole house upside down without success. Disgusted at the prospect of spending the night in the lounge, we solemnly sat down to the light cold supper he had laid out. As I opened my table napkin, the missing key fell out on to the floor.

The Japanese raiding planes came from Formosa, and flew direct to Hankow. Here they refuelled and embarked their bombs, the manual work being done by the Chinese, who on their way home would send a message to Chungking giving the time of departure of the planes. The progress of the raiders and their direction would be regularly reported to Chungking by observers *en route*. Consequently the authorities could forecast the time of the raid with great accuracy. The Government had been energetically providing free public dug-outs in the shape of tunnels blasted out of the solid rock on each side of the river, but there was not enough shelter for all.

In tackling the refugee problem, the Chinese were greatly helped by the missionaries. On one occasion the Salvation Army managed to get a huge consignment of nondescript clothing shipped to Chungking. The consignment came from England and, to judge from many of the articles, Victorian England, for among the gifts were plaid Inverness coats, fawn-coloured overcoats, and grey bowler hats. The feminine modes of the period were also represented by satin gowns with leg-of-mutton and balloon sleeves.* It was not an uncommon sight to see beggars sitting at the wayside with little on save an evening-dress white waistcoat, or peddlers wearing hunting pink.

When the urgent signal sounded, usually half an hour to an hour after the first alarm, everybody was required to be off the streets,

---

* The writer was fortunate enough to secure at an auction a long, white, flounced night-gown, made of linen. It had long sleeves, and inside the high neck was the name of the owner with the date – 1870. It was transformed, by the local Chinese tailor, into a shirt and a pair of pyjamas, which lasted for eight years.

preferably in dug-outs, but failing that in their own flimsy houses or under cover of some sort. A few minutes after this second alarm all the electric lights in the town would be switched off at the main, though before that it was fascinating to watch the multitudinous lights of the city die one by one. Anyone found in the streets now was liable to instant arrest as a spy; or worse, for the armed police patrols were quite 'trigger-happy'.

One had to be most careful of the police. Two things were expressly forbidden: first to make a noise and, second, to wear white. One unlucky goose-owner was forced by the police to destroy his particularly noisy gander, as it unwittingly broke both these rules. White helmets, too, were regarded as a particular danger, and one grew used to the curious spectacle of sun helmets encased, like soft cushions, in detachable dark-blue cloth covers. Even caps of thermos flasks were the subject of various rules. They were supposed to flash in the sun, and were regarded with the gravest suspicion. Smoking or loud talking was also not allowed by the police, on the grounds that it would give away to the Japanese (at 12,000 feet or more) the fact that there were human beings below.

Toiling up the last few steps to the dug-out, under a brilliant moon and a quiet sky of stars, and drifting, fleecy clouds, one knew that tonight, through no fault or action of their own, an unknown number, but never less than 500, of harmless and innocent people would face disaster; some to die instantaneously, others less fortunate to be maimed and mutilated. Because this was a 'Coolies' War', the main burden of death and misery was borne by the poorest classes, just as it was with the soldiers, since no one with sufficient money to buy himself out need be conscripted.

Since the raiding planes required good weather for their three-hour flight from Hankow, these nights of alarms were paradoxically peaceful, bright and calm. Not a leaf stirred in the hot night air. Feathery acacias and the slim pine needles stood out in delicate black tracery against the luminous sky, contrasting with the hard shapes of the banana palms' bold leaves. The approach of the Japanese planes was heralded by a heavy, droning throb, which at first was almost felt rather than heard. Soon the searchlights would start groping about the skies, nervously swinging their long, shining fingers from side to side in their search for the invaders. Since the aircraft flew very high, all that was visible of them was a small, compact cluster of bright, white, flashing lights: the Japanese kept close and steady formation, usually arriving in three batches of three at a time, their total varying from eighteen to thirty-six. Shivering flashes like sheet lightning showed where the first large bombs were falling on the silent city, which lay helplessly exposed on its rocky promontory.

A vast concourse of people would walk out into the country and hide under the trees. One of my Chinese friends, who had previously stayed in his house and had survived all the raids, suddenly one night felt an urge to walk out into the country for greater safety. Together with his wife and some forty villagers they hid under a large tree. Unhappily the returning Japanese jettisoned a superfluous bomb. From a height of some 12,000 feet it fell on the tree, killing all but my friend. 'I am so sorry,' I said to him the next day, 'to hear of the death of your wife.' 'It is most unfortunate,' he replied, 'but it might have been worse – they might have killed me.'

The defence plans seemed to have been rather unevenly carried out. Sometimes the anti-aircraft guns would keep up a brisk fire, while the stammering of machine-guns was heard now and then, and the sky was spectacularly lit up with red tracer bullets. When these were fired by planes, they followed a picturesque curve. The 'All Clear' was sounded from half an hour to one hour later, usually when the last Japanese was clear of the province. The whole period of alarm lasted for two to four hours. Then the Chinese would stream home in an orderly fashion from their hide-outs.

On the 3rd September we listened to Chamberlain's very moving speech, announcing a state of war between England and Germany. Later that night, after the First Alarm had sounded, we sat in our little drawing-room with all lights out except for the glow from the indicator face of our radio set, hoping against hope that the Japanese would delay a little longer so as to enable us to listen to King George's speech. But at seven minutes to midnight, the hour set for it, the lights in the city were turned off at the main and we had to turn our attention to the war on our doorstep. That night in Chungking more than a thousand innocent people were killed, either being

Bombs over Chungking

buried alive or trapped against the city wall in a raging inferno of flames. In the morning fallen masonry, plaster, shattered glass, broken telegraph wires and poles littered the streets, while flames and smoke rose high over Chungking's jagged ramparts.

With hardly a breathing space the raids followed each other. One in particular, on 5th – 6th September, caused the greatest panic because it took place during an eclipse of the moon. The Chinese idea of an eclipse is that a Heavenly Dog – some say the Three-Legged Toad – is swallowing the moon, and they try to frighten away this monster by beating gongs and drums. The Heavenly Dog was no legend that night. It roamed free, too powerful for gongs, drums or fire-crackers.

Although the Chinese were terrified of the raids, they faced them, perhaps because they seemed to be inevitable, with that dogged endurance which is one of the most remarkable features of the race. Far from accomplishing their purpose of terrorizing the Chinese people into submission, the Japanese bombings heightened their determination to resist. A peasant near Hankow was conscripted by the Japanese, and forced to carry petrol. Somehow or other he managed to escape from his captors, still carrying his burden. By devious means he walked nearly 300 miles, and finally delivered the petrol to the authorities at Chungking. Such was the morale of the people at this time.

Scenes of horror had been grim enough up till then, but they could not be compared with the devastation which fell on the city on the 14th September, when again both banks of the river were bombed. Fires were still burning from two earlier raids, in which thirty-six planes had taken part, when at 4 p.m. an alarm was sounded. This started a flight of refugees from the city, while the remaining inhabitants disappeared in an orderly fashion into caves, dug-outs or hide-outs. Dusk came, but no Japanese bombers; and slowly the dug-outs emptied. For months past the Chungking shop-keepers and merchants had done all their business late in the after-noon, in order to limit the danger from air raids. By 6 p.m. the main streets were crowded, when suddenly out of the leaden sky twenty-seven Japanese planes swept in from the north. In the twilight, soon made more brilliant by a full moon, the bombers manœuvred into position, and on this congested area they dropped more than 150 explosive and incendiary bombs, destroying everything that lay in their path and starting nine huge fires in various parts of the city. Civilian casualties were placed at 5,000 killed and 2,000 wounded. The high casualty list was attributed to the streets' being crowded at the time of the raid, and the fact that most of the dwellings in that part of the town were made of wood. The city was without light and water for a week.

The Loh Han ssu Temple was badly damaged. It stood on an eminence almost at the highest point of the town. After the raid the entrance steps were intact, and the front portion of the main gate was still standing; but inside there was utter chaos on all sides. The shrine exactly facing the gate was still there, and the large, seated idols remained together. These figures, in pairs, on either side of the first shrine are the Kings of the North, South, East and West. One had lost an arm, another a leg; but the black-faced Tu-Shih, King of

Above: *A Coolie's hat for protection against the sun*

Below: *The troops were called out and worked well*

Hades, was almost unharmed. His convulsed expression and attitude of ferocity, with one clenched hand above his head and one knee drawn up as though dancing in a frenzy of rage, served as a fitting comment on the scene of destruction; it was as if he were shaking his fist and calling down the wrath of heaven on the work of the raiders.

It was difficult to pick one's way through the rubble and débris, past the ponds of the sacred fish, now half filled with masonry, and across a lumpy stretch of waste ground where once the courts and shrines and cloisters of the temple had meandered. A vast bronze bell lay on its side close to a deep twenty-foot crater, now half filled with rain-water. The bell was bright green from the fire. Nearby lay a huge gilded Buddha, also bronze, broken into two halves, while the head lay apart, its bland face tilted to the sky, the thick lips set in the same inscrutable, secret smile.

The whole structure of the temple was levelled to the ground, yet, unaccountably, at the far end of this large waste plot the main altar stood up bravely, surmounted by its three golden Buddhas. This must surely have seemed a miracle to the faithful. As they were in the open, the Chinese had provided each Buddha with a coolie's straw hat for protection from the sun. The other altar was not itself injured; the little painted plaque below the images retained the colours and contours of the stilted Chinese landscape, the little supporting imps continued to hold up the pedestals, although one or two were deficient in a limb or a foot. The only damage was that all three figures were headless; the three incarnations of Buddha had been decapitated with equal precision. It was curious that the flames and blast had had no effect upon the gold, which shone brightly yellow, 'refined by the fire'. Underfoot in the mass of broken material glowed the deep green of the temple roof tiles and the cheerful colours, mainly red and white, of the thousands of small porcelain Buddhas the monks had formerly sold.

Vividly I recollected my last visit to this temple, when I had seen the tall walls, lined from stone-flagged floor to rafter ceiling with glass-fronted shelves containing a quite bewildering number of these little china Gautamas, and how, on a festival day, I had watched three young women making their bow on the fibre foot-stool below these now headless figures, presenting their offerings of flowers and food, burning the square sheets of coarse brown joss paper in the bronze incense burner now lying broken and neglected, whilst a single note was struck on the bell by a priest to warn the gods that they must wake up, for a petitioner had appeared with candles and gifts and worship. One of the girls had made her deep genuflections in all earnestness, another with awkward, jerky movements, as if shy; the third had eyed me in a mischievous way, as if she were subscribing to a barbarous custom. Giggling, but excited, they had each in turn drawn a numbered strip of bamboo from the bunch in the container proffered by the priest, and then thrown the wooden hooves to see if this were the number decreed to prophesy their destiny. When both hooves fell inauspiciously, exposing either their polished exteriors or their roughened inner sides, they selected a new bamboo slip and threw the hooves again until they lay, one right and one wrong side up. The corresponding number was found amongst flimsy, oblong, yellow paper strips a few inches wide, and from this the priest read out the answers to their questions, so cunningly wrapped in classical phrases and vague allusions that an ingenious priest could easily give an allegorical answer on nearly any question. It had been amusing to study the girls' faces, bashful and eager, and to speculate as to what lay nearest their hearts and what comfort, if any, they drew from the yellow fortune-telling strips of paper which they folded so carefully and stowed away in the recesses of their sheath-like gowns.

Buddhist Priests

The priests had now all vanished. There was nobody to tend the altar, and I wondered if the headless Buddhas would ever again savour the thin smoke from the incense sticks stuck in the sandy trough before them. Returning from the temple through the stricken area, I passed a youth lying with his knees drawn up near the gutter of the broad Ma lu; there was a pool of blood not far from his head. Dead, or just dying, he lay there, one of the million nameless tragedies of China, and it was nobody's business to care for him. No one knew, and no one cared, though many stopped for a few minutes to stare in that soulless, open-mouthed Chinese curiosity that is so typical and so exasperating in this pleasant and on the whole kindly, but infinitely irritating race.

CHAPTER 12

Alas, Poor P'o P'o

EVERYBODY in Chungking knew P'o P'o. She was a curio
dealer, and no account of Chungking would be complete without a reference to her.

Old P'o P'o, as the servants called her, was quite a character. Her
nickname means 'Old Granny'. Although she was old, she was not
at all decrepit. Another name for her amongst the foreigners was
'Old Hsieh-hsieh', for she would continually interpolate this
Chinese word for 'thank you' or, more accurately perhaps, 'thanks',
in her endless discursions.

On the summons, she used to step briskly into the room with her
packages tied up in dingy cloths and would bow and smile and talk
all at once. When the prolonged greetings were over, she would
settle herself down and proceed to unpack her wares.

Shapelessly rolled up in clothes as a protection against the cold
weather, she made an amusing figure, seated on the floor. Her short
legs in padded trousers tied at the ankles stretched out in front of her,
like an elderly child's, ending in those absurd bound feet, which
were painfully crowded, below the bulging instep, into five-inch
long cloth shoes. Her hair, which was growing rather scanty on the
top, was concealed, except for her chignon, in the black turban bonnet worn by all middle-aged Chinese women in the winter. Her
face, framed between the close velvet flaps, would beam in anticipation of an hour's bargaining, and her beady eyes were lost in the
folds of her laughter, as she cackled triumphantly, like a hen, over each
treasure she produced from her dirty little bundles and laid at my feet.

First a pair of blue and white porcelain vases depicting the graceful, wind-blown shapes of Chinese ladies in fluttering garments.

'K'ang Hsi!' declared P'o P'o.

True, the blue chop or mark on the bottom bore the name of that
famous Ch'ing Emperor, during whose glorious reign Chinese por-

celain attained a delicacy of perfection since unequalled; but these chops can be, and usually are, counterfeit.

'New imitation!' I would reply with studied scorn.

P'o P'o would look shocked and pained and would put aside the vases and pick up a blue silk skirt brilliantly embroidered in gold and blue or a darker shade, with a medley of other colours.

'This is old indeed,' she would say; 'it belonged to an old mandarin family, who have lost money and must sell.'

Age must certainly have mellowed those colours to such a delicious blending. I held the pretty thing and savoured its musty aroma, felt the papery texture of the thin, green silk lining, and examined the elaborate pattern of red and gold dragons sprawling among the embroidered clouds. Whose young fingers, I wondered, had put in each careful stitch? What was the occasion for which it was made? Was it not most likely a wedding garment? Inwardly deciding it must be mine, I casually placed it on one side.

'How much then for this old and poor piece of work?' I asked.

P'o P'o studied it with fictitious care, as if she hadn't long ago assessed its worth, what she hoped to get, and what she would finally be content to accept for it.

'Eight dollars would not buy it,' she said.

'Eight dollars would not indeed,' I replied, 'for none would be so foolish as to give it. I might perhaps offer three.'

P'o P'o shook her head in denial, but was careful to leave the skirt where she hoped, and I feared, it would form the nucleus of a pile of my choosing. Tactfully she changed the subject. 'Here are the shoes to go with it.'

She held up an incredibly small pair of shoes in red satin, with tiny embroidered toes, rather shabby from use, the thick soles and minute blocked heels being made of fine black material pressed and stitched. She measured the forlorn little bits of finery against her own bound feet, which appeared quite large in comparison.

'Chinese lady's shoes. Very cheap, as they are old and worn; only fifty cents a pair.'

She put them away as I did not want them.

'See, this is something good!' She placed an oblong trinket-box in my hands. It was made of some sort of mud composition, lacquered over with red, and a tracery of gold design still showed on the surface. It was the cunningly-shaped brass hinges and hasp fastener, however, that attracted me most. Inside, gleaming against the ebony walls, lay a jade blob, spurious but pleasing, hanging from a filigree plaque in gold-washed metal.

'How much?' I asked weakly.

Once more the little ritual was enacted. First her reply, much in excess of all reason, and then my amendment to a figure below that which I was really prepared to give. She made her usual mechanical protest, the article was deposited with the blue skirt beside my chair, and a fresh interest was immediately provided.

'Look,' she tittered, 'an old-time wedding head-dress for a young girl, worn thus.' Held in place with both hands, the stiff, pointed panels of embroidery were cocked rakishly in a half-diadem above her homely face. Herself amused at the incongruity between this gay symbol of youth and her wrinkles and drab clothing, she minced and posed for my regalement. This piece of buffoonery beguiled me into adding the head-dress to the pile at my side, from which my attention was quickly diverted by a chinking of metal. This proved to be a collection of old coins of varying sizes, all without milling and with round or square centre holes. The rubbed inscriptions in ancient script were as intriguing as the embellishments. One bore an imperial five-toed dragon, and another showed, beneath the distorted branches of the symbolic peach-tree, a crudely prancing deer; 'Lu' the Chinese word for deer being a homonym for Official Power.

Leisurely the game proceeded. In as detached a manner as I could assume I inquired the price of what I fancied, and transferred it to the growing heap until I had a selection ranging from richly-worked sleeve-bands, cases for fans or spectacles, and green-lined porcelain sweet-dishes, to a gargoyle of a bronze imp balanced on one foot with the other crossed high above the knee, giving him an air more Tibetan or Indian than Chinese, and a pair of small swords made of brass cash coins joined together by red cord strung through their square centre holes. These swords are still used in remote country places by mothers, who lay them under the mattresses of their children's beds to protect them from evil or disaster.

'How much for this lot of worthless things?' I asked. 'All are old and will require cleaning, many are torn or broken, all are useless save as emblems of ancient customs.'

This was the crucial moment of P'o P'o's afternoon. In silence she fingered and turned over the different articles.

'Twenty-two dollars for all,' she quoted at last, and already this was less than the total of her original figures.

'Impossible!' I affirmed in simulated horror. 'Do you think I am a rich tourist? I will give you . . .' I hesitated, and we eyed each other, mutually indulgent over our little charade, 'I will give you ten dollars.'

I had come up on my first quotation by about the same amount as she had come down. With a spirited show of refusal, she began to pack away all the things I had not chosen.

'My master would never sell so cheap.' In the crisis of a bargain this mysterious 'Master' was always dragged into the argument. 'See,' her tone became coaxing, 'this sewing is most excellently done. The silk alone is worth more than what you offer for the whole.'

'Ten dollars,' I repeated firmly.

Again there was a pause while she tallied the things over, murmuring the price of each aloud, and they had again fallen considerably.

'Eighteen dollars for you, as you are a good customer . . . thank you.'

'As you are old, and I like the things, poor as they are, I will give you twelve dollars,' I conceded.

In some unaccountable way we both realized the bargain was concluded, and this was to be the final figure. Automatically, as she knotted her bundles, she continued her protestations; but they carried no conviction. Tired at last of the little interlude, I moved away with an indifference not altogether assumed.

'Twelve dollars. Do you want it or not? I have now no more time to spare.'

'A little more, Master, thank you,' she pleaded.

'No more,' I returned.

P'o P'o knew when to give in. She rose with amazing agility for one of her years and figure, and laid the things out on the table.

'Truly, I lose money!' she wailed.

'Then do not sell,' I said, dropping the twelve crisp dollar notes into her ready palm. She counted them, folded them away into some obscure corner of her clothing and bowed profoundly.

'Hsieh-hsieh, hsieh-hsieh!' she repeated, sidling towards the door. 'Soon I shall return, and I shall bring many even better things for your most honourable inspection.'

But she never did return. Soon afterwards, on a bright moonlight night in September, at twenty minutes past eleven, the Chungking sirens sounded the last warning of an air raid. P'o P'o had arrived late at the dug-out, off the Street of Perpetual Peace, only to find that one of her grandsons was missing. Although the Japanese planes were by then overhead, she left the dug-out and went back to the house to look for him. This cost her her life; on the way she was killed by a Japanese bomb.

She had a wonderful funeral. In the procession there were many banners (the Chinese equivalent of wreaths) carried by street urchins with dirty faces and in embroidered gowns. There were two large lanterns giving the family name, three big gongs, a pig roasted whole, carried on a huge wooden tray by four men, a motor-car and a sedan chair for the chief mourners and a band playing, 'When Johnny comes marching home again, hurrah, hurrah!'

White storks are always placed on the coffins of worthy old women. Their function is to carry the souls from this world to Paradise. In P'o P'o's case the storks had an easy task.

CHAPTER 13

A Few Gods and Some Beggars and Thieves

FROM Chungking I moved on to Ichang, where I lived in the Customs Compound in safe seclusion, for the most part, from the busy life beyond the high, surrounding walls, over which intermittently there came sounds of the outside world. The most insistent noise came from a nearby temple; it was the resonant clangour of a Chinese gong being beaten at frequent intervals. This was known locally as 'Gonging for Rain', for the child-like oriental mind pictures the Rain God fast asleep, and has devised this method of rousing him to a proper sense of his responsibilities.

Here, in the heart of China, a thousand miles from the sea, it was a curious constricted life, shared by a handful of foreigners hemmed in by teeming millions of Chinese, who regarded us mostly with hatred, curiosity or indifference. For Ichang at that time was probably the most anti-foreign place in China. To me, however, Ichang had always a great attraction. Ceremonies and festivals, so ancient that their beginnings are lost in the mists of time, and which I had come to like so much, were far more strictly observed here than they were in the sophisticated large cities. It represented, too, the gateway to the magical province of Szechuan and its wonderful junks.

*   *   *

Once, when I had nothing very much to do, I started collecting the names of gods. In a short time I got quite a number – about three hundred if I remember correctly. Some were very curious: the god of lice, the god of brothels, the god of smallpox scars, and so forth.

The junkmen say that the gods and the immortals live in a palace made of clouds, beautiful beyond belief. It has ramparts of gold 300 li round, with twelve jade towers and battlements of precious stones; and in the garden are peaches of immortality. Once a year the gods have a birthday party. It is held on the third day of the third moon,

Szechuan Junk

and all the gods are expected to attend in their state robes. The subsequent dinner party is quite remarkable. There is no rationing, and no food cards are required. Monkeys' livers and the marrow of phoenixes figure prominently on the menu. Unhappily, no mortals are invited.

Once a year, too, the idols are taken from the temples and given a good wash. They are usually taken out into the courtyard and scrubbed down with hard brooms. Before all this takes place, strips of paper are pasted over their eyes, so that they shall not see each other being bathed; for gods are exceedingly modest.

Books could be written on Chinese gods. The few outlined here are those favoured by the junkmen. Many of them are misty figures, little known to the man in the street; but there are some who are immensely popular. Many are historic figures of a bygone age, while others are figments of the imagination.

As regards the junkmen, the priests say in effect, 'you accept our gods with all their funny little ways, their likes and dislikes, their foibles and shortcomings; and we, for a small charge, will show you practical methods of outwitting them'. The Chinese, therefore, worship their gods, and they neglect them. When there is anything in particular they desire, be it sons, money or guidance, they go to the temple and carry out a certain routine in a particular way, with no thought but that of securing certain practical results in the process. It is a case, more or less, of commercial enterprise; so much worship for so much benefit. It is quite in order for the suppliant to take advantage of the god's inexperience or inattention; and indeed the priests do this invariably. A good example of this is the case of the God of Fire. He is one of the most unpopular; he travels on a very fast black horse, punishing people by setting their houses on fire. A black crow is his assistant in these acts of arson. Actually he is one of the easiest deities to outwit, for his chief characteristic is propriety; and so, in order to protect their homes from fire, all that it is necessary for the owners to do is to paste indecent pictures on the walls. Shocked and scandalized, the god avoids the house, and the inmates are safe.

It is good fun deceiving supernatural beings, and the familiar case of the Kitchen God is a typical instance of the ease with which one's celestial superiors can be deceived. No matter how small, no matter how shabby the boats are, they are the homes of the men, women and children who live in them; and no one loves his home more than the junkman. In the large junks the galley or kitchen is quite a spacious apartment, but in the small sampans it is no more than a few pots and pans on top of the bottom boards; but there, sure enough, will be found a shrine to Tsao Wang, the Kitchen God. It is often tucked away behind the stove, surrounded by cockroaches, which are known by the junkmen as Tsao Wang's horses. Usually it is a gaudy picture, but in humble boats a piece of red paper with the god's name and title will suffice. He demands great respect. No woman, for instance, may comb her hair within sight of the god, or sharpen knives on the stove, or drop chicken feathers in the fire.

He was first worshipped in the Han Dynasty, and few gods are older than he. His birthday is on the third day of the eighth moon, when cooks all over China burn incense at his temples. His name means 'Prince of the Oven', and his role is of exceptional importance for he is responsible for the good behaviour of everybody in the boat or household. On the twenty-third day of the twelfth moon – that is, just before the end of the year – the Kitchen God makes his ascent to the celestial regions to report to his superior, the Heavenly Emperor, on the conduct of all the members of the home or crew of the boat.

Everybody assembles for the great feast. First offerings are made to him. This is a simple matter, for the Chinese say the smell of food is enough to satisfy gods, spirits, ghosts, and ancestors; they therefore eat it themselves. So important is the god that none but the head of the household can be trusted to supervise his worship. He, and he alone, can apply the match to the paper portrait, when the god ascends on high. At the propitious hour, further food offerings are made to him. Only sweet things may be served, so a sticky sweetmeat of rice and sugar is offered. With this his lips are smeared. There is good reason for this: Kitchen Gods are notoriously talkative, and the sticky concoction is used so that he will not be able to speak too freely. In any case the only things he will be able to say will be sweet things – that is, he will only report on the good deeds. Foreign culture has even invaded the spirit world, for some modern Chinese give him chewing gum. Sometimes, too, he is given a little opium to make him sleepy and not infrequently his portrait is dipped in wine, so that he will arrive in heaven quite drunk.

After the feast his portrait is carried out on deck, or into the courtyard, and placed in his means of transport. The head of the household then applies the match that will send him skyward. In the good old days this mass flight of the Kitchen Gods used to take place in decorous sedan chairs or in junks, but in line with modern ideas of transport their place now is taken by an up-to-date four-engined aeroplane, or a stream-lined limousine, all made of paper on reed or split bamboo frames. In old-fashioned families Tsao Wang still uses a chariot of fire. When this is so, a handful of straw is thrown in for his horse, who also gets a cup of tea. Dried peas are then thrown on to the mat roof of the boat, or on to the house; sound effects to represent the clatter of hoofs. Lastly come the fire-crackers, which evil spirits dislike intensely.

The well-known story of the man who suffered grief because he was unable to say whether he kept his beard inside or outside the sheets when he went to bed, has its counterpart in China; indeed it may be possible that the story originated there. The Chinese version is that when the Emperor Jen Tsung, who lived in 1023–1063, saw Kwan Yu, the God of War, he said to him, 'you have a very fine beard; where do you put it at night, inside or outside the sheets?' Kwang is supposed to have replied that he did not let the problem worry him at all, for he always kept it in a bag to avoid the risk of its freezing. Indeed he is said to have folded the bag most carefully every night in order to keep the entire length of beard close to his chin when going to bed. The god is a historic figure and hero of the Three Kingdoms. He is described as having a red face, eyes like a phoenix and eyebrows like 'sleeping silk worms'. He always prefers wearing green clothes. His birthday is on the thirteenth day of the fifth moon. It usually rains on this day, because it is said that the god showers a few drops of water on the grindstone to sharpen his favourite weapon.

From a nautical-research point of view Lu Pan, the Carpenter God, is by far the most important of all the gods. Opinions differ as to when he lived, some placing it as far back as 506 B.C. and others some hundreds of years later. He had a wife and a concubine, and images of these two, one red and the other black, are objects of veneration by the varnishers. Twice a year, on the thirteenth day of the fifth moon and the twenty-first of the seventh moon, the guild members meet at the temple dedicated to Lu Pan. On the latter date they celebrate Lu Pan's birthday, and make food offerings on a plate with nine compartments.

Besides being the cleverest man of his generation, he is credited with founding the art of carpentry and with inventing oars, paddles, and many improved types of boat, notably the crooked bow and the crooked stern junks. He is said to have designed various mechanical tools, including the irrigation pumps still used by Chinese farmers. He also made a 'self-moving chariot, or automatic wheelbarrow, for his aged mother-in-law; a forerunner, no doubt, of the modern taxi.

It is said that his skill was so great that he never wasted any wood, and could cut or saw a plank without the help of a guiding line. Many are the stories of his exploits. It is believed by the junkmen that when the pillars upholding the sky were in danger of collapse, Lu Pan successfully repaired them. One of his most notable inventions was a ladder which reached the sky and raised and lowered itself as required when he attacked his enemies from the air. He also carved magpies out of wood with such skill that they flew into the air and remained away, some say for several days and others for three years. The Chinese might doubtless claim this as the first artificial satellite.

Nor was this his only venture in aeronautics, for the Carpenter God invented a wooden machine into which his father climbed. On his knocking three times on the door, it rose into the air and transported him to a place near Soochow, whereupon the men of Wu, taking the visitant for a devil, killed him. Under the circumstances they can hardly be blamed. The indignant Lu Pan, however, avenged his father's death by carving a wooden effigy of one of the immortals and placing it to the south of the town. The image was represented as shaking an angry fist towards the south-east, and this produced a three-years' drought which only ceased when the proper apologies were sent to Lu Pan.

\ There are other legends to show how air-minded was this ingenious deity. It is said that he journeyed alone to the sacred mountain of Li, and there acquired marvellous secrets, including the power to travel on a cloud. His end was dramatically in keeping, for he was transported to heaven in broad daylight, presumably to live in retirement for he left his axe and saw behind him.

*　　*　　*

In the good old days of Yao and Shun, who lived between 2357 and 2208 B.C., there was, we are told, no necessity for closing one's doors at night, for there were no thieves. If an article was lost on the highway, it was the duty of the first comer to stand guard over it until the next one came along, who took his turn until the owner arrived to claim his property.

Unhappily, the virtues which are believed to have flourished in the days when the 'Model Rulers' existed have sadly deteriorated. The sages of antiquity would have wept with disappointment at the trend of modern morals in China; for when it comes to predatory devices, the Chinese have developed the theory and practice of thieving into a fine art. For instance the Imperial City at Peking, surrounded by high walls pierced by four triple gates, enclosed the even more exclusive Forbidden City, with its own high walls, for centuries a mystery to the outside world. Nevertheless thieves for years did a roaring trade in yellow porcelain tiles removed from the Emperor's palace.

In former times, too, pigeons were trained to steal rice from the Imperial granaries. These birds were called 'Food Distributors'. They flew straight from their lofts to the granaries and fed until their crops were quite full. On their return they were given a shallow bowl of water with alum in it. This caused them to bring up their food, which was washed and then sold. A hundred birds would collect fifty pounds of rice a day. Well housed and fed, they were highly prized. They were never fed until the day's work was over, and then only in the early evening so as to keep them hungry and ready for the next morning's work.

Thieving in China is a highly-specialized profession, and is very carefully controlled by the Thieves' Guild for the benefit of the majority – of the thieves. The main object of the controlling body is, naturally, to provide a respectable living for as many people as possible. The advantage of this centralized control is obvious, for the Guild is in a good position to know the state of the market and the most likely areas in need of thieves. Moreover it is able to appoint thieves whose professional knowledge is suited to the type of work to be undertaken. For instance, it would be inefficient and wasteful to detail a man capable of removing a safe from an office during working hours to a district where hat-snatching, or removing the brick facings of city walls, is the most skilled type of work. Therefore thieves are appointed by the Guild to definite spheres of influence, and thereafter are not permitted to practise in another area.

Under the present Communist rule, doubtless, thieves have to be careful, but in the days of full employment it was customary for the professional thief, on arriving at any new place, to visit the Magistrates' Yamên, calling on the minor officials in charge of thieving and offering a present. The officials in their turn would brief the thief as to the course he should pursue, which houses were thievable and which were not. The work of these Magistrates' Runners was no sinecure, for in places where no Thieves' Guild was in operation they would have to be in touch with all the thieves in their locality. Moreover they had to be exceedingly wary; for, should a thief wish to spite one of these representatives of Chinese justice, he would commit a substantial robbery and immediately leave the town. Whereupon the Runner would be seized and bambooed – or worse.

It is not easy to enter the ranks of thieves, and the number appointed is governed by the ordinary laws of supply and demand. There is, usually, a long waiting list of applicants, and the newcomer will be expected to pay 'Key Money' and give satisfactory guarantees of good conduct and proficiency.

At Shanghai the Chinese brought the art of thieving to a pitch of perfection which – perhaps fortunately – is almost unimaginable in any other part of the world. Here giddy heights of efficiency were reached, with the result that nothing moveable was safe in the Shanghai Harbour. Merchants of all classes and nationalities had recourse to the Thieves' Guild which would, for a retaining fee, guarantee that nothing was stolen. The cost was little more than that of taking out an insurance policy and was vastly more effective.

The river thieves of Shanghai have a very high standard of technical efficiency, and the rigidity of their etiquette is bound by an intricate unwritten law; indeed they may be regarded as the high priests of chicanery. There are countless instances of the successful activities of these thieving, nautical technicians. On one occasion a gang of thieves with an urge to acquire a two-ton anchor tied up their boat exactly over the site of one of the anchors of a moored ship. As the tide fell and the boat swung, she settled down over the anchor the ship was not riding to, and a diver passed a rope round it while at the same time sawing through the cable. When the tide rose again, the boat made off with the anchor to a quiet reach and slipped it there, to be recovered later. Meanwhile the steamer was riding to the other anchor; but when the tide again turned and she found herself drifting, she hove up and discovered her anchor cable cut and the anchor gone.

I was anxious to obtain first-hand information regarding the activities of these river thieves, so I telephoned to a detective of the Water Police. 'Meet me on the wharf at noon tomorrow,' he said, 'and I will introduce you to some of the finest thieves in Shanghai.' The next day I went down to the waterfront by rickshaw. There I found a large crowd of longshoremen and others, and while paying off my rickshaw coolie I was jostled. I did not mind this – I had been jostled many times in China – and I heard one of the crowd ask my rickshaw coolie how much I owed him. I heard, too, that it was five dollars. I put my hand in my pockets only to find that they were completely empty. My handkerchief had gone; so had my sketch book, my pencil, rubber and, of course, all my money.

I turned to the rickshaw coolie. 'I'm sorry,' I said, 'I can't pay you, my pockets have been picked.' He looked at me with an air of amused interest, combined with deprecation, and pointing to my hip pocket said, 'My fare will be in there,' and sure enough it was, the exact amount – five dollars.

My friend the detective laughed heartily when I told him of my misfortune. 'You should bring your amah with you next time,' he said, adding with a gesture of thinly disguised contempt, 'I'll lend you five dollars to see you home.' This, as it happened, he was unable to do, for the next minute he discovered that they had picked his pockets too.

*   *   *

The beggars of China are world-famous. They have their own god and, of course, their own guild. The god is called Chu Yuan Chang. He started life in quite a humble way; indeed he may be said to have risen from the ranks. So successful was he as a beggar that he soon became a merchant, and this in time enabled him to become a general – the aim of all successful business men in China. The beggars tell a story about him. Long, long ago, when he was still a poor man and had had nothing to eat for many days, he came to a deserted garden, and here he came across a tree covered with luscious fruit. He satisfied his hunger and went his way. Years later, Chu Yuan Chang passed the same garden, this time at the head of his victorious troops. He stopped, dismounted, and turning to his soldiers said, 'Observe this tree; when I was hot, it offered me shade; when I was hungry it offered me food. Gratitude,' he continued, 'is a very good thing,' whereupon he took off his cloak, which he threw over the tree, begging it to accept the title of Marquis of Ice and White Dew.

Begging in Shanghai, as in the rest of China, is a profession with a code of ethics as rigid as that of the medical profession in Europe. The Beggars' Guild is well known. It has its headquarters in the Temple of the Daughter of Heaven on North Honan Road. Here the council and staff of the Guild tabulate reports on shops about to open, and discuss terms with those about to hold a wedding or a funeral. Agents are sent up country to collect likely recruits. Men and women with sores or spectacular defects of the body, or some showy disease such as leprosy, are in great demand. After a short period of training, beggars are appointed to the districts most suited to their individual needs and professional accomplishments.

Shopkeepers pay considerable sums to the Beggars' Guild in their district. This, of course, is nothing short of blackmail, but it is almost universal throughout the country. A generous subscription, promptly paid, frees them from the attentions of the beggars. Failure to comply after a reasonable length of time will result in formidable reprisals. For instance, the shopkeeper who refuses a donation is liable to be invaded by a horde of beggars in the most filthy clothes, some lame, some blind, some cross-eyed or physically deformed. While soliciting alms, they will beat gongs so noisily that the shopkeeper is unable to hear his customers speak, and the transaction of any business becomes impossible until their constantly rising demands have been met. Householders and others also subscribe liberally to the Guild, to ensure that no beggars interrupt the proceedings at a wedding or a funeral.

The Beggars' Guild also fills its coffers through a monopoly of the carrying privileges in wedding and funeral processions. The family concerned must arrange with the Guild for an adequate number of bearers suitable for the occasion. If non-union mendicants are employed, the proceedings will be marred by trained beggars, who by constant annoyance will drive away all the guests. A feature of the beggars' code is their absolute honesty in transporting elaborate wedding gifts or presents for the dead. They never betray a trust when given articles of value to carry in a procession.

Shippers and godown keepers are also prominent supporters of the Guild. A wharf or steamship company which pays them regularly will be fairly safe from sabotage, but a firm ignoring the Guild must reconcile itself to a large proportion of gashed sacks, broken crates and damaged goods.

Some years ago the beggars of Shanghai went on strike in order to show their sympathy with the students, who were agitating for an anti-Japanese boycott. Both the Beggars' and the Thieves' Guilds voted to refrain from their customary occupations for forty-eight hours. Their action, however, did not cause a commercial panic in the city. This is by no means the only time that the Guild has shown an interest in public affairs. Several of the beggars' organizations made substantial contributions to the Famine Relief Fund, and there is a case on record of the Beggars' Guild presenting a grandfather clock to a retiring official who had won their favour.

A missionary doctor, living in the interior, was once asked by a native gentleman to do a kind act for a poor beggar, who was totally blind. It proved to be a case of cataract, and after the operation excellent vision was restored. When the result was certain, the missionary doctor was called upon and told that, as he had destroyed the only means by which the blind man could secure a living, it was his duty to make it up to him by taking him on as a gatekeeper in the hospital.

Most Chinese beggars are considerable artists. They will sit or lie by the roadside, and break into a whining recital of their woes whenever they see a likely subject approach. I remember one beggar who used to sit outside my gate in Golden Duck Lane. He was a very happy individual, and would sit on the ground holding up his legs, supported under the knees by his hands, so that the two foot-less stumps dangled before him. Both ended neatly at the ankles. Resting on the ground beside him were his two missing feet, neatly placed side by side, and with a string through them for convenience in carrying. The flesh had mostly rotted away, save for a few black-ened fragments clinging to the bones. It must have been gratifying for him to know that they could be buried with him eventually, so that his spirit would have the full walking use of them once more.

CHAPTER 14

Something about Rafts

I T is reasonable to suppose that prehistoric man was, at first, afraid to venture on the water; but at length, at a time computed by some to have been about 25,000 years ago, he overcame some of his awe of that moving element and began to take liberties with it. To begin with he must have imitated the animals he had seen swimming, and a floating tree trunk doubtless gave him much moral support in crossing a river or stream under his own power. Then it was that it must have occurred to him to experiment with a log as a conveyance. Next came the need to improve on it; and finally, with dawning intelligence and the aid of crude flint tools, he learned to hollow out the log and build the first dug-out canoe. But there are no dug-outs in China, and it is thought that the craft in China today are descended not from the dug-out but from the raft – doubtless the bamboo raft.

Bamboo consists of the hollow stems of a gigantic grass, cultivated in groves throughout China. It grows best in damp places, sometimes attaining a foot in diameter and 100 feet in height. A valuable feature is its great tensile strength in proportion to its weight. The many uses to which the Chinese apply the bamboo are amazing. It is pressed into service both on water and on land. It is used for building a house and for clothing its inmates. It is used, too, for making buckets, brooms, kitchen utensils, mats, baskets, hats, pillows, musical instruments, bridges, bows and arrows, token money, chopsticks, ropes, pipes, fences, combs, walking sticks, carrying poles, furniture, fishing rods, tool handles, containers, fans. It is indispensable in the school-room and in the police station. Its young shoots, too, are used as a vegetable in many ways. On the Ya River, however, it is used to provide one of the most interesting and perhaps the most efficient forms of raft to be found in China.

Bamboo rafts being of such importance I began making a detailed study of them; and, directly I learnt of a new type, I was not satisfied until I had not only made a plan of its structure, but had made a voyage on it as well. I had, of course, heard of the famous Ya River rafts in the 'Wild West' of China, but that area was too bandit-infested even for me. And then one day, with an air of importance, my No. 1 Boy in Chungking handed me on a tray a striking looking folder, dashing black characters on a red ground, which I examined with interest and curiosity. It was, of course, a New Year's card; and it came from 'Accumulated Virtue', my cook of former days in Kiukiang.

In order to prevent unwarranted excitement, Chinese letter writers usually mark their envelopes with well-known phrases, so that the receiver will not suddenly be scared to death. The most usual phrase is 'Safe Tidings'. Sometimes this can be misleading. A man once received a letter to the effect that his wife had suddenly died, and that the neighbours had helped themselves to every article in the house. Yet on the exterior of the missive were inscribed the somewhat inaccurate words, 'A Peaceful and Happy Family Letter'.

Those writers who believe in neatness have evolved a system whereby their private seals will convey the nature of the contents of the letter. One seal denotes bad news, two seals indicate some good news, and three seals denote ordinary 'safe' information. It was obvious from the two seals on my former cook's letter that I was in for something interesting. On the back of the document was an important message. The writer said that he was no longer a cook; he had changed his job, he was now rich, happy and prosperous – he had become a bandit; and, it continued, if I cared to study the rafts in his area, would I let him know, for as he was now one of the leading bandits he would be able to guarantee my safety.

'Accumulated Virtue' had been, when I knew him, a great rascal, who drank like a fish and beat his wife. Of all the servants in a foreign establishment in China, there is none who so entirely holds the peace of the household in his hands as the cook; and, in spite of his many failings, 'Accumulated Virtue' was a very likeable fellow. He combined extreme faithfulness with extreme iniquity. Although he would swindle me without mercy he would never allow any of the other servants to do so. In short one never knew whether to sack him or to raise his wages. Whenever we invited people to dinner, they almost invariably accepted, for 'Accumulated Virtue' was by far the best cook in the port; but he was chancy – one never quite knew if he would be in our kitchen or in the local jail; indeed many a time have I had to bail him out before an important meal.

I left Chungking long before dawn the next day, and through the kindness of my friend the Postal Commissioner, I was on my way in the general direction of Lung Chang in a lorry carrying the registered post. In course of time I met 'Accumulated Virtue' at the rendezvous, and together we travelled on horse-back to the head waters of a tributary leading to the town where the large rafts of the Ya were located. The river here is extremely shallow and runs at a very great speed through half-covered boulders in the stream. Although sampans are in use at favourable ferry points, the river is so unsuitable for navigation that everything has to be carried on rafts of special design.

We were fortunate to find a raftman who would take me as a passenger. 'Accumulated Virtue' did not wish to risk becoming a 'Toast for Neptune' and so travelled down-river by the land route. The raftman said he was going down-river to attend his grand-father's ninety-first birthday party. The family had subscribed quite a substantial sum for a birthday present, and he was going to take it down with him on the raft. While we were talking, the present arrived carried by two men. It was a large and handsome coffin, painted red – red is the colour for happiness in China. The raftman said that, for a small extra charge, I might occupy the coffin and so avoid getting my feet wet. He added that at our first stop his aunt would be boarding the raft as a passenger; and, he continued, 'she is a most unpleasant woman.'

I duly entered the coffin, which was extremely comfortable and permitted an all-round view of the proceedings. The first stage of the short voyage was without incident, and, when we banked-in, I noticed a nondescript crowd gathered round two old women in paroxysms of fury, both screeching themselves red in the face. It was a hot day, and at intervals the revilers would suddenly stop and proceed to refresh themselves by fanning, afterwards returning to the attack with renewed fury. It is well known that Chinese women use much viler language than men and that they continue doing so much longer, thus justifying the aphorism that what Chinese women have lost in the compression of their feet seems to have been made up in the volubility of their tongues. And then quite suddenly two peace-makers arrived and, each seizing a roaring belligerent, proceeded to tranquillize her with good advice. The less bellicose combatant was finally led away from the battlefield, yelling back scorn and defiance at her opponent as she went. The woman who remained turned out to be the raftman's aunt.

Having been a silent witness of the scene I judged it prudent to offer her as gracefully as possible the hospitality of my coffin, which she accepted without acknowledgment. Her contribution to the birthday party consisted of a goat, which she insisted should also be accommodated in the coffin. A cargo of dried vegetables had meanwhile been stowed on the fore part of the raft, and on top of this the raftman's son was precariously perched. Just as we were about to start there was great excitement on the bank, and presently a small boy appeared carrying a bundle of chickens tied together by their legs, looking like a bouquet. This, it was explained, was the gift of the younger generation to the forthcoming festivities. The aunt directed that these also were to be given room in the coffin, which by now was so crowded that it was next to impossible even to break stowage.

The Chinese have carried the art of denunciation to the point of perfection, and one of the worst forms of abuse is to observe, 'May all your relatives be stuffed into one coffin!' It was with this thought uppermost in my mind that we again proceeded down-river at a very high speed, with the goat sitting on my knee. All went well for a time when suddenly, while we were rounding a bend, a weir loomed up ahead. The drop was about four feet, and the raft went over this, still at sickeningly high speed, and at an acute angle. The result, of course, was that the coffin with the old woman, the goat, the chickens and myself, with the addition of the grandson who had fallen off the vegetables and joined us in the coffin, charged to the far end of the raft. The raftman had left us by disappearing involuntarily and quite hurriedly over the stern, and was now racing down the bank in an effort to catch the raft; indeed, so alarming was the situation that it looked as if the overloaded coffin and the raft would be proceeding to our destination separately. Happily, without effort on our part, the raft took a sudden sheer and ran into the bank, when the breathless raftman caught up with us. At the end of the voyage I was not sorry to rejoin 'Accumulated Virtue' and tranship to a larger raft, one of which was almost ready to sail.

The Ya River is a swiftly-running, little-known tributary of the Min Kiang, which it joins a few miles below Kiating, a town on the Upper Yangtze. The river, which rises in the mountainous country north of Yachow, is about two hundred yards wide and is plentifully bestrewn with boulders, shingle and sand-banks. It is extremely shallow in winter, but in summer becomes a raging torrent when the stream, which is clear, runs at a rate of six knots or more, while in freshets it is vastly increased. At its junction with the Tung-Ho, another tributary, it produces whirlpools and eddies of great variety and number. In addition the river runs down a steep gradient. It is by no means the sort of waterway that one would choose to navigate; but the trade between Yünnan and Kwei Chow is so important that it is imperative to negotiate the hundred miles of intractable river between Yachow and Kiating, which is a vital link in the chain.

The Yachow Raft consists of a long, narrow bamboo platform of great strength and flexibility. The bamboos used in its construction are the culms of the Giant Bamboo (*Dendrocalamus giganteus*), which is the largest type of bamboo in China. The growth is rapid; in one season a height of 20 feet to 100 feet may be reached. The trees are hollow between the joints, which gives great lightness and elasticity. These bamboos have a thin siliqua cover, which is scraped off with a special tool consisting of a curved knife fitted round a small bamboo tube, the tube being pushed backwards and forwards over the stem of the bamboo. Before being made into rafts the nodes are hardened over a slow fire.

The bamboo poles are 5 inches in diameter and 15 to 18 feet in length, laid side by side; and as with smaller rafts, the joints are so spaced that no two ever coincide. The lengths of the rafts vary somewhat, the largest type being 75 to 100 or more feet long with a beam of 12 to 15 feet. The bamboos are securely lashed to each other and to numerous cross beams of bamboo spaced at intervals of about three feet. These are, however, less in diameter than the remainder, and they are not treated in any way. The lashings are made of withies half an inch wide. Protection and extra strength are provided by a continuous fender on each side from bow to stern.

Starting at the 6th frame, and running down the median line, is a platform supported on legs a foot high. This platform is 4 to 5 feet broad, and the supporting legs are secured to the bamboo crosspieces. Cargo is stowed on this superstructure, suitably dunnaged, to a height of 4 feet and protected by bamboo mats. The largest rafts will carry up to 7 tons of cargo and/or passengers. When light, the raft draws 3 inches; when under way and fully loaded its draught is about 6 inches – which puts the main deck of the raft an inch under water.

The upturned bow is tapered with 20-foot, specially-selected bamboos, which are braced by 10-foot cross-pieces securely lashed to the main structure. The bow is supported by a rope bridle leading from either side of the projecting cross beams to a central fore-and-aft iron bar, terminating in a hook and situated on the 5th frame, to which it is made fast by a lashing. In order to ensure a better lead, the bridle rests on a towing horse 4 feet above the deck. Below this there is a small, low platform of five bamboos, and from here the laodah cons the raft. The stern, which narrows slightly, is flat, and has a small lean-to shelter for the normal crew of seven men. Of these, four are quanters or oarsmen according to circumstances; one man is employed renewing worn-out withies, one man cooks, and the laodah superintends the steering. The cook has his clay stove and gear near the stern, and mans the midship oar when this is necessary.

The raft is tracked up-river, at the rate of about five miles a day, by hired trackers who are not normally part of the crew. The tow rope, which is made of bamboo, is secured inboard to bamboo bitts situated just abaft the towing horse. The raft is steered by a sweep, which is augmented at times by some of the crew entering the water and pushing with an 8-foot pole, or alternatively, by oars which operate from thole-pins situated in the fore part of the raft, one on the starboard side and one on the port quarter. The downward trip takes one and a half days, while the upward journey takes two to three weeks or more.

Anyone in search of a new sensation is recommended to take a trip on one of these rafts.

CHAPTER 15

Chungking to Chengtu — The Salt Wells
of Tzeliutsing

AFTER studying the Crooked-Stern Junks of Fuchau I felt that
there must be other salt junks in Szechuan with something
curious about them. Then one day, quite by accident, I came across
a travel book by a dauntless woman named Mrs. Bishop, who mentioned that she had seen a 'Crooked-Stern Junk' at Tzeliutsing. This
was good news. I put the book down and went upstairs and packed
my suitcase.

Tzeliutsing, or 'Self Flowing Wells', is situated near the centre of
the Red Basin of Szechuan on the Yentsingho, a small tributary of
the Lu River, which in turn is a tributary of the Yangtze. Even
from Chungking it is a tiresomely inaccessible spot, which probably
accounts for Marco Polo's failure to mention it when he passed
through Chengtu about 1283. The journey from Chungking to
Tzeliutsing by river is indirect and tedious, necessitating changes
from one uncomfortable form of travel to another, while overland
from Chungking it takes several days by motor-bus, wheelbarrow
and chair, over indifferent roads. The provincial highway is left at
Neikiang, some 156 miles from Chungking, after which the branch
road continues in a south-westerly direction for another forty miles.

All my travels in Szechuan had been deadly uncomfortable, but
this trip promised to be the reverse, at any rate as far as Neikiang,
for I was to share a half-loaded lorry, hired by the Canadian Mission,
with a bishop bound for Chengtu. Never had I travelled in such
luxury before, or with such exalted company.

Chungking was just stirring when I left my house in Golden Duck
Lane. In torrents of rain my secretary and I picked our way in the
dark down the long street to the foreshore. Coolies carried our bags,
and skipped lightly ahead down the precarious and uneven flights
of steps without any light and without a single slip. Arrived at the

186

water's edge we had to rouse a drowsy boatman to take us across the river. It was rather a pleasant and eerie experience to cross in the dark, slipping quietly through the slack water until we entered the fierce current. With one man at the heavy stern sweep and two others at the oars, we shot out into the current, our only light a paper lantern, the only sound the rushing of the water rising to a roar as we breasted a race.

Chungking looked grim, dreary and depressing in the cold and rain as we touched the further shore. A twenty minutes' walk up what seemed an endless street of steps to the Gate of Eternal Peace, sadly damaged by Japanese bombs, brought us to the centre of the city. For Chungking the truck was remarkably punctual, arriving only an hour late. The rain had stopped by this time. The truck was typical of those in use all over this part of China at that time. It was a Dodge, with a Chinese-built body, mainly of kerosene cases and oddments of wood from bombed houses. In the rear were placed two wicker chairs, with inviting-looking cushions, for the comfort of the Bishop and myself. I always travelled light, with at most a couple of suitcases which I was prepared to abandon if need be, or lose, and the canvas bag I had acquired at Haiphong from the Consul. The Bishop had a number of heavy trunks, which were all stowed in the fore part of the truck, together with various packing cases of stores for the Mission at Chengtu. When all this gear had been stowed, covered with canvas and securely lashed, we were ready for the road.

The Bishop and I had taken our seats and had said what I hoped were the final farewells, when two giggling Chinese lady converts made their appearance and it was explained to us that these also were to be accommodated in the truck. With the greatest gallantry the Bishop gave up his comfortable chair and sat on one of his trunks, and I was compelled to do the same. The truck took a good deal of starting; but, with the help of the large crowd that had by now appeared, we started off at a handsome pace down the uneven road to the police examination point, a mile away.

To an old traveller like myself it was quite obvious what was going to happen, and it did. The police held up the truck and refused to allow it to move until several of their private passengers had been given a lift. So many of these 'gold-fish passengers', as they were called, had demanded space that it became necessary to remove some of the packing cases and finally some of the Bishop's personal belongings. A vast crowd had collected, and all were loudly taking part in the controversy. The Bishop was undoubtedly the loudest of all; and, as he waved his umbrella, he seemed a classical example of the Church Militant here on earth.

I had neither the time nor the inclination to join in the unequal struggle; and, after saying good-bye to the Bishop and luxury travel and collecting my scanty belongings, I left the battlefield and departed for the bus station, now a long way back. At the bus station we found that the bus was a very dirty and decrepit truck; and, although it was an exceedingly easy matter to buy tickets, it was quite another matter to enter the bus, which was being invaded by a fighting, yelling mob. After it was filled long past the safety point, the only exit in the rear was fastened to prevent the passengers from falling out. All superfluous luggage of the usual bed and bundle and enamel basin type was then lashed all over the outside, so that no one could possibly get either in or out. Odd bits of extra luggage, and some babies, were passed up through the aperture in the side curtains. One baby was held out of the window by its mother to relieve the calls of nature.

After an immense amount of talk and persuasion, and finally a disgusted affectation of indifference which proved oddly effective, we managed to exchange our bus tickets for seats in a lorry laden with hundreds of motor car tyres stacked on top of each other in regular rows. These tiers reached a great height, and it was possible to wedge one's behind into the circle of the topmost tyres and sit in a sort of armchair, with an unbelievably fine view; indeed, so elevated was the position that we narrowly escaped decapitation by banners tied across the street or by sagging telegraph wires. We had to take on a drum of petrol as there were no filling stations on the route, and after a delay of three hours we were off again. This time we managed to get through the police check point without much trouble, owing largely to the judicious expenditure of dollars, and had just time to wave to the Bishop – still negotiating – as we passed.

We left the city about noon, which, in the circumstances, was good going. As we approached one of the villages we were fired upon without warning. The shots came from soldiers at the road-side, who had several gold-fish passengers they wished to introduce. The local rules at the time allowed no more than three passengers in lorries; and, as we had by now accumulated twenty, it meant delays at the check points, for the gold-fish passengers had to be disembarked before the lorry arrived for the police inspection, and we had to wait on the other side until they could be re-embarked. After leaving one of the check points, all traffic on the road was held up by the military owing to an air raid. The queue of stationary vehicles extended for several miles on both sides of the road, while the passengers and drivers stampeded far out into the country. The Japanese planes flew low along the road, firing machine-guns into the sitting targets, while the soldiers on the ground returned the fire when the planes had passed out of range. It was rather like a 'Western' in Children's Hour; there appeared to be no casualties on either side, but there was a great deal of noise and excitement.

Soon after leaving Chungking the road started to climb, and there were many hair-pin bends; in one place the road crossed itself over a bridge, a very creditable feat of engineering. We then traversed valleys of hummocky little hills, with high mountains always in sight somewhere. We passed through many fascinating towns, an interesting feature being the covered bridges, of which we passed at least four. Just at dark we reached the Lu River, and crossed it in a boat like a gigantic sampan. The lorry was driven on board down the foreshore mud and on to a deep, long car-ferry junk.

The lorry stopped soon after dark, and we slept the night in Neikiang in an inn, supposedly an hotel. My room which was upstairs, was a cubicle, dark and dirty, with beds at the far end draped with grimy curtains. I slept, as usual, in my clothes. The bed in a Chinese hotel is nothing more than a few boards on two trestles. This does not worry the Chinese at all, for they can sleep anywhere, lying across seats or baskets of ducks, with head downwards, their mouths wide open and probably a fly inside. A quilt is provided, and also a pillow, if such it may be called: it is merely a support for the neck, either a miniature stool of bamboo, a block of wood, or more commonly a brick. To foreigners a Chinese pillow is torture, but it is no less certain that no Chinese would tolerate under his head the "feather-filled bags" we use for the purpose.

Chinese inns in the interior are always badly lighted at night. The oil used in the lamps is made from beans, cotton seed or peanuts: it has a most disagreeable smell, and affords only sufficient illumination to make darkness visible. The lamp consists of a crude iron dish containing the oil, soldered on a tripod, while the wick is generally made from the pith of a rush. A large nail is usually laid over the wick to keep it submerged in the oil. The making of glass is a comparatively recent innovation in China: in the interior, oiled paper, silk or half-grown sea shells are used instead for the window; these will not keep out the rain, wind, sun, heat or dust. In the large towns electric light is often to be found. Chinese invariably go to sleep with the light on, and so in the inns and hotels the electric light switches are always placed outside the rooms in the corridors, so that the servants can, for the sake of economy, put out the lights when they judge the guests have gone to sleep.

The floors are usually of rammed earth, which makes the ground-floor rooms extremely cold and damp in winter. The upstairs floors are made of wooden planks, which seldom fit and are usually loose and readily admit the cold air from the downstairs rooms. The door frames are so low that a person of average height must either bend his head or bump it.

The champing of the mules in the courtyard is varied by kicks and squeals from the pigs. These sounds, and the hooting of the horns of arriving buses, alternate with the huge watchman's rattle (which he sounds to warn thieves of his approach) and by the almost incessant yelping of what seems to be a congress of hundreds of dogs. This reckless and irrepressible barking of a vast army of dogs does not worry the Chinese in the least.

Very few Chinese in the interior seem to regard parasites as a preventable evil, even if they recognize them as an evil at all. Mosquitoes and sandflies are considered a nuisance, and occasionally faint efforts are made to keep them at bay. The nets which are sometimes supplied are usually full of holes and extremely noisome. The normal practice is to burn aromatic weeds, and one can well understand the insects' desire to keep away from the choking fumes.

Accustomed as I was to sleeping in Chinese inns, the night was a sleepless one, due chiefly to the activities of hordes of bold and hungry rats. I had left the remainder of my sardine sandwiches at the foot of my bed, and the rats ran along the rails of the bed within inches of my head and proceeded to remove the packets with the utmost audacity. I moved the food to the far end of the room; and, when the noise and squealing grew beyond endurance, I flashed my torch on the scene and saw the rats fighting over the division of the spoil.

I had planned to go on to Tzeliutsing in the same bus, but early the next morning the conductor came up and told me that the bus was full and there would be no room for me. This meant, of course, that I should be stranded in the far interior of China for more than a week. Hardly had he said this when the driver came up to me and said, 'If you are interested in a seat in the bus, I will see that you get one for a consideration.' This I agreed to; but when we were due to start I noticed that the bus was quite empty. When I commented on this, the driver advised me not to ask too many questions, but to get in without delay. This I did, and the bus immediately started. We rounded a bend in the road, and there came into view a fighting crowd of expectant passengers. The driver then proceeded to auction the seats inside the bus; he then dealt with the roof, the wings and part of the bonnet; and, when these had been knocked down to the highest bidder, baulks of timber were inserted in the rear of the bus and planks spread thereon, and these were likewise auctioned.

We stopped at many check stations on the route, and each time an inspector signed the form presented by the driver certifying that the bus was empty. When finally we came to the last mile of our journey the bus stopped, and we were told to get out and walk, for, said the driver, 'the bus must arrive at its destination quite empty.' The quite considerable sum collected was the monthly perquisite of the driver and was what the cricketers of England would call 'a benefit'.

The scenery was charming. For a long time the road skirts the Lu River, the valley being amazingly fertile. The farmers were preparing the warm brown fields with little furrows, in which they laid short sections of sugar cane, kept over from the last crop. The road then climbs, by means of hair-pin bends, the dividing range of low mountains. After three more nights on the road we finally arrived at Tzeliutsing.

The specially-constructed salt junks and sampans here have a peculiar interest of their own. So bound up are they with the life of the salt-producing district that no description of them would be complete without an account of Tzeliutsing itself, and of the cumbrous, crude, and curious methods of obtaining the salt. The first mention of the wells of Tzeliutsing occurs during the Minor Han Dynasty, A.D. 221 to 265, and, in a reference dated about A.D. 347, it is stated that there were wells to a depth of 800 feet and that natural gas had also been discovered and was used then, as it is now, for the evaporation of the brine. In this district there are an enormous number of salt wells, estimated by the local merchants to exceed 1,200,* surrounding a city, or what may be described as twin cities, known by the Chinese as the Upper and the Lower Market.

The district covers an area of about 10 miles by 17 miles, and has a population assessed at from 800,000 upwards. Some authorities assert that there are half a million workers alone, and that the sum total is nearly four million souls. Certainly the twin cities present all the bustle and alertness of prosperity and enterprise. The huge derricks, which can be seen from ten miles away, the myriads of ropes stretching from them in all directions, the bamboo aqueducts leading from hundreds of wells, the numerous low buildings sheltering the brine pans, are the outward expression of one of the great industries of China.

In the crowded streets may be seen caravans of coolies and pack-animals laden not only with salt, but with food for the men, fodder for the beasts, and coal to supplement the natural gas used at the wells. Processions of water-buffaloes ceaselessly arrive, to be drafted to the wells. A feature of the thronged streets is the prevalence of the white turban or bandeau, wound round the head, or even round the ordinary black Chinese hat; for here in the heart of Western China this distinctly Szechuanese head-dress has not yet given way

* The number varies greatly; some authorities give a much higher figure.

to the unlovely head-gear adopted from foreign styles by the workers in the larger cities. The wearers assert that the bandeau is worn in perpetual memory of, and in mourning for, their great hero of the days of the Three Kingdoms, Chu Ko Liang, who lived about seventeen centuries ago.

The usual noise of a busy street is dominated by other sounds: the whining of the great drums of the capstans, the doleful creaking of the wheels on the derricks, the roaring of the flames of the natural gas, the yelling of the muleteers, the clatter of the ponies' shod feet on the hard road, and the bells of the caravans. All leave an ineffaceable impression.

The methods used in digging the wells have probably changed very little down the ages, and are still unbelievably primitive and equally ingenious. The selection of a site is determined by omens or portents, as interpreted by experts in Fêng Shui. As these advisers are quite without geological knowledge, wells are often bored in unsuitable localities and not necessarily near existing gas supplies. An auspicious start is secured by the usual ceremony of 'Killing the Cock' and letting off fire-crackers, which in Szechuan accompanies every undertaking of importance.

After the geomancers have indicated the precise spot the well is sunk, being only from 9 inches to 1 foot in diameter. It is lined for the first 200 or 300 feet with cypress-wood in 6-foot lengths, and the long and expensive operation of deep-drilling then commences. The Chinese method is basically simple, and makes use of a cutting tool suspended from a flexible line, which is alternately raised and dropped, the percussion serving to cut and crumble the rock at the bottom of the hole. Scaffolding 10 to 12 feet high is erected nearby, on which is balanced a drill-beam – that is to say, a baulk of hardwood 12 feet or more in length and about 6 inches in diameter, which acts as a see-saw lever, the shorter end being over the well hole. When required, the axis about which the beam pivots is moved nearer the well, but despite this the suspension of a heavy drill from the shorter end serves to keep it depressed. As the boring deepens, and heavier lengths and rods are added, a considerable weight in the form of a large stone, or stones, is attached to the far end of the drill-beam to give it more lifting power. The drill, however, still remains in a depressed position in the well unless artificially raised.

The raising of the drill-beam is effected by means of very ingeniously employed man-power. The scaffolding is so arranged that the beam rises and falls between parallel platforms, on each side of which stand four men who, with automatic precision, perform a continual simultaneous interchange of position. This performance consists of five steps. The second stride, using the beam as a stepping-stone, lands the weight of eight feet together on the free end of the beam, which immediately sinks beneath them, raising the drill in the well. Instantly the men spring off the beam on to the opposite platform, thus again releasing the drill, and then turn ready for the next step back with the other foot. At each jump the drill is lifted and dropped about two feet, and in falling strikes a crushing blow of great force at the bottom of the well. An iron cross-piece at the far end of the scaffolding prevents the free end of the drill-beam from flying up too far. A man stationed at the well-mouth is employed in giving a quarter-turn to the bamboo cable, which thereby imparts a rotary motion to the drill at the moment of its impact with the rock. The cable is so adjusted that, when the lever is horizontal, the drill rests easily on the bottom of the well. The men's timing in jumping on and off the beam is perfect, as indeed it has to be, for the smallest error in judgement entails a serious accident, the man near the end of the beam being in the position of the greatest danger.

The initial drill used, an iron rod which ends in a sharp flange, can be as long as 14 feet with a weight varying from 150 pounds to more than double that amount. Various types of drill are used, some being roughened with incisions at the lower extremity. All have a ring at the upper end for attachment to the bamboo cable. As the boring goes deeper, other rods are bound tightly together so as to strike as one.

An average of 3 feet can be drilled in a 24-hour period, for the work is carried on day and night. Much delay is caused by the need to change the drills, which soon become blunted. The methods of removing the debris from the bottom of the well are varied and slow, for this operation takes longer than the drilling. Tins are

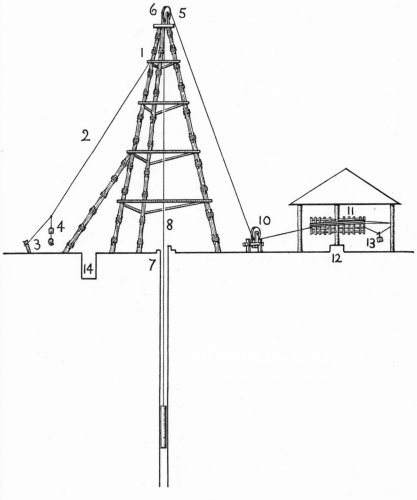

Raising the Brine

lowered down in the hope of raking up the loose earth or rock, and iron rods with spikes and barbs, and other contrivances such as bamboo tubes fitted with suction valves, are also used. Sometimes the rope breaks and the drill falls down the well, and then it takes five or six months to crush the old drill and get it out piecemeal.

The men work in shifts, timed by means of incense-sticks hung from a beam. After ten minutes the end man is changed and a new man comes on at the other end, while the others move down a place. It is a life-time occupation, and the men seem remarkably cheerful and contented, despite the literally boring nature of their work.

The drilling of a well may take anything from three to twenty years, though in rare cases brine has been found after only a few months. Time is normally of small account to the Chinese, who will labour at an enterprise in the hope that it will be brought to a successful conclusion a generation or so hence. This patient anticipation is taxed to the uttermost at Tzeliutsing, where every irritating form of delay combines to retard progress. The work, too, is so expensive that a change of owners often occurs before it is completed, the originators having used up all their capital before striking brine or gas. Moreover, a well that flows today may be dry tomorrow, continue dry for days or years, and then mysteriously be renewed.

Brine boiling may sometimes be started while the drilling is still in progress. The first essential to the raising of the brine is the lofty derrick[1] (see page 195), of a height varying from 60 to 175 feet over the well-mouth. This tripod is composed of a multitude of sha-mu poles lashed together to a considerable thickness, and so disposed that no two joins ever coincide. The lower sections have five or more poles lashed together; the second, four; the third, three; and so on. The bamboo-rope lashings are tightened up by wedges, and additional support is provided by numerous cross-pieces and an extra leg. The structure is stayed by the use of bamboo ropes[2] attached to buried stones,[3] often as many as ten of these guys being used. When they get slack, adjustment is made by hanging heavy stones[4] to them near the ground. This dangerous practice seems to escape the nemesis it richly deserves.

At the derrick-head is a grooved wheel[5] about $2\frac{1}{2}$ feet in diameter and running on a $1\frac{1}{2}$-inch axle, which rests on heavy timbers mortised into the cross-beam.[6] This is situated directly over the well-head, which, when completed, is covered with a square stone[7] with a central aperture less than one foot across. Over the central wheel[5] passes the cable[8] supporting the brine-pipe,[9] or bucket, which is made up of lengths of hollowed bamboo. A short distance from the derrick is a fair-lead[10] consisting of another wheel supported on an axle slung between two uprights, which in turn are wedged into a cross-beam resting on two more supports and heavily weighted with stones. The whole contrivance creaks and wobbles alarmingly, but nevertheless is astonishingly efficient.

The brine cable[8] passes under this wheel and thence to an enormous capstan[11] which supplies the motive power. The drum of the capstan, which is about twelve feet high and will wind about sixty feet of rope on its 16-sided circumference, is placed on a vertical axle tipped with iron, on which it revolves in a hollow in a large stone[12] of hard consistency. The upper end of the axle engages in a hole in a heavy beam built into the structure of the shed, which covers the whole. The spokes of the capstan, which are about eight feet long, are let into the rim, and all the component parts are lashed with bamboo rope.

Formerly mules and horses were used in considerable numbers to haul up the brine, but nowadays the well cable is wound round the capstan by water-buffaloes of any number up to five, harnessed to its circumference at equal intervals by a bamboo rope attached to a wooden yoke and pole. Each animal has its own driver, who controls it with a bamboo rope through its nose and a length of discarded cable used as a whip.

The work is arduous, and it is said that the animals are soon worn out, rarely lasting for more than four or five years at the most, after which they are sent to the butcher. During their reportedly brief lifetime these valuable workers are well fed and looked after. They are chiefly imported from Chungking, and it has been estimated that 10,000 are in use in the salt industry in Tzeliutsing alone. They are fed on hand-cut grass, rice straw in winter, and a daily ration of beans. Water baths are supplied for them to wallow in at least once daily, as it is found that this increases their powers of endurance. At a properly-run well the buffaloes are changed every twenty-five minutes, and do about ten shifts in the twenty-four hours.

The height of the derrick varies according to the depth of the well and the length of the bamboo-tubing bucket in which the brine is raised. In a big well with a depth of 3,000 feet* the derrick would be some 170 feet or more in height and the bucket as long as 130 feet.

* The deepest well is said to be 4,200 feet.

A bamboo rope 2 inches in diameter and over three-quarters of a mile in length would be used to draw the bucket to the surface. This rope has to be renewed every ten days.

The process of raising and lowering the bucket takes twenty minutes or more, and 10,000 catties (5¾ tons) of brine are brought to the surface in the 24-hour period. This highly concentrated brine yields from one-fifth to one-fourth of its whole weight in salt. A total complement of sixty water-buffaloes and a staff of more than thirty men would be kept at an important well.

The bucket, bound with hemp cord at the natural sections and with iron clamps at the telescoped joins, is a very ingenious device. Made from the giant bamboo it is fully 6 inches in diameter, with a wall ¾ inch thick. The outer skin is removed, and the bamboo is hollowed throughout its length. The base is provided with a buffalo-hide non-return valve, which on immersion opens to admit the brine and closes on leaving the level of the brine.

On reaching the surface a rope is thrown round the lower extremity of the bucket so as to draw it over an adjacent reservoir[14] sunk into the ground. Here a man is stationed with an iron rod, with which he forces open the leather valve, allowing the brine to gush out. A bucket of these dimensions is capable of holding about 350 pounds of the dark, dirty-looking, and evil-smelling fluid.

The water buffaloes are now unhitched and the bucket is placed back in the mouth of the well and let go. As it falls, the great, lumbering capstan at first unwinds slowly, but after a few seconds it revolves about fifty times a minute, and this high speed causes a tremendous current of air in the shed, which rocks with the vibration of the clumsy machinery while the bucket makes its 1½-minute descent. The revolutions are controlled by an improvised brake consisting of a band of split bamboo running round the upper end of the capstan. The standing part is made fast to a beam, while the other terminates in a bamboo rope. A large stone with a hole into which a wooden fork has been driven[13] rests on this rope and acts as a throttle, the operator moving the stone away from the capstan to obtain acceleration and towards the capstan when braking is necessary. This brake, although it is a most primitive device, is yet most efficient in the hands of an expert, and represents touch control developed to a nicety. The buffaloes, meanwhile, with amazing agility and sagacity, step deftly aside and stand immovable not more than a foot away from the capstan, which unwinds with such force that a blow from it would have a most damaging effect even on these enormously strong beasts.

Where the gas and brine occur in the same locality there are no transport problems, but normally the transportation of the brine from the well-head to the boiling pans forms the second important and remarkable part of the industry. After the brine has been run into a temporary reservoir some 25 feet from the well, it is allowed to settle. It is then necessary to raise it to a sufficient height so that gravity will convey it to the boiling pans. The general method is to

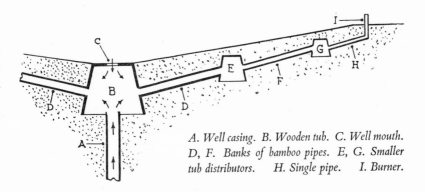

A. Well casing. B. Wooden tub. C. Well mouth.
D, F. Banks of bamboo pipes. E, G. Smaller tub distributors. H. Single pipe. I. Burner.

Plan showing well mouth when gas and brine occur. Natural gas being lighter than air seeks the higher level and goes to burners. The well mouth, C, being open, air flows down and mixes with gas in B which becomes a giant carburettor. Mixture to burners is, therefore, not pure gas, but air and gas—not quite an explosive mixture. If the supply of gas from the well diminishes, the danger point is reached, and E is opened and some of the pipes plugged with clay to reduce flow. The whole system is, therefore, a very delicate balance. If too much gas it will escape from the mouth of the well and there will be an explosion. If too little, an explosion will take place caused by flash-backs from the burners. The mixture must be exactly right.

hoist the brine by means of another capstan and team of buffaloes to the top of a derrick, whence it is decanted into a funnel, which feeds a system of bamboo pipes supported on high trestles. Another plan is to install a treadmill in a shed on poles some feet above the ground. Here men pedal the brine up into a tub, from which it flows down until lack of gravity requires a repetition of the operation. This is known as a dragon lift.

On arrival at the boiling site, the brine is diverted into various small reservoirs suspended on bamboo poles over the pans. When possible the natural gas is utilized to heat the pans, in which the brine crystallizes in about 24 hours, whereupon the process is repeated. If gas is not available the evaporation is carried out by heating with coal brought in from neighbouring districts by junk and road; but the salt thus obtained, owing to the coal soot which discolours it, is not considered to be equal to that crystallized over a gas flame. Moreover, it takes about three times as long as when gas is used.

As the brine hardens it is removed and set in baskets to drip, the drippings being carefully collected and returned to the boiling pans. The boiling pans are of the usual shallow, cast-iron type in use for various purposes all over China, but of extra large size, being about 5 to 6 feet in diameter and weighing sometimes over half a ton. Contrary to what one would expect, they are not manufactured locally. They can only be used for about seventy heatings, after which they crack.

The ideal, of course, is to find brine and gas together. The gas is said to be deeper than the brine, and when a brine well runs dry and is dug again it is not unusual to strike both brine and gas together, a combination which, with a steady output, ensures a fortune to the owner. Gas in a brine well is allowed to flow out from a side aperture into iron pipes, where it is set alight, burning with a bluish flame and very little odour. These pipes are increased as needed, each burner being sufficient to keep one pan boiling. The pans are arranged in parallel rows in ascending order, so as to permit the lighter-than-air gas to flow upwards. A large factory may have 100 pans in use. Flaring gas jets illuminate the working sheds, and as all the burners are more or less permanently alight, the waste of valuable gas is considerable.

Many of these 'fire wells' are said to have been in use since A.D. 347. The gas from a well, if directly ignited, will, it is said, throw a flame 20 or 30 feet high, which can be readily extinguished by placing a piece of clay over the opening. The mouth of the well is then closed with a small bamboo tube through which the gas is led away as needed.

It is interesting to note that 1,700 years ago the people in this far western province possessed sufficient skill and enterprise to bore down through rock for a depth of from 2,000 to 3,000 feet and the acumen to perceive that the brine was there to reward their efforts. The salt wells of Tzeliutsing deserve to be associated with the Great Wall and the Grand Canal as monuments to the industry and foresight of the ancient Chinese. Actually these wells are in a class apart, for the two other undertakings, prodigious as they were, required little engineering skill, whereas the wells afford unique evidence of Chinese ingenuity and perseverance.

CHAPTER 16

The Crooked-Bow Junk – Tzeliutsing to Chengtu

ALTHOUGH the salt wells were interesting enough in their way, it was the Crooked-Bow Junk that I had come to study, and so I made my way as soon as possible to the Lu River. My stay in Tzeliutsing had been an exciting one; for, in my haste to be on the trail of this, to me, thrilling junk, I had neglected to bring papers establishing my identity. This was a military zone, and it was not long before I was arrested as a spy. I spent two days in custody, which was a sad waste of valuable time. When I was finally released, two armed soldiers were detailed to shadow me wherever I went, and at night they or their reliefs stayed outside my room. Their chief duty was to prevent me from sketching, so I was compelled to evolve a method of drawing in my pocket. By removing the lining of my rain-coat pockets I was enabled to hold a small pad in one hand and a pencil in the other beneath my coat. The little finger of my right hand travelled up and down the edge of the pad as a guide to position. With a little practice I soon became so expert that I was able to carry on a conversation with my watch-dogs while making sketches.

It was sometimes possible to divert their attention. For example, my secretary would stroll away and then stare fixedly at an object such as the top of a telegraph pole. Soon their curiosity would get the better of them, and they would move away from me and stare at the object of my secretary's gaze. Soon a crowd would collect, which would only serve to increase their curiosity. My secretary would then withdraw.

Finally, when I had made all the notes and sketches I required, we parted on most friendly terms.

And then one day a great misfortune happened to me. I broke my spectacles, right across the bridge; and foolishly I had brought only one pair. Using one lens in the form of an eyeglass had many disadvantages; but then, while passing through a remote village, my eye chanced on a packet of 'Ten in One' Rations on sale in one of the shops. I bought the packet, which must have travelled, by devious routes, more than 1,000 miles and into the black market of the interior. Enormous shiploads of these rations, as well as other luxuries, came over from America for the use of the Chinese hospitals, but they were sold by the officials, who had built up a most efficient black market. In time Post Toasties and boned turkey from America became cheaper than locally-grown rice and vegetables. As far as my recollection goes, my packet contained what the biochemists considered a suitable breakfast for a G.I. on active service; a packet of cereal, milk, sugar, two rashers of bacon, a powdered egg, two cigarettes and a packet of chewing gum. The last item on the menu was my salvation; after the requisite mastication I planted it firmly on my nose and it held the two broken ends of the frame fairly securely in position, until I came upon an itinerant dentist who drilled holes in the frame and secured it with thin wire.

The Weiyüanho and the Junghsienho unite a few miles above Tzeliutsing and proceed, as the Yentsingho, to the Lu River. On this short stretch of 120 li, there are four formidable rapids. The first is the weir and dam at Chungt'an, and it was here that I first saw the Lu-ch'uan or Oar Boat. This, the Chinese name, is such an inadequate description of the craft that I prefer to call it the Crooked-Bow Junk.

The junk was lying secured to a rock some way out, and could be approached only by crossing to an adjoining sandbank. No sampans were in sight, and so anxious was I to reach at last the object of my search that I immediately waded out in the general direction of the junk. I had hardly got more than half-way across the stream when there were excited and incoherent shouts from the crowd on the opposite bank. Disregarding these I carried on, until my secretary very gallantly dashed into the water after me and, seizing me by the coat, begged me to return; for, said he, 'they have just opened the dam, and in a few minutes this stream will be a torrent.'

A tale is told in Tzeliutsing that Lu Pan built several types of junks for that turbulent little river the Yentsingho, none of which, however, was successful. One day while he was engaged on a new design, a large hawk swooped down close to him and he noticed how, as it came out of its dive, it banked at an angle. This inspired Lu Pan to build the bow of the junk leaning obliquely to one side, while the planks forming the stern were slanted to match, after the manner in which the feathers of a hawk's tail were disposed as it flew away from him. The junk when completed proved the most successful of all his efforts, and the type has been perpetuated ever since.

The Crooked-Bow Junks are built on slender and pleasing lines, tapering gently to bluff bow and rounded stern. Despite their graceful appearance they are, however, of exceptionally strong construction, as they must be for their passage through the dangerous rapids. The length is supposed to be standard, that is to say, 57 feet, but they are sometimes a little longer. The junks work in convoys of five, each group being known as a *tsai*. The leader, or flagship as she might be called, of each group is known as *tso-ch'uan*, and is always slightly larger than the others. They all draw only a few inches when light, and one foot when loaded.

It is noticeable that for use in comparatively deep rapids the Chinese have in nearly every case designed vessels with an under-water line, or flare, more or less rounded, and this deep draught makes for greater stability in broken water. As the rapids of the Yentsingho, however, are abnormally shallow in the low-water season, the craft built to negotiate them must draw the minimum of water; they are, therefore, with the exception of rafts, probably the lightest cargo carriers in the world. To achieve this end they are flat-bottomed and, moreover, represent more markedly than any other Upper Yangtze craft a vessel in its very simplest form, that is to say, a long, four-sided box. This method of construction indicates the origin of these junks, and the primitive manner in which the building is still carried out supports the junkmen's claim that they have been thus fashioned, without change in design, for many hundreds of years.

It must be appreciated that the work of the Yentsingho shipwrights, though ingeniously conceived and skilfully carried out, is of the crudest. This necessarily makes the caulker's task a formidable one. Gaping apertures between the planks, deficiencies in the wood, careless clinching of nails, and other minor errors of omission and commission not only demand a lavish use of chunam and bamboo shavings, but frequently graving pieces have to be inserted to fill up the larger holes.

The Chinese shipwright's tools are far inferior to those of his brother in the West. The axe, the chisel, the drill and the saw are all different in design and they are all used in a different manner. All Chinese tools are hammered out by hand from mild 'bamboo steel'.*

The most outstanding of all the uncommon features of these craft is, of course, the crookedness of the bow, which tapers from the water-line upwards. On the port side the height from the water-line to the stem-head is 4 feet 8 inches, while on the starboard side it is 5 feet 11 inches. The angle of ascent is also markedly different, and the planking, as it runs at right angles to the stem-head, is therefore aslant, although to a lesser degree than the stern planking. Seen from the end-on view, this gives the vessel a most odd appearance, as if she had a heavy list to port.

The closest questioning of the junkmen and trackers was on the whole disappointingly fruitless. A few vaguely affirmed that the channel in some places is so narrow, being little more than sufficient for the junks to pass through, and so steeply bounded by rocks, that a cut-away and very distorted shaping of the bow averts collision. Others, who seemed better informed, claimed that the bow forma-tion alters the balance of the junk, deflecting the current in such a manner as to gain the fullest advantage from it when proceeding

* Many years ago a large consignment of steel was very urgently required from Europe by a Chinese merchant. The order was given to a British firm, who, on coming to roll the steel, found that their rollers were not exactly suited for the particular size required, and that there was no time to make or procure new rollers. Accordingly, small grooves or notches were made in the old rollers to enable them to get a better grip on the metal bars, with the result that the finished bars all bore small transverse ridges on the surface. The consignment was sent out and proved to be a great success. Later on the same Chinese firm ordered more of the same class of steel. In the meantime, the firm in Great Britain, who were rather ashamed of the rough state in which the former shipment had been turned out, had pro-cured new rollers, and were able to deliver the next consignment in perfectly smooth, well-finished bars. The Chinese merchant, however, refused to take de-livery of the shipment, on the ground that as the bars were quite smooth they could not be of the same quality as those formerly sent, which were marked like 'a bamboo'. Since that time, this class of steel intended for shipment to China has always been prepared with the transverse ridges on the surface, and is still known as bamboo steel.

down-stream, while, when proceeding up-stream, it facilitates towing and makes for easier handling in the sharp turns of the rapids. The free flooding device doubtless plays its part here too.

The claim that the whole balance of the vessel is so affected by her unsymmetrical lines as favourably to influence her passage through the water raises an interesting problem and one difficult to solve. Before lightly dismissing such claims, however, it must be remembered that the ancient Chinese methods of trial and error have always been carried out with some ingenious, if unusual, end in view, which has presumably always been attained, though often by methods strange to Western eyes. Moreover, in favour of this theory, it should never be forgotten that the Chinese understand the art of balance better than any other nation in the world.

From personal observation on board a Crooked-Stern Junk, both in rapids and in calm water, it would appear that there is some justification for much of what the Chinese claim. Unquestionably, when proceeding down-river in the quiet reaches, the elevation of the starboard side of the bow enables the quanter to get a better purchase on his pole.

The above notes were written in 1940; seventeen years later, at my home in Windlesham, I put a model of the Crooked-Bow Junk in our duck pond, to amuse my grandchildren. I discarded the giant sweep, because it invariably came off, but rigged the tracking ropes in exactly the same way as is usual on the Lu River for hauling junks up-stream. The children represented the trackers. To my astonishment I found that, provided the 'trackers' were not too energetic, the junk proceeded on a perfectly straight course without the aid of rudder or sweep, even with the tracking rope leading broad on the port bow. This then is the undoubted reason for the crooked bow.

The rapids of the Yentsingho have to be negotiated by crossing from the left to the right bank of the river when descending, and conversely when ascending. The peculiar type of bow would appear to be of help in meeting the requirements of the upward journey, for, as the trend of the channel through the rapids is then always from right bank to left bank, the distorted port bow serves to maintain the trim of the vessel and ensures that the tow-rope will always lead clear of any fouling on that bow. This could ordinarily be achieved by mastheading the tracking-line, but such a procedure would be dangerous, if not disastrous, in a rapid.

Dams are built at each rapid so as to maintain sufficient water in the low-water season. These dams are opened on suitable dates selected by a joint meeting of the representatives of the Salt Administration, the Rapids Controlling Bureau and the Junk Guild. During the low-water season the last dam at Laoyat'an cannot be opened, and this means discharging the cargo and reloading it onto other junks below the dam. High water is also unsuitable for navigation, which is entirely interrupted from July to August. When water conditions are favourable, the salt junks can berth opposite the town of Tzeliutsing and load their cargoes direct. During the low-water season, however, they have to bank in about a mile below the town, and the salt is brought to them from the factories in open-decked boats known as Yen-ch'uan, or Salt boats.

These craft, which are exceedingly interesting, are 43 feet long, of 8 feet beam, and 2½ feet in depth. Although they are never called upon to negotiate rapids, and carry the salt only for a distance of little more than a mile, yet they are true to the local tradition in that they all have crooked bows. Indeed they are in most respects miniatures of the larger salt junks. No explanation is forthcoming from the junkmen as to why this pattern is used for these ferry craft.

Early on the morning of my arrival at Chungt'an the leading junks began to arrive. The Chungt'an dam consists at low water of a rocky ledge crossing the river, into which wooden boards have been built to form a dam, leaving an aperture slightly more than that of the beam of the junks. Although there is no particular danger, great care is required to keep each boat in the axis of the current when approaching the weir, over which there is a fall of probably 3 feet at dead low water. Before making the passage two or three men are taken on board to assist the helmsman. Once fairly in the current, the junk gathers considerable speed, and the combined efforts of all the men are necessary to wield the heavy stern-sweep. After passing the weir the surplus men wade ashore and proceed to the next boat. The long line of junks then drifts slowly down with the current to Hsient'an. On arrival they bank-in and await their turn. This, at low level, is a very formidable rapid, and the passage down it a most exciting experience, for there is no turning back once the craft has started her mad rush.

Again two or three extra hands board each boat, which moves slowly with the current, 200 feet astern of the next ahead, and crosses from the left bank through a flagged channel to mid-river at the point A on the plan opposite. Here a dam extends two-thirds of the way across the river, essentially the same as at Chungt'an, and similarly leaving only a narrow aperture capable of admitting one junk at a time. Gradually gaining momentum, the junk appears to be heading directly for the dam, but partly by the force of the water and partly by the action of the great stern-sweep, it is suddenly diverted as it strikes the axis of the current, and at the point B curves round the end of the dam to come finally to rest, banked-in, at the point C. Here it again awaits its turn for the ordeal of the main Hsient'an.

Keeping perfect station, the boats leave in succession from point C. Each boat's crew now consists of four men at the sweep and a bow-man with a boat-hook. Having gained a speed of about six knots, the boat arrives at point D, where a long line of men can be seen wading out to meet the boats in mid-stream. As each boat rushes past, three men nonchalantly slip on board. Instantly one takes up his station at the foremost bollard, while the two others leap to the stern-sweep to direct and assist the men already there. These three are local pilots, of whom there are ninety-six, and they receive $1 for each junk they pilot. Trained by their fathers for this hereditary work, they start their careers at the age of 12.

From the point C to D, and thence to G, is a straight course, and the boat is now travelling at a very high speed. Across the surface of the river is a perfect shoal of scattered rocks that seem to bar all passage; but as the junk gets nearer, an opening between two of the largest groups of rocks can be seen. What, however, is not apparent is how the boat on arrival at G can possibly be turned almost at right angles, where the channel is only a few feet broader than the junk itself, and where the stream is at its swiftest.

The men at the stern-sweep direct their entire attention to keeping a straight course through the various eddies and races. The sweep is kept in the water, and is used as a rudder. There is a moment of

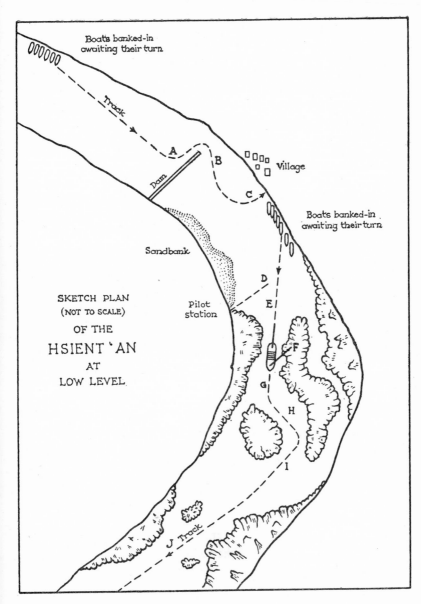

Boats banked-in
awaiting their turn

Track

A

Dam

B

Village

C

Boats banked-in
awaiting their turn

Sandbank

D

SKETCH PLAN
(NOT TO SCALE)

OF THE

HSIENT 'AN

AT

LOW LEVEL.

Pilot
station

E

F

G

H

I

J Track

Plan of Hsient'an

tension as the boat, moving with what appears to be the speed of an express train, heads directly for a rock some two feet above the seething waters. The river flows down with a mighty swing, and the rocks at a distance of 2 or 3 feet seem to be flying in the opposite direction. The supreme moment has arrived, and the man on the bows braces himself for his important role. As the junk flashes past point F, a man standing on the rock neatly hands him the end of a rope whose other end is made fast to the rock. In a few seconds the bow-man has cast three turns round the foremost bollard, and as swiftly starts to surge the rope in short, sharp motions – that is to say, he allows it to slacken in jerks. So deftly does he perform this operation that the 50-foot length of rope slips smoothly and quickly round the bollard until it finally runs out and falls over the side. On being asked what would happen if the bow-man failed to grasp the rope, the junkmen replied that the man on the rock has been passing the rope in just this manner for twenty years, that no accident had ever occurred, and that there seemed to them no reason why one ever should. This rope, which is renewed after five boats have passed down, takes only about fifteen seconds to run out, but the restraint has been just sufficient to alter the course of the boat from headlong collision with the ugly, jagged-looking rock round which the current foams.

The boat is still in the grip of the rapid and appears to be steering a course directly for another rock and utter destruction. Its safety now depends entirely on the men at the sweep, which not only acts as a rudder, but can be used as a powerful lever. The five men bend all the weight of their shoulders against the heavy loom, and with a single movement wrench the junk round at the critical moment when a crash seems inevitable. To achieve this, the sweep must be put over once only and at precisely the right moment, when the junk is only a few feet off the rock. Diverted as if on a pivot, the junk now careers away in comparative safety, still at a fairly high speed, through the narrow gutterway, with the dangers fast disappearing astern.

The current slackens somewhat at the point I, where the junk emerges into an open stretch; but as the channel narrows she again begins to fly down the lower part of the rapid until eventually she

Model of the Crippled Paru Junk

enters a long, even reach which, after point J, becomes smooth water. In the low-water season the pilots do not wait to reach the bank. When sufficient way is off the junk, these intrepid men slip into the icy water in the same unobtrusive way as when they boarded her.

Lying snugly banked-in in a convoy, or hauled up on the bank for repairs, the Crooked-Bow Junks of Tzeliutsing display in their odd yet trim outlines evidence of an antiquity of design which probably reaches back to the time of the origin of the salt wells themselves, some 1,700 years ago; but to be fully appreciated they should be seen in operation in the wild waters of the little river for which they were designed. To the sailor's eye there is little to surpass in interest and beauty the sight of a well-handled Crooked-Bow Junk descending the rapids of the Yentsingho at dead low water.

The junkmen of the Yentsingho are as conservative as it is possible to imagine. To any inquiry as to the reason for any particular device, or method of construction, nothing is more common than to receive two answers: the first, is that everybody does so. The second, that the design for the particular custom has been evolved by Lu Pan, the Carpenter God, who lived c. 506 B.C., who handed it down to their forebears, who in turn passed it down to them, and must, therefore, be on the firmest possible basis. 'Who knows more about it, you or Lu Pan?' said a Chinese shipwright to me once when I suggested an alternative method of strengthening the stern. Good or bad, my method was certainly more modern.

So attracted was I by the Crooked-Bow Junks that I stayed on and made a detailed study of them which included a model, constructed under my personal supervision. It was made by two junk carpenters, who were, incidentally, very sceptical as to the desirability of such unproductive labour, and who were so entirely unversed in the art of model-making that it was necessary to provide them with cardboard patterns cut from carefully drawn-up plans. Such patterns were provided of all the component parts, and from these the carpenters made the faithful copies in wood. All the appurtenances, furnishings and fittings were made to scale, and nothing of the least importance was omitted. The model is especially interesting, as it embodies many features which it would be difficult, if not impossible, to give in a plan and therefore shows these strange craft in all their detail.

It was built to the same scale as the model of the Crooked-Stern Junk, to be described later, and was intended as a companion model. Unhappily, however, Sir Frederick Maze would not accept it for the Maze Collection in the Science Museum on the grounds that it measured only 4 feet 9 inches, whereas all his other models were never less than 6 feet.

The model is now in my possession, and I hope it may be possible to find a museum where it may have a happy and peaceful retirement.

*   *   *

From the Lu River I went to Chengtu. The owner of one of the transport companies took such an interest in me and the model of the Crooked-Bow Junk I had had made that he offered to place a car at my disposal, provided I did not object to taking some dried peas with me. After a delay of a few hours an enormous lorry arrived with the sides boarded up. It contained three tons of dried peas in bulk. From the large, expectant crowd which appeared it was obvious that the lorry was not entirely at my disposal; and so, after paying my fare, which was not inconsiderable, I climbed up and lay down with my effects beside me, taking up as much room as possible in order, selfishly but understandably, to keep others out. My example was followed by several others. The lorry started with a jerk, and three passengers fell off; they had paid their fare, and so it did not matter greatly, and it certainly reduced the congestion.

The grey hairs I possess all started as a result of this journey from the Lu River to Chengtu. Even the slightest curve in the road was enough to shoot all the passengers, and my model, over to one side. The effect resembled a rugger scrum on ball bearings. As we slid over, trying to defeat the laws of centrifugal force, we would all seize any part of our neighbour's anatomy that happened to be nearest. I was not sorry when the curved roofs of Chengtu hove in sight.

Chengtu, about 1,400 feet above sea-level, is the capital of Szechuan, and lies in a fertile plain, where rice, silk, China grass, ground-nuts and opium are the principal crops. In the south-west part of the city stands the old palace, now in ruins, where the Emperors of the Minor Han resided.

I stayed for the most part of my time in Chengtu in a temple about four miles out from the North Gate. It is said to be one of the most famous in Szechuan. The monastery lies among huge groves of tall cypress trees. It was very pleasing to walk through court after court, with here and there an old monk idling in the sun. There was a soothing air of peace and meditation here after the rat-infested inns of the past three weeks.

The Abbot was certainly a power in the land, for the military had left the precincts alone, except for the outer courtyard. The Laughing Buddha, whose fat and bulging form in porcelain is to be seen everywhere in China, is said to have once lived here as a monk, and through his cheerfulness won his immortal place in the Chinese Pantheon.

Whenever I come across one of these Buddhas, I go back in my mind to the days of my youth. My father was stationed in Malta, and I used to go out to stay with my parents for the school holidays. The island was a schoolboy's paradise. There was bathing and tennis, and at 17 years of age I was playing polo tolerably well, for my father was a great horseman.

Some little time before, my father had been given a Buddha. Its history was obscure, but it was said to have a bad reputation. 'It must never be dusted,' said the donor, 'otherwise misfortune will overtake the household.' These instructions were duly passed on to the servants by my mother, who was a very religious woman and thoroughly disapproved of having idols in the house.

Several minor mishaps occurred to my father; he fell from his horse, he missed his footing on the gangway of a ship when going on board to dine, and there were other annoying episodes of like nature. On each occasion suspicion rested on the Buddha, and on investigation it was always found that, in spite of every precaution, and directly against orders, someone had dusted him. When my school report arrived and turned out to be extremely bad, I lost no time in pointing out to my father that the Buddha probably had something to do with it.

My mother, sceptical but co-operative, suggested a glass case as the best way of preventing the idol from being dusted. When this had been installed, we all wondered why we had never thought of it before. We wondered, too, how the Buddha would react to his new quarters. Would he suffer from claustrophobia and wreak his vengeance upon us all, or would he settle down and make the best of a bad job? Would the glass cage prevent his communicating with the powers of darkness? We all hoped so. He seemed happy enough; his stupid, inane smirk gave no indication of any intended acts of aggression. A great friend and admirer of my father came out from England to stay with us. When told about the Buddha, she pooh-poohed the whole affair. She put us to shame. Were we ignorant heathens that we were so concerned over the comfort and happiness of this so-called god? Perhaps, she suggested, we had better do what the Chinese did with their gods, propitiate him, make a bargain with him, purchase felicity by subscribing to a temple – if one could be found – and a great deal more besides.

My mother was greatly shocked by all this. She explained that none of us believed in the Buddha; he was just an idol and a very bad one at that; but, in spite of her Christian beliefs, she could not help feeling that we could ill afford to take any chances with this wretched, dominating thing.

Before she left for England Mrs Frampton, for such was her name, gave us a final lecture on the stupidity of associating minor misfortunes with what was after all merely a piece of porcelain. To prove her point and to show her complete disbelief in the powers of this image, she placed her photograph, which always stood on a table nearby, directly against the glass case of the Buddha and the next day sailed in high spirits for England.

But we were soon to hear from Mrs Frampton. The intelligence came in the form of a wire from Gibraltar. It ran:

I AM IN HOSPITAL HERE WITH MALTA FEVER. REMOVE MY PHOTOGRAPH FROM BUDDHA IMME-DIATELY. PLEASE CONFIRM.

Left to his own devices, the Buddha behaved reasonably well for the next few years; and in course of time my father died. My mother, when selling up the house, was confronted with a problem of the very first magnitude. What was to be done with the Buddha? She did not wish to take him to England for obvious reasons, neither did she wish to dispose of him with his, by this time, well-known unsavoury reputation. Then a brilliant idea occurred to her. She consulted a missionary, who happened to be staying in the island with his wife. 'Would it be possible,' said my mother, 'to destroy it in some way, could it be "sunk without trace"?'

This was what was done. The missionary took the Buddha out to sea in a hired boat and threw him overboard. He disappeared below the waves and was no more seen; glass case and all. We all heaved a sigh of relief.

And that was the end of the Buddha – but not the end of the story. Thirty years later my mother came out to stay with us in China. It was not long before we started reminiscing about the good old days in Malta. The picnics, the wonderful parties and old friends. What a long time ago it all seemed.

'What happened to that old missionary pal of yours?' I said to my mother.

'It was awfully sad,' she said, 'he murdered his wife and then committed suicide.'

'Wasn't that the man who dumped the Buddha?' I said. My mother turned deadly white and did not answer; she had fainted.

That Buddha was a terrible hater.

CHAPTER 17

The Chengtu Plain Irrigation

ACCORDING to the Chinese the Min, and not, as is commonly held by other authorities, the Kinsha, is the parent stream of the Yangtze. From a navigational point of view there is everything to support this opinion, for the Kinsha is navigable only for fifty-eight miles above Sui Fu, whereas the Min is navigable at high water for 133 miles to Chengtu, the provincial capital. Its source is situated near the edge of the Tibetan plateau, 13,000 feet above sea-level: after passing Sun pan, 9,500 feet above the sea, the Min crashes down through a 100-mile long gorge until it finally emerges from the Szechuan mountains on to the Chengtu Plain at the mountain town of Kwanhsien.

This most picturesque and attractive city stands at the clear-cut boundary between east and west Szechuan, and has all the diverse features of a frontier settlement. Here the Chinese, the tribesmen and the Tibetans mingle in the narrow streets. Coolies with unbelievably heavy loads bring down medicinal herbs, skins, wool, deer horns and musk, and take back salt, cotton, sugar, tools, straw sandals and tea.

The plain of Chengtu here is amazingly fertile, thanks to an irrigation scheme which has been in operation for a thousand years. The ceremony of the 'Opening of the Waters' is a most important event for all those who live on this fertile tableland. I had received an official invitation to the proceedings, and so immediately set about arranging for a wheelbarrow to take me to Kwanhsien on the following day.

Kwanhsien is the centre of the irrigation works and is only ninety li from Chengtu, but Chengtu is 120 li from Kwanhsien. In terms of li, it depends on which is the starting point. This may sound strange to us, but to the Chengtu wheelbarrow man it makes great sense; for the li as a unit of measurement represents not only distance but

Carrying Coolies

the difficulty of getting over the ground. To the carrying coolie a li represents the distance a man carrying a fair, average weight slung over his shoulders will travel before he stops to rest his load against a sort of rough shooting stick. Moreover in Szechuan the li is subdivided into 'large' and 'small' according to whether it is over good or bad roads, or whether the road is up or down hill. One mile is roughly equivalent to just over three li on level ground, and to as much as fifteen li over mountainous country.

The Chinese day begins so early that it is not often a great remove from midnight. So that it was very early in the morning that the wheelbarrow I had booked arrived at my door to take me to Kwanhsien. Even so, the streets were full of traders waiting for daylight to begin the sale of their vegetables and other foods.

The narrow passages which serve as streets in most Chinese cities are choked with every form of industrial obstruction. The butcher, the barber, the cook with his travelling restaurant and countless other dealers all do their best to block the streets. It can be said that there is little that the Chinese do at all which is not at some time done in the street. In this part of China, where the roads are very narrow, the most usual means of transport is still the wheelbarrow. Although these vary very much in design from those used in Chekiang and elsewhere, the general principle is always the same, namely a single wheel surrounded by a frame guarding the upper part of the wheel from contact with merchandise or persons carried.

Wheelbarrows are said to have been invented as long ago as the Han Dynasty. They were originally designed for the transport of food and military supplies from Szechuan to Central China. The Premier Chu-ko-liang, struggling for supremacy over the Kingdoms of Wu and Wei, is said to have built a huge fleet of wheelbarrows, which he used effectively along the zig-zag, narrow and muddy paths. They have earned poetic names such as 'Lone Wheel Car' and 'Goat Horn Carriage'. In the old days women were not encouraged to ride in them because, in doing so, they were apt to allow their small, bound feet to be seen. Women in those days wore long skirts to conceal their feet, for the display of these limbs was considered bad taste if not actually immoral.

The ingenious Chinese wheelbarrow is the classical example of abundant motion with little progress; nevertheless it is the only conveyance that could stand up to the considerable bumping over the unbelievably bad road to Kwanhsien, which in places is only broad enough for foot passengers. Besides transporting immense loads, the wheelbarrow is used for carrying pigs, goats and passengers. A full capacity load consists of two passengers sitting side by side on the framework, facing in the direction they are going, with their legs resting on the curved, wooden guard which covers the wheel. The passengers lean against a backrest. Trunks, furniture and/or babies can be carried in addition.

Actually these wheelbarrows are not as perilous as they look, except when they are going down a steep gradient. Here, when the heavily-loaded wheelbarrow, quite innocent of brakes, has gained momentum it charges forward at such a high speed that the driver's feet are off the ground for the most part, as he literally flies through the air in his wild efforts to catch up with his charge. The endurance of the wheelbarrow men is quite amazing. They rise early and they work late. They will undertake journeys often of months in duration, they transport their heavy loads over steep mountains or difficult fords in all seasons of the year, and in all weathers. All this is done on two meals a day of coarse rice, with perhaps some fried cabbage, for sustenance. The work must be exhausting beyond measure, but they carry on as a matter of course cheerfully, happily and without grumbling.

My wheelbarrow man lashed a light bamboo pole mast to the framework of his vehicle and hoisted a yard and sail. Expectorating noisily he took up the shafts and, long before daylight, with a fair wind and the sail drawing well we set off on the 120 li journey to the Kwanhsien Plain.

From time immemorial the bearer of the heaviest load is entitled to the right of way. This applies equally to men-carried burdens, wheelbarrows, water-buffaloes and even junks on the creeks and canals. Approaching traffic, on narrow roads, start waving wildly to each other to claim precedence long before they meet. In my case it was unflattering to me to note that he affixed a hat at the mast head to denote he was carrying a particularly difficult load.

We made the passage, which must be about thirty miles, in some ten hours, with two waits of half an hour, and one or two short ones. I walked in snatches for a few miles at a time, but as I found it difficult to keep up, the wheelbarrow man, who did not wish to be delayed, soon stopped this.

The Chengtu Plain through which the Min, under various Chinese names flows, is part basin, part alluvial delta. It was known in the old

Imperial days as the Prefecture of Heaven, and is still called the
Garden of China. It is the only large expanse of level ground in the
mountainous province of Szechuan. Nor, indeed, is it really level,
for it slopes gently down towards the south, comprising a total
area of nearly 3,500 square miles.

Nowhere in China, some go so far as to say perhaps nowhere in
the world, is there a more fertile, productive or densely-populated
agricultural area of similar size. The many water channels are lined
with poplars and other trees, and the large farms and country residences which are thickly scattered about the landscape are set in
groves of cypress, bamboo or the tall, handsome Nanmu trees. The
wooded aspect of the countryside prevents any extensive view, and
adds to the general air of productive prosperity. Every foot of the
land is used, soil culture has been intensively developed, and crop
failures are unknown.

All this luxuriant prosperity is due to the irrigation system, whereby the fertility of nature and the industry of man is effectively
supplemented by an elaborate regimentation of the waters of the
Min. By a bold project, excellently conceived and carried out, half
the waters of the Min are diverted from the river into an artificial
passage carved out by hand through a rocky spur of the foothills.
From there it is distributed through three main channels and a network of canals. But for this, most of the Chengtu Plain would be
a swampy marsh to the east and west, and a waterless, stony desert
to the north.

The man to whom the Chinese give credit for the hydraulic feat
that makes such fertility possible is Li Ping, who was Prefect of
Shuh soon after its conquest by the state of Ts'in in 215 B.C. Shuh
was the old name of part of the present province of Szechuan.

The main feature of the whole irrigation scheme, which shows
that the first principles of the great work were fully appreciated
over 2,000 years ago, is contained in Li Ping's often-reiterated instructions to clear the channels at regular intervals from all silt and
boulders brought down from the mountains by the force of the
current. This injunction has been preserved on a stone tablet bearing
six Chinese characters: 'Sheng Tao Tan di Chia Yen'. That is to say,
dig the bed of the channels deep, and keep the dykes low. Two

similar tablets carry a proverb with four characters on each with another maxim for river control. 'Yu Wan Chieh Kao Feng Ch'ou Hsin', meaning take off the corner where there is a bend; and cut through where there is an island or middle ground.

All these instructions have been faithfully observed. The work involved each winter in clearing out the bed of the river by hand is enormous. The yearly cleaning begins about 1st December. Even in a dry winter the western half of the river is still a stream of considerable force, with a width of about fifty yards, and a depth of over

The Bamboo Bridge at Kwanhsien showing trestles beyond

six feet. A dam is built from the west bank to the Fish's Mouth, and all the water of the outer river is sent down the inner river. The damming is accomplished by means of a series of tripods which support the main structure. These roughly-made tripods are lashed together with bamboo rope, particularly at the apex, with slats duly spaced to give rigidity. The tripods are placed at intervals across the stream. Strength and stability is provided by fitting bamboo basket trays, filled with cobble stones, at the bottom of the tripods, and again higher up on the cross bars above the water level. Double layers of bamboo matting resting vertically against the tripod legs have soil closely packed between them. In this way a solid wall of mud cased in matting is gradually built up, until the flow of the stream is finally completely cut off, the leakage being surprisingly small. The exposed corners are further reinforced by means of wooden piles and, in some cases, great stone flags clamped together.

When the natural bed of the river is thus laid bare, it exposes the deposits of silt and small boulders. The speed of the river slackens considerably in the vicinity of Kwanhsien, where more or less level ground is reached, and the stream accordingly deposits its heavier loads on the bottom of the channels. This accumulation of the past year is laboriously dug out by hand, for a distance of about half a mile. The banks are then revetted and repaired, and when all is ready the gangs of coolies working in the water remove the tripod dam and allow the stream to flow back into its course. The barricade of tripods, matting and pebbles is then re-erected across the entrance to the Inner River which is similarly dried off.

At last, with the coming of spring the river, which has been permitted for most of the winter to flow through its newly-cleared bed on the west side of the plain, is divided so that it passes down the cut and the irrigation channels, and thence into the empty ditches which the farmers have been busy cleaning out in preparation. The date of the opening of the waters is never fixed until shortly before the ceremony by the geomancers who determine the most auspicious date in accordance with the principles laid down in the classical books on the subject. Generally speaking, however, it takes place round about the first day of the fourth moon, soon after the Festival of the Pure Brightness. The Intendant of Circuit is always invited to come and perform the ceremony. On the day of his arrival at Kwanhsien he is met by the city officials, and taken to inspect the work. He also receives any complaints from the farmers as to the supply of water to their fields. The next day, after paying honour to the memory of the famous Li Ping and his son, he proceeds to the barrage to perform the opening ceremony, in the presence of a great concourse of people.

On 2nd April we were up before dawn and filed through the streets of Kwanhsien to the Temple of the Crouching Dragon. An open area leads up to the Temple steps, and on this wide space a fair had been in progress. This morning, however, it had all been cleared away to make room for the enormous crowds of uniformed school children assembled to greet the Governor and the President of China, Lin Sen, who was to be present at the ceremony. The Temple is built on a projecting spur of the split hill, Li Tu, and forms the apex of a peninsula, with the stream running round it to the north, while the vast, uneven shingle bed of the Min meanders by to the south. It is an immensely picturesque site. From the balcony of the temple one looks sheer down to the swift, green waters in the cut below, where, deflected from the side of the mountain opposite, they form a dangerous whirlpool.

Our tickets entitled us to a position in the porch of the Temple, and here we took our stand. No one but those actually officiating were allowed inside. The ceremony was disappointing from a picturesque point of view. It was shorn of all but a minimum of the old ritual, which the intelligentsia regard as barbarous, and was brought up to date by choruses sung by the children, neat and uniform in their identical dresses, and

Buddhist Priest

although eminently praiseworthy, utterly devoid of atmosphere or local interest. The only relic of the ancient ritual seemed to be the presence of the Buddhist priests and the carcases of a pig and a goat which served as offerings, and were precariously poised on rough frames not unlike saddle racks on either side of the altar. Formerly these sacrifices were made amidst the fumes of incense and sounds of prayer, drum, and gong, in the hour before dawn. But on this day the animals arrived killed and skinned direct from the butcher. The pig's portly and comfortable carcase adapted itself well to its stand, but the goat, which had had its throat hacked in a disfiguring way, looked quite indecently dead, and created a diversion by falling off its stand.

Lin Sen, the President of China, a very stately, white-bearded old

gentleman, performed his task with pleasing dignity. This office
consisted of holding up the various offerings of food, flowers, wine
and so on, and repeating the dedication phrases at the prompting of
the Master of Ceremonies. The oblations having been made, the
whole concourse of people filed out and, passing to the south of the
temple, plodded along the high exposed bank of shingle in the bed
of the river.

Another large temple dedicated to Li Ping overlooks the dam, and
to this spot the long procession wound its way. The pig and the goat,
carried by coolies, accompanied the procession, and were arranged
in position on either side of the shrine containing the great golden
figure of Li Ping. The same offerings were made by the President
with the same intoned formulae, to the shouted choruses of the
children. The great crowds which had here congregated were swelled
by more and more onlookers; for all the farmers for many miles
collect to see the opening of the dam which means the welfare of
their crops.

The procession then moved off to the dam where a shelter, draped
in national flags, had been erected for the officials on a high shingle
bank. The view from the heights here above the south bank was
curious and striking. A vast mass of many thousands of people lined
the edges of the river, and covered the central shingle bank. Now
that the moment was at hand, men climbed up on the trestles forming the dam, and cut through one supporting arm. A length of
bamboo rope was passed through about twenty trestles, and a gang
of coolies, at a given signal, with a shout bent to the task of pulling
these away. At last the long line of men pulled as in a tug-of-war and
the trestles forming the barrier cracked and finally gave way. The
water began to pour through from the higher level, to the accompaniment of a loud burst of shouts and calls from the thousands of
spectators, some of whom waded into the water for luck, while
others threw in stones, for it is believed that those who strike the
water will be free from sickness during the coming year.

Immediately after the ceremony the Intendant leaves for Chengtu
in a time-honoured race with the waters, which, if there is a good
supply, may get there before him as he travels by chair.

The main feature of the Inner River has always been the raft traffic. Early in May, about a month after the opening of the waters, there is another, smaller ceremony, and the Inner River is formally opened for rafts to navigate. Over 2,000 are said to pass down yearly. They always carry a certain amount of cargo, and the passage through the bottleneck of the gorge is fraught with excitement and danger. More than fifty men are drowned here each year. In 1905 a life-saving service was instituted in the gorge. It consists of a pair of ropes crossing the river at some little distance apart, each being supplied with rings hanging from vertical ropes at intervals across the stream. When a man falls in, the cross rope is dipped so as to enable him to grasp the ring nearest to him.

This ancient irrigation system has been a complete success, and probably ranks as the greatest of China's public works and engineering feats, not excepting the Salt Wells of Tzeliutsing and the Great Wall. Despite her age and continuous civilization, China has few such remaining monuments, and this is one of the few that has not only survived but, instead of being allowed to fall into decay, has been very well looked after. The reason is to be found in the remarkable co-operation of the people themselves, their willingness to be taxed for their own and the common good. But for their co-operation in the essential work of clearing out the channels and repairing the dykes, the scheme must, long ago, have failed.

* * *

It was now time for me to return to Chungking, and so I retraced my steps to Chengtu where I took the first available bus back.

When the new and wonderful highways first came into being all over China, drivers were required for the thousands of vehicles which poured in from England and America. These were mostly lorries, which ended their lives as home-made buses. Most of the drivers came from Shanghai, and were paid a king's ransom; but, in order to keep pace with the huge demand, others were recruited locally from cart drivers and rickshaw pullers. The mountainous roads with their hairpin bends and unprotected shelf-like highways, incredibly narrow in places, sometimes blasted out of the live rock with no parapet and a precipitous drop of several hundred feet, required in their negotiation more skill than was possessed by the usual run of rickshaw coolie. The standard of driving was extremely low and accidents were frequent, particularly in the mountains, where whole buses, full to bursting, were wont to disappear over a precipice into the valley below.

It was useless to draw up rules and regulations. The drivers were for the most part illiterate, and, even if they could read, with that inevitable Chinese gift for evasion they would quickly devise methods of getting round, or through, the regulations. The military, therefore, stepped in and introduced a highway code with but a single rule. The rule was that both drivers were always equally to blame, and the punishment was, 'Off with their heads, and no questions asked.' This was simple, easily understood, and quite a brilliant idea, but it had its disadvantages, not only for the drivers, but for the passengers; for, when an accident happened to a bus, the driver would vanish into the country at high speed and be no more seen. Moreover no new driver would take over the bus for fear of being regarded as the offending driver and of losing his head.

Nevertheless, this firm action on the part of the military had the desired effect in a few months, and the standard of driving improved out of all recognition.

CHAPTER 18

Chungking to Fuchau and the Crooked-Stern Junk

TOWARDS the end of the summer of 1941 I received a letter from Sir Frederick Maze, the Inspector-General, saying that he wanted me to go to Fuchau to make a scale model of the Crooked-Stern Junk for the Maze Collection in the Science Museum at South Kensington.

Fuchau is some sixty miles below Chungking, and must not be confused either with Foochow, a town in Fukien, or with a town in Kiangsu which is usually spelled Fuchow. It is not the sort of place that law-abiding citizens would normally visit; for not only is it well off the beaten track and difficult to approach, but it has always possessed a very bad reputation for bandits, opium dealing, drug smuggling and other forms of vice so dear to the hearts of the average Szechuanese. Indeed the place is so well known for all forms of depravity that it has been said that even the junks have crooked sterns.

I took a sampan to the north bank of Chungking and an hour later, at about 6 a.m., found myself on board the *Ming Chu*, one of the best and largest of the Chinese steamers operating on the Upper Yangtze. I arrived in good time, to find that it had been decided to postpone the sailing for a few hours. The ship actually possessed a saloon, and here I took refuge from the arriving hordes of Chinese passengers. Later, after we had got under way, the Captain invited me on to his comfortable covered and glassed-in bridge.

The Captain, a bluff, thick-set man in baggy shorts, was, the Chinese steward informed me, English. But in fact he turned out to be half-Chinese. Getting on for 60, and with grown-up children, he said he found his interest in life in his work on board, in navigating the ever-changing channels of the treacherous Upper Yangtze, and in studying the face of the stream, which only after years yields up its secrets. This ship had only two rudders and was unpopular with

Chinese captains, but he said he understood her, and knew how to supplement her lack by the judicious use of his engines. He had been in her for ten years without mishap, a record indeed in these waters where accidents are so prevalent. He was the most honestly devout Christian I have ever come across. He gave me tea in his cabin at a large round table, which, set in a bay, filled up most of the room. This table and all the seats round it were half-filled with large biscuit tins and Bibles. He seemed to have innumerable versions of the Chinese translations, some with the English text alongside the Chinese.

In his unregenerate days, not so many years before, he had been given to drinking and smoking, and was not even above using opium; but through his daughter, now in Shanghai, he and his wife had both become ardent Christians, and had found a new peace and happiness. I did not see his wife. 'Very peculiar, the old woman,' he said with a wave of the hand. 'She don't come out to see anyone; she just lives quietly on board in my quarter and prays.' When the ship had been bombed by the Japanese on the last voyage, he said, 'she prayed harder than ever,' but otherwise took no notice.

There was an air raid alarm while we were on board. The news came through by wireless from Chungking. Of late the Japanese had been making a determined attempt to bomb all Chinese shipping, particularly below Wanhsien. The Captain said that normally he paid little attention to the planes; he relied on the small target his ship presented to them at the height at which they flew, as well as on her speed. He felt now that discretion was becoming more necessary, and so he took his ship into an arm of the river at a point where he knew the raiders generally cut off a corner and flew overland. Here we lay under a leafy bank, with hawsers laid out ready to pull her in shore if need be, to let the passengers scatter for safety. It turned out as he had predicted; I must say I was greatly impressed by his bluff and cheery toughness – no nerves or panic here. After a two hours' siesta we got under way again, and slipped swiftly down the red-brown stream.

The Chinese pilot stands near the wheel and watches the water intently – motionless and expressionless; his only movement is when he makes the faintest signal with his hand, which rests on the rail. Sometimes he merely flexes a finger, at others he extends one or two, or half raises his thumb, to indicate to the helmsman how much to alter course. A pilot takes upwards of five years to qualify on the Upper Yangtze.

The ship stopped at the little town of Li Tu, once known as Old Chungking. It shelters attractively under a steep scarp on the north bank. At the summit is a temple, below which the natural rock forms a bastion. From here, looking down the river, which takes a sharp turn, the hills march right across the horizon in strangely symmetrically shaped pyramids, seeming to form an impassable barrier to progress.

There was a busy ferry service from here to Fuchau, which is a large town at the junction of the Yangtze and the Kung T'an Ho. This stream, which is placid enough in midsummer at its mouth, where it is fully 200 yards broad, is higher up compressed by a succession of turbulent and dangerous rapids; so much so that the local legend says that its control was considered a very pleasant sinecure for any retired dragon, since there was no traffic for him to concern himself with. The Carpenter God, however, who seems to have been an interfering sort of deity and disinclined to let sleeping dragons lie, was so moved by the Dragon's boast that his labours were so light that he proposed to find some work for him by building a junk that would be able to navigate the Kung T'an Ho. Consequently he devised the famous Crooked-Stern Junk, which by its peculiar formation was able to employ two huge sweeps and so negotiate even the terrible Goat-Horn Rapid. The Dragon, annoyed at the presence of this craft, which increased his responsibilities, begged the Carpenter God to build no more. Eventually, so the legend runs, they came to an understanding whereby, if the Carpenter God should prove himself clever enough to build a wooden pagoda without employing any nails at all, the Dragon would own himself worsted and would agree to the building of more junks. The Carpenter God appears to have performed the miracle of cabinet-making without the least trouble; and the small wooden Pagoda still stands as a monument to his skill, and as a sign that the Dragon has had henceforth to resign himself to his task of looking after the mariners of the Kung T'an Ho.

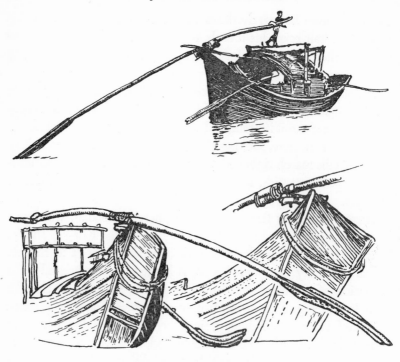

The Crooked-Stern Junk

The Crooked-Stern Junk is generally called by the Chinese the Wai p'i ku ch'uan, but by the junkmen who operate it Lu-ch'uan or Oar Boat. The eccentricity of its design has excited considerable speculation concerning its origin. As the scope of its activities is in a remote region of the Upper Yangtze, it is seldom seen by the outside world and is little known.

The outstanding feature of this junk is that its hull is devoid of bilateral symmetry. It has no rudder and is steered by means of two powerful sweeps, one of which is usually longer than the junk itself. The after part of the junk is curved to such an extent that the port quarter is placed in a position exactly amidships. The corresponding starboard quarter is considerably lower, thus permitting the sweeps to be handled independently of each other. The twisted shape of the hull provides sure foundations on different planes for the fulcrums of the sweeps and is the factor in determining the original design of the junk. The main sweep, sometimes as long as 120 feet, although beautifully balanced by stones placed at strategic points along its length, is necessarily heavy and slow in action. The small auxiliary sweep, therefore, is kept ready for immediate use in case of sudden emergency, which may arise at any moment amidst so many physical obstacles and navigational dangers.

I stayed at the only inn in Fuchau, the Inn of Ethereal Virtue, which sadly belied its name. At inns in this part of China one retires to rest certain of more bedfellows than comfort demands. Rats in search of food jumped through the paper windows with the skill and agility of circus clowns. On this occasion I had brought with me some hard-boiled eggs, and the rats rolled these off the table and along the floor between their front paws like professional footballers. When travelling in the interior I always went to bed in a long leather coat to protect myself from the rats. But we will draw a veil over Chinese inns, I have already tried to describe them.

There was, of course, no water of any sort for washing; but, happily, there were a number of floating bath-houses moored to the bank a short distance away. One never knows how dirty one is until one has been to a Chinese bath-house. These floating establishments employ experts who are specialists in rubbing a customer's back until it is quite crimson in order to remove all dirt. All you have to do is to sit in a wooden tub – with your legs out – and let the professional back-scrubbers get to work on you. While this is going on another man will massage your feet, another will punch you all over with his fists, while a third will serve you with a cup of tea and wipe your head and feet with boiling wet towels. This, of course, is a bath-house boat of the first class. If you are not so rich, you can go to a hot-water shop and buy a few ladles of boiling water and hire a tub.

The next morning I went to the tea houses to try to engage a carpenter who would be prepared to make a model of the Crooked-Stern Junk under my supervision. The tea house of China is an institution closely woven into the fabric of Chinese daily life. In addition to being a centre for social intercourse, fulfilling the functions of a club, it is closely associated with the commercial side of life. The average man from every class of the community patronizes his own particular tea house, where he spends a leisure hour or so, transacts some bargain or merely looks round for an opportunity to do so. Others who frequent the tea houses are the pedlars and beggars and, more welcome than these, the professional story-tellers who sit on stools and recount their stories of a bygone age. The tea house also serves as a sort of labour exchange; each has a regular clientele of customers, who attend at different times of the day.

When I began to make inquiries about having a model made, the local people scoffed and explained that a junk as small as seven feet in length would not be profitable, as it would not carry enough salt. The explanation that it was wanted in London caused even more amazement. 'Surely London,' they said, 'if it required salt, would have its own salt junks.'

It was difficult to find a junk carpenter willing to undertake the work, and capable of doing it, for the Szechuan carpenters are the worst in the world, and those of Fuchau the worst in Szechuan. An additional handicap was their complete inability to grasp what was required.

Eventually, however, two experienced carpenters agreed to try their hand at a model. They, like the model-makers at Tzeliutsing, had no conception of working to scale. And so the first thing to do was to make cardboard patterns scaled down from an actual junk and subsequently scale cardboard patterns of all the important parts, none of which was cut out or fitted except under my supervision. Frequently in the early stages I nearly gave up in despair at their clumsy methods. Twice they threatened to abandon the work, twice it had to be re-started from zero; and three attempts were made at the crooked stern itself before it was correct enough to be passed. Finally we managed to get a correct representation, and in addition the extra twist, or wave, in it which is so sought after by the Kung T'an Ho carpenters. They were pleasant, if rapacious people, and after a time took considerably more interest in the job, co-operating to the best of their ability. They were less efficient than those at Tzeliutsing.

Despite all roughness, there is a great appeal in their direct, if slip-shod workmanship, a charm which grows on one, and is difficult to describe, unless under the heading 'Utilitarian'. The only tools normally used are the axe, saw and a prehistoric form of auger. None understands the use of a plane, and my feelings may be imagined when watching the chief carpenter with a cataract in one eye, and acute trachoma in the other, trimming the bulwarks of the model with a large axe. Several times I stopped the work, believing the carpenters were making technical mistakes, only to find by verification that they were correct.

The model, like the originals, was made of Hung Ch'un, a very attractive hardwood, only obtainable on the Kung T'an Ho, and in favour with the carpenters because it yields readily to their curious methods of bending under heat. The bulkheads, however, were made of Cypress, and the bridge of Feng Hsiang, another local wood. Hung Ch'un wood is a bright, light red in colour, which made the white wood of the bulkheads show up in startling contrast, even though some of them are hidden by the deck planks. In the original junks the wood of which they are made is never painted, but after accumulating the dirt of ages this difference in colour is not apparent. Successive coats of wood-oil add to the general dinginess, so that one may say the colour of all Crooked-Stern Junks is a faded grey-black. The bulkheads of the model were, therefore, rubbed over with mud from the foreshore. When completed I was not sure if the model was too well finished to look real, or too rough for a museum piece; but I was satisfied that it was absolutely accurate.

Timber for timber, and plank for plank, all had their scale prototypes, even down to the last wrought-iron clamp, and flared-over nail. No detail had been too small to reproduce, and the cooking-stove, grindstone, bunks, bedding, strops, oars, sweeps, trackers' harness, and furnishings are exactly similar to those in daily use. The miniature bamboo rope was made by the men who had made the original rope.

From the point of view of nautical research the model is of the greatest interest. It is unique in that it was not only built in the place of origin of the species, by the two most experienced foremen-carpenters of the Crooked-Stern Junks, but that our workshop was on board its prototype, a junk approximating closely to the scale measurements, namely, 1 inch to 1 foot. By a happy coincidence a full-sized craft was also under construction on the foreshore nearby, and kept pace with the work on the model, both being completed in two weeks. I was thus able to study the real article in course of construction, and make detailed notes throughout.

When completed the model was the subject of much conjecture, interest and amusement. The general opinion seemed to be that no one but a lunatic would have so unprofitable a junk built; but that, as it had been built and was now to start on its long voyage to London, at least it should be given the benefit of being launched in the traditional fashion by 'Sacrificing the Cock'.

Accordingly on the day appointed a large crowd assembled. The magistrate and general graced the occasion with their presence. When a small altar had been erected, gifts of fruit and vegetables were grouped round it. Candles and incense were burned, together with joss paper, and fire crackers were let off. Then the priest cut off the head of the cockerel he had been nursing and sprinkled its blood in the prescribed places on the bow and each side of the junk and, plucking a few feathers from the neck of the bird, stuck them in its own blood on the fore side of the big bow sweep and also on the sides of the fore part of the house. He then folded his hands together, and performed the kotow, bowing to all four directions of the compass. Next a few grains of rice were picked up with chopsticks and placed in a bowl half full of water, the mixture then being poured into the river as a libation to the gods invited to take part in the ceremony. These included, of course, Lu Pan, the Carpenter God, and Yo Fei; but there were others, too. Kuan Ti, the God of War, was there in blue, Shou Hsiang, with his long beard, Tu Shih, the King of Hell, Yao Wang, the God of Medicine, and many others. The junk was then launched and a crew of frogs placed on board. Unfortunately, when the crowd clapped their hands with joy, the frightened frogs dived overboard and were seen no more.

When it was time to go down to the ferry boat which would take us off to the river steamer for the return journey to Chungking, the whole town seemed to have joined us. The procession was led by a coolie with the junk on his head. He was followed by myself, my secretary, the important people, and finally the delighted inhabitants. It had been a grand party, and everybody went home delighted.

Our river steamer on the way back was heavily bombed by Japanese planes, returning from an attack on Chungking. The ship was caught practically stationary in a rapid, and a stick of bombs hit the high cliff and brought down a shower of rocks and stones, which fell on the ship. Chungking itself was burning fiercely when we got back. When our own casualties had been landed, the Crooked-Stern Junk was taken ashore. For days it was a constant source of joy to the inhabitants.

Among the first visitors to see the junk was the shipwright of the British gunboat, H.M.S. *Falcon*. He was delighted with it, but begged to be allowed to make a few improvements. As I have said, the Chinese carpenters do not use a plane, they work with a crude axe, which often misses its mark. In our search for accuracy we imitated these blemishes. When we again saw the junk, it had been neatly sandpapered, and varnish had taken the place of wood-oil.

The completion of the model coincided with the end of my work on the junks of the Upper Yangtze, and so I was able to take it down to Shanghai myself. From Chungking I flew to Hong Kong over the heads of the Japanese, and then went up the coast by steamer to Shanghai. Sir Frederick Maze had planned that I was to write the remaining volumes of the *History of the Boats in China* under his eye there. The Emperor of Japan, however, had made other plans for my future.

On 7th December, 1941, Japan bombed Pearl Harbour, and soon afterwards occupied the International Settlement of Shanghai. A very limited number of privileged people were able to get repatriated with the Diplomatic and Consular bodies; but, together with some thousands of my countrymen, I was trapped.

When the Diplomatic Body and the Consular authorities had given their last cocktail parties to each other and, with their large staffs, grand pianos and furniture, had sailed down the Whangpoo for England, fighting to the last over precedence and the best cabins, we who remained felt sadly neglected and abandoned. We did not expect the exalted ones to share our sufferings and misery; but all of us did resent the flowing champagne and the farewell parties they gave when we were in such dire need.

The Japanese had taken over the Chinese Customs and discharged the British employees with pay to the end of the month, and we were left, practically without resources, to fend for ourselves in a nominally neutral, though extremely hostile town, which was occupied by a ruthless and implacable enemy. We were compelled to wear distinctive and numbered armbands, our movements were severely restricted, and we were under constant observation by a host of tireless spies. We sold those of our possessions we were permitted to dispose of to keep ourselves in food; and, when we had almost reached the limit of our resources, we received a week's notice to prepare for internment in a 'Segregation Centre' at Yang-chow, in the very heart of China, on the Grand Canal.

I had just time to pack my manuscripts, notes and sketches, and with the greatest secrecy carried them at night and on foot to Sicawei Observatory. My friend, Father Gherzi, an Italian Roman Catholic priest in charge of the Observatory, kindly agreed to keep them for me until after the War. Together we hid them in a disused locker.

The model of the Crooked-Stern Junk and the Crooked-Bow model, wrapped in blankets, were placed in a large wooden box which under cover of darkness was secretly buried in the garden of the Customs Library. It was rather like the burial of Sir John Moore at Corunna.

CHAPTER 19

Internment

THE 4th March, 1943, was a cold, rainy day, when my wife and I rose in the dark and, after a hasty breakfast, left our flat for the last time. It was a sad parting, for all our various pieces of furniture, my typewriter, all my books of reference, my nautical library, our stoves, electric fans and almost all our possessions had, with Japanese thoroughness and efficiency, neat little labels attached to them saying in English, 'Strictly prohibited to remove. One violating this notice will be severely punished.' All motor-cars and radios had already been sequestrated.

We had been ordered to take into internment 'things of daily use': a mug, knives, plates, spoon, and, in addition, a bed, three 'approved' books and one 'cabin size permitted trunk'. All this was to be regarded as heavy luggage, which we had already delivered to the assembly point the day before. We were told that we should also be allowed to take into the camp as many bundles or possessions as we could carry ourselves, and that we must take with us provisions to last three days. These, too, I had delivered to a house close to the assembly point, which was the Anglican Cathedral. This extra luggage was the occasion of grave anxiety, for all depended on how far we should have to carry it. If too far, we would doubtless collapse under the weight and be forced to abandon some on the way. I had rehearsed and practised carrying the various weights and contraptions for several days previously, and these had been packed so that the least important could, if absolutely necessary, be abandoned. *En route* I carried two suitcases slung over my shoulder on a strap in the manner of a French porter; a bucket, containing three days' rations, in one hand, and a Chinese paper umbrella in the other. I wore dungaree overalls over a lounge suit, an overcoat and a raincoat on top of it, and on my shoulders two blankets. Two hats, shoes tied together by the laces round my neck, and gumboots with

237

spare socks stuffed into the tops, completed the ensemble. By dint of a week's practice I found I could carry this amount for half an hour without a rest. My wife carried lighter burdens, including the invaluable sack I had acquired from the British Consul in Haiphong, which now contained all the money and valuables we possessed.

We fell in on the wide cement pavement in front of the English Cathedral, according to our groups, which had been marked out in chalk squares previously. Here we were kept standing in the rain while the Japanese guards called the roll.

During the 1914 War the Germans living in Shanghai had been repatriated by the British authorities, and had marched for a short distance down Nanking Road, the principal thoroughfare of the town, to the Customs jetty, where the embarkation had taken place. The present German consul, apparently, had remembered this and so had begged the Japanese to make us walk over the same ground.

The order came at last to move off, and we shouldered our heavy packs and filed out, 200 or more, supposed to be in fours, surrounded by menacing-looking Japanese soldiers with fixed bayonets. Everybody was equally loaded, the pace was slow, and we crawled along down Nanking Road through the jeering crowds of Chinese. An attempt was made to sing, 'Pack up your troubles in your old kit bag'; this, however, was instantly stopped by the guards. When nearing the jetty, I was jostled by two Chinese with soft hats drawn down almost over their eyes and felt something being thrust into the pocket of my coat; they vanished almost immediately, but not before I had recognized my cook and his son. The gift was a bottle of water which was to prove invaluable later on.

The march proved shorter than anticipated and I managed to get all my possessions to the jetty, but many prisoners were not so fortunate and the discarded gear was eagerly pounced upon by the Chinese crowds milling round us. Three unfortunates had their pockets picked as well. One incident I particularly remember. M., a lawyer, was moving from platoon to platoon, dressed in a black overcoat over pyjamas, surmounted by a bowler hat. He was a small man and incredibly thin and very frail indeed. The evening before, his last in Shanghai, he had spent as the culminating night of a fortnight's celebrations, in preparation for the drinkless years of imprisonment before him. Determined not to lose a moment, he had sat up all night in the company of a suitable number of bottles. He was, moreover, quite heavily laden himself. He came up to me, removed his absurd bowler with a flourish and said in his precise and charming manner, 'you seem grossly overloaded, sir, allow me to assist you.' I came to know him well in the camp, and it was a great grief to us all when he died, a year later.

After a long wait on the jetty we were crowded into the two tenders, which to our astonishment moved up-river. We travelled in the *Victoria*, which had so often taken us off to the P. & O. steamers in which we went on home leave. What a grotesque change of destination now! After a further delay we were decanted into a Japanese river steamer, painted a wartime grey. There was great chaos on board, but we were eventually herded down into the hold. There was an open arrangement of deep shelves, four-abreast and in two tiers, on which the women and some of the more fortunate men lay down.

We arrived at Chinkiang about 6 a.m. the next day, in pouring rain, and were literally packed into three lighters and towed by a Chinese launch. So tightly were we stowed that there was not room enough for all to sit down. The Japanese guards then put on the hatches and battened us down. Below the water-line and in the bowels of the lighter we were in complete darkness. It was cold and wet, and in crossing the river the sea was choppy and most of the men and all the women and children were seasick. Finally we entered the Grand Canal and smooth water.

I knew the country through which we were passing well, indeed I had had many a narrow escape there from armed thieves. We had been told to carry as much money as we could muster, and so I felt very apprehensive, for there were now only two Japanese guards on each lighter, and they did not appear, as far as I could see through a crack in the hatch, to be greatly on the alert.

After a passage of five hours and twenty minutes we arrived at Yangchow. Our new guards were more humane and allowed us frequent rests. After an hour's march, shuffling along with our luggage, we arrived at Camp A, where we joined the 200 other prisoners who had preceded us, and who gave us a rousing welcome. The very first action of the Japanese was to relieve us of all our money and valuables. The seams of the Haiphong sack were unpicked, and this served me as an apron throughout my time in the camp.

The discomforts of the journey were certainly no worse than those I had often willingly experienced when travelling in the interior in search of an interesting junk; but, somehow in the present circumstances I resented them, and it was most distressing to witness the sufferings of the women and children, who were far from used to this mode of travel.

The camp was a Baptist Mission Hospital not fully completed, and we occupied the small wards; men, women and children with complete impartiality. The beds in the room touched each other, except where a small passageway was necessary. We had to be in bed by 7 p.m. At first all the men in the room would retire while the women got undressed; but in course of time by mutual agreement this formality was dispensed with. M. slept in our room in a bed close to me. He was a pleasant companion at all times except for the circumstance that he invariably snored like a giant foghorn. A lady of the same name was also in our room, and owing to the arrangement of the beds she had to crawl across M.'s bed each night *en route* to her own. There were always hearty exchanges, seldom complimentary, during the operation, for he invariably retired to rest early.

It was only after his death that we learnt that the lady was his late wife, from whom he had parted many years before. An irony of fate had decreed that she should come into the same camp, the same room and practically the same bed.

The country round Yangchow is extensively cultivated. Rice, vegetables, particularly yams, with the ordinary cereals, grow in great abundance. This was also pig country, as those of us who worked in the kitchen were soon to find out. Donkeys and water buffaloes also figured on our menu. Considering that we were in the heart of the agricultural country, there was no reason why the Japanese should have kept us so short of food.

All water had to be carried in tubs on wheelbarrows from the Grand Canal, and we were, therefore, very strictly rationed. This was a great hardship, particularly in the heat of the summer. Coal was unobtainable, and we had to cook on reeds on home-made brick stoves. A small mountain of reeds would be necessary to cook a meal for 400 persons, and the labour of its transport presented quite a problem. We wrote letters once a week, but none reached its destination, and no letters or newspapers came into the camp; and so, in the far interior, we were completely isolated from the outside world for more than a year.

The guerrillas had been particularly active, and several of the prisoners had received notes to the effect that we were to be liberated. Being liberated meant being held to ransom and sold to the Allies. Our Japanese guards had as little desire to be liberated as we had and were just as apprehensive. In due course, therefore, we were told we should be moved and split up among the various Shanghai Concentration camps. My wife and I were drafted to Pootung. This was the roughest and the toughest of all the camps, but it had by far the highest morale. Hitherto it had been a men's camp; now it was to receive 250 women and children.

Our arrival at the Pootung Camp was quite unbelievable. The small, stunted trees, oleanders and young willows were almost hidden beneath a vast, untidy dump of coal dust. A lake of sewage stretched its slimy tentacles over the lower ground near the dining-room wash-troughs. The four-storey warehouses in which we lived had been condemned twenty years before; they were now littered with débris and looked immeasurably forlorn.

The camp contained a collection of all types and races: British, American, Dutch, Russians, Negroes, Greeks, Jews, Hong Kong Chinese and mixtures of them all. They were drawn from every trade and profession in Asia. Cabaret entertainers, sanitary engineers, doctors, nurses – they were all there; and if one desired it one could have been professionally hanged. Sometimes one wondered if it would have been a good thing. In spite of it all, perhaps because of it, there was hardly ever a row, and I cannot remember a fight.

There was a dining-hall only large enough to accommodate about one-third of the prisoners. The dormitories, which each contained about 200 men, women and children, were so crowded that the beds were often touching. In course of time ingeniously contrived screens separated the more modest inmates. At first, however, one had to undress (if one did undress) where there was sufficient space, and then walk over other people's beds to one's own.

Sunday in the camp was a day of rest. On this day work was confined to the essential services only. The day was also noteworthy for the variety of the costumes which made their appearance. Many of these reflected in one way or another the character and interests of the wearer. A white mess jacket, without shirt, and corduroy shorts; plus-fours and a dinner jacket and many others. My lawyer friend always wore his bowler hat. During the heat of the summer the most popular costume, for those that had them, were pyjamas. For myself I preferred to relax in bathing slips and a kimono, which was also the costume I changed into in the evenings.

While out for a walk one Sunday I was approached from behind by three Japanese guards, two of whom were armed, and without the slightest warning suddenly found myself on the ground locked in a Ju-Jitsu embrace. I was taken before the Commandant. The reason for my presence in his office seemed to me an insoluble mystery, and I listened with something like awe (without understanding a single word of what was being said) to the imprecations which were being levelled against me by the Commandant and ably supported by my captors.

Presently the Commandant, fixing me with an icy stare, said in perfect English, 'I suppose you understand the serious nature of the offence you have committed?'

'No!' I said, 'but I should like to.'

'Well,' he returned, 'you are being charged with a very grave violation of the civil code law of Japan, in that you are wearing a kimono to which you are not entitled. Since when,' he bawled, pointing to the characters on my back, 'have you been the Senior Judge of the High Court of Japan?'

The illegal garment was torn off my back and destroyed by the guards; and I was led away to my quarters a sadder, but a wiser man. I had often cause to regret that I had not blocked out the offending characters.

Some, indeed most, of the men went to bed fully dressed. A large percentage grew beards, which, with their unkempt appearance, ragged clothes and broken shoes added to the general air of poverty and dirt. Some of those whom one would have expected from their background to set a high standard of leadership were often dismal failures, while often quite humble and insignificant little men came out in an emergency as giants and leaders. Of the 2,000 men in that camp, drawn from every walk of life and ranging from leaders of the Church, society, and the learned professions to drug-fiends, professional thieves and murderers, I don't think there were more than half a dozen who could be described as really bad. Many gave freely of their talents for the good of all. The nurses and doctors were magnificent. The camp started from absolutely nothing, and everything, lavatories, baths, sheds, cookhouses, etc., had to be built or improvised from the most unpromising materials.

From being on the Women's Committee my wife rose to be the Women's Representative, and I well remember her sitting, with her secretary, on the doorstep of the Commandant's office for a whole day until he finally agreed to provide the women in the camp with a necessary article. Although in very bad health she refused to give up her very exacting duties.

Some of us had friends outside the camp, and we were allowed sometimes to receive parcels of food and little luxuries. Just as a generous ration of pea-nuts saved us from starvation in Yangchow, so a ration of cracked wheat, sent by the Red Cross, probably saved our lives in the Pootung Camp, where the food was desperately bad both in quality and quantity. Although Red Cross parcels were regularly sent from England, we received only one issue, and this most of us hoarded against possible emergency when the war ended. In two years of imprisonment we received only one letter from home, and this was to say that both our sons were serving with the Forces, and that the youngest had been very badly wounded and was a prisoner of war.

From among the many 'human interest' anecdotes of life in the camp I select two. The first is of the man who acquired an egg; he probably bribed a guard. This egg he wrapped in cotton wool and he took the most extraordinary pains to keep it at the correct temperature for incubation. He slept with it in his bed each night, it was rumoured that he sat on it, and all of us laughed at the care and attention he gave to it. But in due course it did hatch out, to his utter delight. It turned out to be a cockerel and was named Horace. It used to sit on the rail of his bed, and he taught it a variety of tricks. It would turn its back when addressed as 'Hitler' and would nod its head when called 'Churchill'. Horace's owner gave up his life to his bird. He would not be parted from him; Horace went for walks about the camp and was spoilt by all who knew him. When the end of the war came, Horace was not allowed to be taken to England, and his owner almost gave up his passage rather than be parted from him. He left him at last with a very trusted friend. Horace became a profitable investment for his new owner, visitors would say, 'Poor Horace! He should have a wife,' and they would follow this up by sending a hen along. But Horace was a confirmed bachelor and would immediately kill the wife selected for him, with the result that his new owner was never short of chicken for dinner.

The second story concerns the camp gardeners. Some horticultural experts had built for themselves minute landscape gardens constructed out of rubble. These were limited by the authorities to seven feet square in area, and no more than twenty were permitted. These gardens would be tended with the greatest care, and their owners invariably guarded their property by 'all means short of war'. Privileged persons would sometimes be invited to join them as guests, partners or lodgers.

Tins in the camp were hard to come by and highly-prized possessions. One fortunate gardener became possessed of a tin of ample proportions, which, after he had punched a few holes in the bottom, he used as a watering can. Normally such a valuable gardening adjunct would have been guarded with the utmost vigilance; but, through action I am not permitted to disclose, the tin was acquired by a short-sighted fellow prisoner, who did not know the purpose for which it had been used.

This new owner of the tin suffered from a weak bladder, which necessitated several visits each night to the only lavatory, which was on the ground floor. Apart from the annoyance of the long trek down one hundred steps in the cold or rain, he had more than once been arrested by the Japanese guards and charged with attempting to escape. To this short-sighted owner, therefore, his new acquisition

represented a heaven-sent alternative, and before retiring he placed
it under his bed.

The next morning the Unattached Ladies, known locally as the
'Loose Women', who lived in the room below, complained that
their roof was leaking.

Various animal lovers in the camp sometimes caused embarrass-
ment to their fellows. One woman for instance acquired a stray
cat, which had come in under the wire. Its progeny multiplied to
such an extent that they became an even greater menace than the
hordes of rats which they exterminated. These wild, half-crazed
cats, working in bands, would raid food lockers during the night
and were a real danger at times. It was quite impossible to get rid
of them.

A student of zoology managed to capture quite a large snake,
which he kept inside his shirt. Unhappily for the snake it died pre-
maturely, as its owner would insist on waking it up for meals
during its period of hibernation. There were few to mourn the
passing of the snake.

One of the minor horrors of the camp was the presence of bed-
bugs. One of the prisoners utterly refused to take the fortnightly
home-made shower to which he was entitled or even to wash his
clothes. His bed soon became infested with the smaller varieties of
insect life. There were two schools of thought in his dormitory.
One held that he should be forcibly washed to prevent the spread of
his insects; while the other school, equally firmly, held that his bed
became a rallying point, and a home from home, for all the distressed bugs in the room, who came to look upon him as their pro-
tector.

From only one point in the camp – a window on the top floor
on the east side of Room 13 – could one get a glimpse of the harbour. I used to visit this spot frequently to watch the Tsungming
cotton junks beating to windward through the harbour crowded
with small craft. This was to me a rejuvenating sight.

From this point of vantage, too, the Italian luxury liner, *Conte
Verde*, could be seen at her buoy when she swung to the flood tide.
She had been interned early in the War with a skeleton crew. When
Italy capitulated and joined the Allies, her Captain, one night, with

Tsung Ming Cotton Junk

amazing courage, opened the sea-cocks on one side of the ship. She took a heavy list and by the next morning lay on her beam ends, her port side just above water, like a huge island in the middle of and almost blocking part of the upper harbour. The Captain and his crew, of course, soon found themselves in a Japanese jail doing hard labour.

Immediately the Japanese started salvage operations. They erected huge derricks on her hull and, using buildings on the Bund as hold-fasts, slowly and with infinite patience in seven months managed to right the ship. Her bottom rested on the bed of the harbour.

Every few days, after the last stages of the work, an Allied plane would fly over the area, presumably taking photographs. We wondered why no bombers were sent, her destruction would have been such a simple operation and would have caused the Japanese much loss of face.

Enormous caissons were next produced and sunk in the required places; and, when the hull had been sealed, compressed air was pumped into the mammoth structure which forced the water out, and the vessel rose gradually to the surface.

The Japanese had no aircraft in the area, and so the Allied plane which continued to view the scene had an easy and undisturbed task. In the camp we said what we thought about the Allied High Command in no uncertain terms. One bomb in the right place would have been enough to undo the twelve months and more of united effort on the part of hundreds of Japanese workmen. Yet no action was taken: indeed, they did not even bother to take cover. It was all too bad. A most valuable opportunity was being missed.

At last the great day arrived – smoke began to come from the huge funnels. It was indeed a sad day for those of us watchers in Room 13 to see the triumphant conclusion of the salvage operations. Tugs and small craft full of excited and cheering Japanese came to see the ship off to sea, now flying the Japanese 'poached egg' flag over the Italian.

About an hour afterwards four violent explosions, coming from the general direction of Woosung, rocked the camp; and soon afterwards clouds of black smoke rose high in the air. This came obviously from the *Conte Verde*.

We were subsequently to learn that the Allies had not been as stupid as we had imagined. The ship had been sunk, as she entered the narrowest part of the channel at Woosung, and had blocked the whole Whangpoo River.

Once again the Japanese started operations with their characteristic zeal and industry and finally raised the ship once more just in time to permit the British ships to enter the Whangpoo River when VJ-Day arrived.

The bread which was supplied was incredibly bad and came into the camp on a large truck with some of the coolies lying on top.

Care was necessary in cutting it up, for bit by bit wireless parts came into the camp inside the loaves. In course of time a wireless set was assembled, and I can well remember the excitement when our wireless experts first received the B.B.C. news direct from London. When we were paraded each day for roll call we could afford to smile when the Commandant proudly announced that five more British battleships had been sunk. The Japanese had spies in the camp, and soon the set was discovered, and three prisoners were taken out of the camp. A few days later a complete set came into the camp, and was in full operation by the time of the Normandy landings.

The end came with startling rapidity. The Commandant paraded the entire camp, and we were informed that the War was going very badly for the Allies. We were then ordered, as we filed past a desk, to write down on a slip of paper the name of the country we thought would win the war. We were told, too, that the result of this Japanese-sponsored Gallup Poll would be announced. This was the result: The Irish won with a large majority, the Italians were a close second, while the Jews came third. No other nationality seemed to have been considered.

After the dropping of the atomic bombs on Hiroshima and Naga-saki an announcement was posted on the Notice Board. It said in effect that a new type of bomb had been dropped on Japan, that there had been some casualties and that if any further bombing of this order was to take place the Commandant felt he would not be able to restrain the guards and could not be responsible for their actions. It was curious that our guards never seemed to sense that the end was approaching. Even a few days before the American troops entered the camp, we were being told that British battleships were being sunk in large numbers.

One evening an aeroplane flew low over the camp. It dropped leaflets saying in effect, 'Keep calm, do not leave the camp; we are coming to your rescue.' The next day three American planes, flying low, dropped wooden rafts, supported at the corners by parachutes. We were then subjected to a friendly, but alarming bombardment. Objects as large as houses filled the skies and descended on the camp in great quantities; in some cases the rafts were dropped at low level, and the parachutes did not open at all, so that they would land with a sickening thud on the roofs or on the parade ground with the prisoners scattering in confusion. Our first casualty was a Dutch vegetarian, who, too uninterested to get up, and asleep in bed, received a direct hit on the head from a tin of bully beef that had fallen off a raft and passed through the roof.

Fifty-gallon drums containing cocoa, porridge and coffee came hurtling down from the skies. It practically rained Grapenuts and Post Toasties. Lux washing soap and tomato juice came down in profusion. A fifty-gallon drum of delousing fluid demolished one building, and from out of the débris emerged a half-crazed woman. I was pinned against the washhouse wall and half-buried by a gigantic bale. Anxious to discover what was inside this mountainous receptacle, which had so narrowly failed to cause my death, I found a label saying, 'the contents of this bale is chewing gum and underpants sufficient for 2,000 men'. One red coloured parachute bore a message, 'If there is anything else you require ring up Lunghwa Airport.' In vain we telephoned back from the defunct Commandant's office that there had already been eighteen casualties and asked for a respite from the dehydrated foods, the 'Ten in one Rations' and the boned turkey which were descending upon us in increasing volume.

Much of the food and clothing which was dropped that day fell outside the camp and was eagerly seized upon by the Chinese, who, in their anxiety to obtain even more, tore down our barbed wire and relieved us of many of our presents and on their way out looted one of the buildings. Meanwhile the Japanese guards had discarded their uniforms and were being hidden by those of us who did not wish to see the Chinese cutting the throats of those who had so lately been our persecutors.

Later what appeared to be motor-cars came dropping out of the sky, followed by four men in parachutes. Within the hour four Americans drove into the camp in a jeep. Thereafter food came roaring in in an endless stream by lorry. Eggs and bacon, steak and kidney pie in tins, baked beans and ice cream. Brick ovens were erected all over the camp, we all became chefs and cooked all the food we could eat, with the result that many were taken ill. From then on the Pootung Camp became a Butlin's Holiday Resort;

indeed the food was so wonderful, and there was so much of it, that we invited many of our neutral friends to share some of our good things.

First to greet us, as the iron gates of the prison swung open, had been our dear friend, Monsieur Etienne Sigaut. He had smuggled in parcels and shown unfailing kindness in innumerable other ways. He brought letters and the good news that our sons, after many adventures in the War, were now safely in England. Sigaut handed me a thick wad of notes. 'This should be enough,' he said, 'to pay your sampan hire across the river. My car will be waiting for you on the other side.'

Back in our quarters my wife and I slowly counted the notes. The result turned out to be no less than $44,000. We looked at them aghast, for less than this amount would have kept us in perfect comfort for several years. Subsequently we learnt that since we had been in custody the ugly spectre of inflation had raised its head in China. From being at six dollars to the pound, the dollar exchange had fallen to about as many millions. The result was, of course, that everybody, both high and low, was busy turning practically worthless paper into tangible articles, from washing machines to cigarettes. It was, indeed, a difficult time for everybody, and even the humblest coolie got caught up in the net of higher mathematics. A meal in a restaurant at this time, costing say $500,000, would suddenly double its price while it was being eaten due to the fluctuating exchange rate.

To return, however, to the Camp. When the Americans had fully established themselves and rounded up all the Japanese troops that had been cut off in Shanghai, the local Chinese general begged to be allowed the pleasure of disarming them. When this had been done, and as our camp was the most primitive and uncomfortable, it was decided to send them there without delay. We therefore received orders to evacuate the camp at once in order to allow the new arrivals to move in.

My wife and I thereupon sewed up the Haiphong sack and hastily packed our scanty belongings. As we left the camp for the last time we paused for a moment to watch the 'disarmed' Japanese troops being marched into the quarters we had so lately vacated. The iron gates closed behind them with the same dull thud with which they had closed on us.

A number of Japanese, however, had managed to smuggle their arms, including some machine-guns, into the camp and, during their first night of internment, amused themselves by firing live rounds into the air in the general direction of Shanghai. The Chinese guards took no notice, for they thought that the Japanese were firing off crackers to celebrate their internment and (which was to them quite reasonable) to frighten and disperse the evil spirits and devils we had left behind. Although a great number of rounds were fired there was fortunately only one casualty, and this was on the opposite side of the river. A bullet passed through a skylight at street level and killed a Chinese who was playing Ma Jong in a basement flat.

Although I shall never quite forget the many hardships, the hunger and thirst, the bitter cold, the intense heat and the ever-present Japanese guards, yet I shall always look back on my two and a half years of internment with some very happy memories. To me this period was not a complete waste of time. I acquired a lot of 'know-how', which has stood me in good stead in my retirement, and I have learned a lot about my fellow beings. The spirit of comradeship in adversity and service without reward was a very fine experience and was of a very much higher order than is commonly to be found in the world today.

My first concern on being set free was to recover the manuscripts and notes I had left at Sicawei Observatory. Father Gherzi could remember nothing about them, but with an unerring direction I led him to the disused locker off the map room. With a throbbing heart I searched beneath the débris, and there lay the cardboard boxes containing the result of eight years' work. They were not exactly as I had left them, for in one corner was a rat's nest which had lately been vacated by its owners.

My next visit was to the garden of the Customs Library, to exhume the models of the Crooked-Stern and Crooked-Bow Junks, which we had buried so secretly two and a half years before. When at last they were unearthed they were found to be none the worse for their long sojourn underground.

Troop ships and a hospital ship had been diverted to Shanghai to pick up the ex-prisoners for passage to England and, until they arrived, we stayed with Monsieur and Madame Sigaut in their lovely flat, perched high up on one of the skyscrapers, overlooking the vast city of Shanghai spread out at one's feet like a relief map. After the squalor of the camp one felt a singular lightness of heart, and we responded without difficulty to the congenial company of our host and his wife.

We had to get used to many things. After being cooped up with more than 2,000 human beings it seemed odd to be sleeping in a room without 300 other people. To hear the clang of the lever, when one pulled the plug for the first time, was an unforgettable experience. It was peculiar too to be clear of bed-bugs. In captivity it was impossible ever to get away from one's fellow beings; now it seemed sometimes very agreeable to be alone – and yet how strange. The exhilaration of sitting in a hot bath almost took one's breath away. Even the simplest sights and sounds seemed of almost overwhelming interest.

So too, with the food. For two and a half years we had not tasted such plebeian delicacies as milk, coffee, butter, white bread, cake and the thousand-and-one little everyday commodities. After living almost exclusively on the everlasting stew consisting of offal, yams and ningpo cabbage boiled together, we had to get used to the new form of diet; and, curiously enough, it was not so easy.

Although I have, normally, a good memory for things nautical, I have completely forgotten the name of the ship in which we took passage to England. She was, however, known as the *Hell Ship* and had become famous because of the mutiny that had taken place a few months before, when some disgruntled troops had been embarked on a previous voyage. There were some highly derogatory remarks about the ship generally scrawled all over the bulkheads and other parts of the troop decks. These *graffiti* were all written in soldiers' basic English, and bore mute testimony to what our discontented predecessors thought of the food and the accommodation provided.

Our women and children and the very sick men were accommodated in the officers' quarters, while the rest of us slept in hammocks on the troop decks. Ill-nourished and ill-clad as we were, the ship appeared as no *Hell Ship*, rather we saw her as an *Angel from Heaven*.

We embarked just before sunset. Many of my Chinese friends were there to see us off. Our guests were not allowed on board, but we foregathered on the jetty. Mr Yuen, who had so often guided my halting steps through the Chinese classics, Mr Whong my ever-faithful secretary, who had been with me off and on for twenty-five years, Mr Chang, my draughtsman, who had 'no children, but only seven daughters', Mr Kung, who really did know something about

The End of a Junk

Chinese history, and several others. Miss Tsung, my typist, who could speak no English but could always be counted upon to read my writing, the Tingchai and the office coolie. The last looked strangely fat in his Chinese clothes.

When it was time for me to go, he suddenly drew from inside his long, silk gown an enormous string of Chinese fire crackers, the essential part of every ceremony. These, with great solemnity, he proceeded to ignite. The crackers continued to explode and bang in the air long after I had reached the head of the gangway. There I looked over my shoulder and saw, through the blue haze of the booming and spluttering artillery, my faithful Chinese friends for the last time.

We were due to sail at daylight, and long before dawn I was dressed and up on deck. The scene was quite lovely. The early life of a great city is always interesting. It was peaceful, and yet there was a strange sense of life, for even at five in the morning the teeming population of Shanghai was beginning to stir. The stars seemed to shine more brightly just before the day broke, and these mingled with the thousands of lights ashore and afloat. From the high buildings on the Bund, just beginning to show darkly in the distance, my gaze swept across the river to the Pootung Camp, our home for two and a half weary years.

As I stood at the stern of the ship still looking towards the great city of Shanghai, now boldly silhouetted by the dawn, and as the ship moved slowly ahead, picking her way down the brown-coloured Whangpoo River, with its twists and turns, its mud flats and reedy banks, past the old familiar landmarks, the numerous creeks and the fishing villages, she finally increased to full speed; and as she gathered way and moved forward, so my thoughts went back to the country I was leaving, in which I had spent more than thirty happy years of my life; and now . . . now it was all over and done with.

I watched the Woosung Outer Bar lights dip below the horizon, Tsungming Island loom slowly out of the dawn, and the sun rise over the summer sea. Then, with genuine sorrow in my heart, I turned my back on China and went below for breakfast.

For me a new life had begun.

THE END

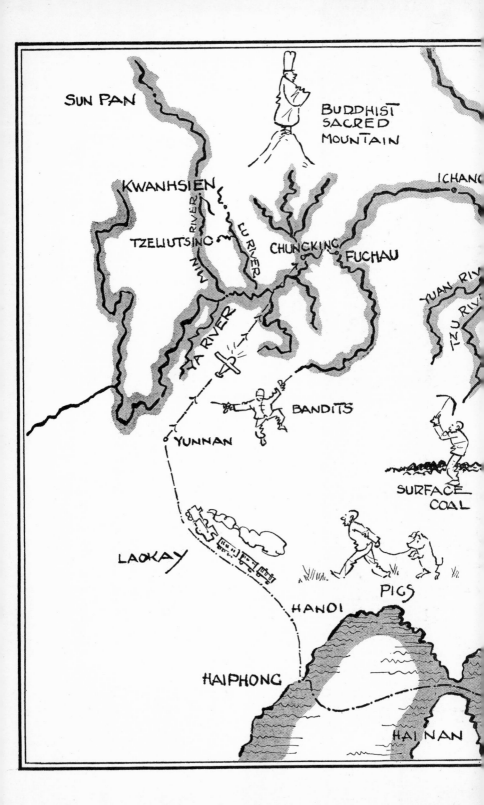